This cookbook is from my charity here. Hope it reminds you of the foods here!! Love and Miss you!   xxoo Patty.

Settings

Sunrise to Sunset

Settings
Sunrise
to
Sunset

A Medley of Flavors, Tastes, and Styles from the Texas Gulf Coast

Settings Sunrise to Sunset

A Medley of Flavors, Tastes, and Styles from the Texas Gulf Coast

PUBLISHED BY ASSISTANCE LEAGUE® OF THE BAY AREA

COPYRIGHT © 2007 BY ASSISTANCE LEAGUE
OF THE BAY AREA
P. O. BOX 591131 • HOUSTON, TEXAS 77259-1131
877-277-3452

PHOTOGRAPHS© BY J. PAMELA CULPEPPER, CPP

This cookbook is a collection of favorite recipes, which are not necessarily original recipes.

LIBRARY OF CONGRESS CONTROL NUMBER: 2006932344
ISBN-10: 0-9668381-1-4
ISBN-13: 978-0-9668381-1-4

Edited, Designed, and Manufactured by
Favorite Recipes® Press
An imprint of

FRP™

P. O. BOX 305142
NASHVILLE, TENNESSEE 37230
800-358-0560

ART DIRECTOR: STEVE NEWMAN
BOOK DESIGN: BRAD WHITFIELD AND SUSAN BREINING
PROJECT EDITOR: LINDA A. JONES

MANUFACTURED IN CHINA
FIRST PRINTING: 2007
15,000 COPIES

Thank you to the membership.

The cookbook committee expresses

heartfelt thanks to the wonderful

ladies of the Assistance League®

of the Bay Area. They, along

with their family and friends,

have continuously supported and

contributed to this project. Settings,

Sunrise to Sunset belongs to all of

you. Job well done! We regret

that we were unable to publish

all the recipes due to available

space or similarity.

Scene from the Jim West Mansion

The cover: The gazebo from the historic Jim West Mansion provides the perfect introduction for a visit to the Bay Area of Texas. The gazebo itself sits to the right of a cloister situated on beautiful grounds of this extensive ranch overlooking Clear Lake in Nassau Bay. This forty-room Italian renaissance-style mansion was built in 1924 at a cost of $500,000 and was considered one of the nation's showplaces. "Silver Dollar" Jim West built the mansion to entertain friends and family when he wanted to escape the pressures of his oil, lumber, and cattle businesses. Locals recall West tossing coins from his chauffeur-driven limo when he visited. He sold the lavish estate in 1938 soon after discovering oil on his Clear Creek property to Humble Oil and Refining Company (the Exxon Company). Friendswood Development Company, a land development subsidiary of Exxon, created Clear Lake City in the 1960s as a master-planned community on this vast property adjacent to NASA's Johnson Space Center.

About the Photographer

Pam Culpepper, CPP, is the owner of J. Pamela Photography, Inc. Pam is a member of the Assistance League® of the Bay Area and graciously donated her time to produce the beautiful photographs found in *Settings, Sunrise to Sunset*. She has pursued her passion for photography since opening her studio in the Clear Lake area in 1983. Her main focus is on family and children portraiture. Pam's unique niche is photographing "Second Marriages."

Community involvement has always been a key part of Pam's personal and professional life. Bay Area Turning Point has honored her as a Woman of Heart for volunteer efforts in the community, and she was the 2000 recipient of the University of Houston-Clear Lake Distinguished Alumni Award. Pam and her husband, Peter, are doting grandparents to a grandson who is a freshman at Baylor, a fifteen-year-old granddaughter who is a ballerina, and, most recently, a little granddaughter who will be walking by the time this cookbook is published.

The members of the Assistance League of the Bay Area count Pam as one of their true blessings and would like to thank her for her vision, her soaring spirit, and her unfailing generosity to our organization.

Preface

ASSISTANCE LEAGUE® OF THE BAY AREA WAS CHARTERED AS A CHAPTER OF THE
NATIONAL ASSISTANCE LEAGUE IN 1994. SINCE THEN, OUR MEMBERSHIP HAS RAISED MORE THAN
$1.2 MILLION AND DEDICATED MORE THAN 82,000 VOLUNTEER HOURS TO PUT CARING COMMITMENT
INTO ACTION THROUGH OUR COMMUNITY-BASED PHILANTHROPIC PROJECTS.

THE GOAL OF THE ASSISTANCE LEAGUE OF THE BAY AREA IS TO MAKE A DIFFERENCE IN SOMEONE'S LIFE.
THE MEMBERSHIP HAS DEDICATED ITSELF TO EXTENDING A HELPING HAND IN TIMES OF NEED BY SUPPLYING
FINANCIAL ASSISTANCE THROUGH OUR PROJECTS, AS WELL AS PROVIDING A SMILE, A KIND WORD,
AND A CARING TOUCH TO YOUTH AND THE ELDERLY. FOLLOWING HURRICANE KATRINA, MEMBERS SHOPPED
FOR 663 SCHOOL-AGE CHILDREN SEEKING REFUGE IN OUR COMMUNITY. ASSISTEENS®, OUR TEEN MEMBERS,
PROVIDED BACKPACKS FILLED WITH SCHOOL SUPPLIES. MEMBERS VISITED WITH VICTIMS OF THIS HORRIFIC STORM,
REASSURING THEM THAT THEY WOULD SURVIVE AND REBUILD THEIR LIVES.

NET EARNINGS FROM THE COOKBOOK SALES OF THE AWARD-WINNING *SETTINGS ON THE DOCK OF THE BAY*
AND NOW *SETTINGS, SUNRISE TO SUNSET* WILL ENABLE OUR CHAPTER TO FUND OUR
PHILANTHROPIC COMMITMENTS IN THE FUTURE. PROJECTS INCLUDE:

OPERATION SCHOOL BELL® PURCHASES NEW CLOTHING AND HYGIENE KITS TO GIVE TO STUDENTS IN NEED
IN GRADES K–12. OUR MEMBERS BELIEVE THAT A STUDENT'S SELF-ESTEEM WILL BE ENHANCED WHEN PROVIDED
WITH NECESSARY CLOTHING, LEADING TO GREATER ACADEMIC ACHIEVEMENT AND PEER ACCEPTANCE.

ASSISTANCE LEAGUE PARTNERSHIP WITH COMMUNITIES IN SCHOOLS—BAY AREA, INC.,
SPONSORS THIS NATIONAL PROGRAM AS MEMBERS PROVIDE TUTORING, MENTORING, AND INCENTIVE PROGRAMS
TO STUDENTS DEEMED AT RISK OF LEAVING SCHOOL.

ASSISTANCE LEAGUE KIDS' U SCHOLARSHIP PROGRAM IN PARTNERSHIP WITH THE UNIVERSITY
OF HOUSTON-CLEAR LAKE AWARDS SCHOLARSHIPS TO DESERVING ELEMENTARY STUDENTS
AND PROVIDES CLASSROOM ASSISTANCE FOR THIS SUMMER PROGRAM.

ASSISTANCE LEAGUE Hands from the Heart sponsors monthly visits at a local care center where chapter volunteers provide the residents with manicures and companionship.

The membership of the ASSISTANCE LEAGUE of the Bay Area is committed to improving the quality of life in our community through projects that have been carefully researched and reviewed. League members recognize the difference one person can make in providing help to an individual. They also realize that as a group they can collectively change lives by sharing their time and talents.

Mission Statement

ASSISTANCE LEAGUE® is a national nonprofit organization that puts caring and commitment into action through community-based philanthropic projects. ASSISTANCE LEAGUE of the Bay Area is a chapter of National ASSISTANCE LEAGUE®.

ASSISTANCE LEAGUE of the Bay Area is a nonprofit philanthropic organization dedicated to improving the quality of life in the Bay Area by providing services, education, and financial assistance to at-risk populations, including children and the elderly.

ASSISTANCE LEAGUE of the Bay Area Motto

Commitment—Connection—Community
Caring for the Children—The Elderly—The Environment

Cookbook Underwriters

SAPPHIRE LEVEL

Nancy and Tom Warren

ALEXANDRITE LEVEL

Donna and George Gartner—GARTNER COATINGS

Dianne and Dick Gilbert—EXXON/MOBILE CORPORATION

Elaine and David Wynegar—NEOCHEM CORPORATION

AQUAMARINE LEVEL

Amegy Bank

Krista and Dan Borgen—USD LLC

Tonya and Eric Collum

Ebby and Jack Creden

Sharon and Dr. Howard Dillard

Tisa and Dr. Mitch Foster

Peggy and Chris Heinrich

Kathie and Randy King

Dan McCarver—

PRUDENTIAL REAL ESTATE

Joy and Charles Smitherman

Deanna and Jack Vernon

Linda and Doug Walt—

DOLIMA PROPERTIES

Jill and Stuart Williams

TOPAZ LEVEL

Pam and Dr. Mike Bungo

Tracey and Dr. Doug Webb

PEARL LEVEL

Jay and Courtney Atchley

Denise and Andy Beakey

Darice and Darrell Davis

Liz and Chris Dooley

Alice Jones—

COLDWELL BANKER PENNINGTON-CHEN

Sheryl and Richard Lane

Joy and Dr. Henry Muniz

Madeline Nugent—SILPADA DESIGNS

Betsy and Jerry Pennington

Barbara and Dr. Hal Rosenthal

Mary and Jeff Smith

Patty and John Whalen—

TURBO COMPONENT AND ENGINEERING

Cookbook Underwriters

Opal Level

Atiya and Dr. Ezzat Abouleish

Sheila and Steve Banovic

Doris and Charles Brown

Linda and Joe Byrd

Cindy and Gerry Castille

Janith Coutret and Joel Lowe

Terri and John Dieste

Sheila and Art Fichtner

Mary Kay and Paulie Gaido

Karen and Greg Gandy

Fran and Mickey Gentry

Elizabeth Glenn

Linda and Dr. Larry Goodman

Jennie and Rob Hampton

Susan and Jim Hart

Patty Hoffman Designs

Marie and Walt Inkofer

Jeri and William (Buzzy) Knapp

Carol and Doug Latimer

Becky and Shawn Lunney

Johanna and Doug Mathera

Elizabeth Clemente-Nelson and Keith Nelson

Marian and Ken Nickerson

Jennifer and Chuck Nutt

Yvonne and Shepard Perrin

Cindi and Karl Priebe

Patty and Dr. Mike Romanko

Belinda and James Scheurich

June and Paul Schladenhauffen

Rhonda and Randy Seward

Diana and Bruce Shuman

Barbara Visser—
Coldwell Banker Pennington-Chen

Dawn Webb—Remax Space Center

Angie and Matthew Weinman

Jennifer and Adam Weinman

Gloria and Tom Wong

Opal Level Restaurants

Bay Oaks Country Club

Mark's Restaurant

South Shore Harbour Resort

The Italian Café

Cookbook Committee

CHAIRMAN *Donna Gartner*   VICE CHAIRMAN *Dianne Gilbert*

PROOFING EDITOR *Jan Parks*

TESTING COORDINATOR *Marie Inkofer*

RECIPE COLLECTION *Barbra Mouton*

COMPUTER *Atiya Abouleish*

MARKETING CHAIRMAN *Sharon Dillard*

NONRECIPE TEXT *Linda Byrd*

ART/DESIGN COORDINATOR *Barbara Rosenthal*

INDEXING *Ruth Beecher*

PUBLICITY *Pat Bertelli*

TREASURER *Mary Smith*

Set Designers

Carol Bergman

Belva Dewey

Jeanne Jones

Sonya Moore

Cathy Osoria

Lori Ray

Gretchen Sheehan

Joy Smitherman

Krista Williamson

Category Chairman

APPETIZERS AND BEVERAGES   *Barbara Dugat*

BREADS   *Lynda Forsthoffer*

BRUNCH   *Barbara Visser*

DESSERTS   *Diane McLaughlin, Ebby Creden*

ENTRÉES (BEEF)   *Betsy Pennington*

ENTRÉES (PORK AND LAMB)   *Sheila Fichtner, Doris Brown*

ENTRÉES (POULTRY)   *Yvonne Perrin*

SALADS   *Sandra Sellers*

SEAFOOD   *Joy Smitherman*

SIDE DISHES   *Belva Dewey*

SOUPS   *Joan Burt*

WINES   *Mary Kay Gaido*

RESTAURANTS   *Dianne Gilbert, Cindi Ditta Priebe*

League Presidents During Cookbook Production

Donna Gartner   *2003–2004*   *Cindy Castille*   *2005–2006*

Donna James   *2004–2005*   *Jennie Hampton*   *2006–2007*

Cookbook Committee

CHAIRMAN *Donna Gartner*　　　**VICE CHAIRMAN** *Dianne Gilbert*

Atiya Abouleish	Rebecca Doxey	Diane Konick
Courtney Atchley	Barbara Dugat	Stephanie Korenek
Janeane Bacon	Carrie Dulmage	Sheryl Lane
Sylvia Balionis	Annette Dwyer	Judy Love
Ana Bearce	JoLynn Falgout	Becky Lunney
Deb Beard	Shelia Fichtner	Teresa Macon
Ruth Beecher	Darlene Fore	Peggy McBarron
Carol Bergman	Lynda Forsthoffer	Darla McKitrick
Patricia Bertelli	Mary Kay Gaido	Diane McLaughlin
Debbie Bonno	Theresa Gardner	Sharon Mendelson
Kristin Boozer	Fran Gentry	Sonya Moore
Pam Bungo	Lil Glynn	Barbra Mouton
Doris Brown	Jeni Golden	Joy Muniz
Pat Burnett	Sue Ann Goodwin	Marian Nickerson
Joan Burt	Lanette Hale	Nancy O'Dowd
Betsy Bush	Jennie Hampton	Cathy Osoria
Linda Byrd	Octive Healey	Laura Parker
Cindy Castille	Peggy Heinrich	Jan Parks
Peggy Clause	Melba Heselmeyer	Eileen Parus
Tonya Collum	Julie Hill	Betsy Pennington
Georgette Curran	Patty Hoffman	Yvonne Perrin
Janith Coutret	Joanne Hogarth	Nancy Platt
Ebby Creden	Marie Inkofer	Cindi Ditta Priebe
Gloria Cruz	Suzanne Jaax	Judy Raiford
Margaret Daniel	Michele Jacobs	Lori Ray
Darice Davis	Donna James	Joy Rayne
Belva Dewey	Donna Jerz	Ann Reed
Terri Dieste	Jeanne Jones	Sylvia Resch
Sharon Dillard	Mary Alice Jones	Rebecca Richey
Renee Dollar	Jeri Knapp	

Cookbook Committee

Lila Rosen	Carol Short	Charlotte Teeter
Barbara Rosenthal	Mary Smith	Rosalyn Turner
Janet Rushing	Joy Smitherman	Tracy Uehlinger
Betsy Salbilla	Betty Squyres	Barbara Visser
Sarah Sawin	Susan Spalding	Terrie Waddell
June Schladenhauffen	Patricia Stallings	Dawn Webb
Sandra Sellers	Paula Stroumpos	Elizabeth Webb
Rhonda Seward	Patti Sulkin	Jill Williams
Gretchen Sheehan	Kathleen Symons	Renate Wood

Acknowledgments

Beecher Chiropractic

Mary Alys Cherry

City of League City

Clear Lake Chamber of Commerce

Peter Cronk

Sabrina Curran

Frenchie's Italian Restaurant

Gaidos

Haak Winery

J. Pamela Photography, Inc.

Patricia and Barry LaChance

Landry's Seafood Restaurants and
the Kemah Boardwalk

Laura's Tea Room

Lynn McLean, Lary's Florist

Dr. Jeff Moore

Beth Morgan

Pappas Brothers Corporation

Robyn Reuhrwein, Republic
Beverage Company

Tommy's Seafood Steakhouse

Mary and Terry Williams

Marlie and Macie Williamson

Contents

Contents

Introduction

Welcome back! Our Texas Gulf Coast is brimming with excitement as we offer a second helping of TEXAS STYLE. Join us as we revisit the multifaceted lifestyles and tastes that were introduced in the ASSISTANCE LEAGUE® of the Bay Area's first cookbook, *Settings on the Dock of the Bay*. Home to a melting pot of the historic, sleepy coastal charms of seaside communities and the aeronautical advances in space exploration from the Johnson Space Center, the Bay Area of Texas beckons all to its shores. Travel with us as we present *Settings, Sunrise To Sunset* and enjoy the sites and tastes of our coastal plains.

Settings, Sunrise to Sunset invites you to enjoy our tested recipe selections. They were chosen to spotlight local favorites, member-family treasures, and area restaurants, while appealing to all levels of gourmets. Experiment with recipes for summer outings and picnics, cozy dinner parties, and quick and easy dinners for your family. Our menu selections, complete with the perfect wine or beverage accompaniment, are designed to help plan special events and holiday parties. Sidebars providing clever tips, hints, and recipe alternatives are sprinkled throughout the cookbook. The discriminating gourmet will revel in the variety of this extraordinary compendium.

Embark on our newest culinary journey and experience the Bay Area through award-winning photographs featuring jewel-toned skies and charming views of the Bay Area. Entertain and savor your celebrations as you unlock the secrets of gracious dining served with Texas Gulf Coast PRIDE and STYLE.

Appetizers and Beverages

Haak Vineyards and Winery

What began as a hobby in 1969 for Raymond and Gladys Haak, has grown into an 11,000-square-foot winery in a Mediterranean-style facility. Their winery is situated on their original twelve-acre homestead where they raised their family. After many years of experimentation, the Haaks decided on two varieties, a Blanc du Bois, white grape and Black Spanish, or Jacquez, a red grape. Their wines have won numerous awards in both national and international competitions since the winery's inception in 2000. Haak Winery hosts many public events, the most popular being Music in the Vines where wine enthusiasts sit outside under the Texas night sky, enjoy a variety of music, and sip Haak wine.

Sunset at Haak Winery

Fresh Mozzarella and Olive Toasts with
Basil and Vinaigrette, page 29

Asparagus Prosciutto Rolls, page 28

Layered Shrimp Dip, page 37

Chicken Wraps with Tomatoes and Goat Cheese, page 31

Caviar Supreme, page 21

Bacon-Filled Cherry Tomatoes, page 26

Wine Pairings
Haak Blanc du Bois
Haak Nouveau Jacquez

Caviar Supreme

Serves 25

2	envelopes unflavored gelatin		1	large green onion, minced
4	hard-cooked eggs, chopped		2	tablespoons fresh lemon juice
1/2	cup mayonnaise		2	tablespoons mayonnaise
1/2	cup parsley, minced		1/2	teaspoon salt
1	large green onion, minced		•	Dash of Tabasco sauce
3/4	teaspoon salt		•	Dash of pepper
•	Dash of Tabasco sauce		1	cup sour cream
•	Dash of pepper		1/4	cup minced onion
1	avocado, puréed		1	(3- to 4-ounce) jar black caviar
1	avocado, chopped		•	Fresh lemon juice for sprinkling

Line the bottom of a 1-quart soufflé dish with foil, extending the foil 4 inches beyond the rim of the dish on two sides. Grease the foil and dish lightly with vegetable oil. Soften and dissolve the gelatin using the package directions. (You may also prepare the gelatin individually for each layer in the amount specified for each layer.)

To prepare the first layer, combine the hard-cooked eggs, 1/2 cup mayonnaise, the parsley, 1 green onion, 3/4 teaspoon salt, dash of Tabasco sauce and a dash of pepper in a bowl and mix well. Stir in 1 tablespoon of the dissolved gelatin. Adjust the seasonings to taste. Spread the egg mixture with a spatula neatly into the prepared dish, smoothing the top and wiping away any of the egg mixture from the foil with a paper towel.

To prepare the second layer, combine the puréed avocado, chopped avocado, 1 green onion, 2 tablespoons lemon juice, 2 tablespoons mayonnaise, 1/2 teaspoon salt, dash of Tabasco sauce and dash of pepper in a bowl and mix well. Stir in 1 tablespoon of the remaining dissolved gelatin. Adjust the seasonings to taste. Gently spread over the egg mixture layer.

To prepare the third layer, mix the sour cream and minced onion in a bowl. Stir in the remaining 2 tablespoons of dissolved gelatin. Spread carefully over the avocado layer. Cover the dish tightly with plastic wrap and chill for 8 to 12 hours.

To serve, place the caviar in a fine sieve and rinse gently under cold running water. Sprinkle with lemon juice and drain. Unwrap and lift the mold out of the dish using the foil extensions as handles. Remove to a serving dish using a long spatula. Spread the caviar over the top. Serve with thin slices of dark pumpernickel bread.

Note: *Use red caviar at Christmas for a very festive dish.*

Smoked Salmon Cheesecake

Serves 30

1 1/2 tablespoons butter
1/2 cup dry bread crumbs
1/2 cup (2 ounces) grated
   Gruyère cheese
1 teaspoon minced fresh dill weed
3 tablespoons butter
3/4 onion, minced
28 ounces cream cheese, softened
4 eggs

1/4 cup (1 ounce) grated
   Gruyère cheese
1/3 cup heavy cream
1/2 teaspoon salt
8 ounces smoked salmon,
   coarsely chopped
2 tablespoons minced fresh dill weed
• Sour cream or cream
   cheese, softened

Wrap a large piece of heavy-duty foil across the bottom and up the side of an 8- or 9-inch springform pan. Tightly seal to prevent leakage. Butter the inside of the pan with 1 1/2 tablespoons butter. Combine the bread crumbs, 1/2 cup Gruyère cheese and 1 teaspoon dill weed in a small bowl and toss to mix. Sprinkle evenly in the prepared pan. Chill in the refrigerator.

Melt 3 tablespoons butter in a heavy skillet over low heat. Add the onion and cook, covered, for 10 minutes or until soft, stirring occasionally. Remove from the heat and set aside.

Process the cream cheese in a food processor until blended and smooth. Add the eggs, 1/4 cup Gruyère cheese, the cream and salt and process until smooth. (Be careful not to process too long or the mixture will be very light and the baking time will be greatly reduced.)

Reserve 1/4 cup of the salmon. Stir the remaining salmon and the onion gently into the cheese mixture. Pour one-half of the salmon mixture into the prepared pan. Sprinkle with 2 tablespoons dill weed and 2 tablespoons of the reserved salmon. Gently spoon the remaining salmon mixture over the layers and sprinkle with the remaining 2 tablespoons reserved salmon. Set the springform pan in a large roasting pan. Fill the roasting pan with enough water to come halfway up the side of the springform pan. Bake at 325 degrees for 1 hour and 20 minutes, checking for doneness after 1 hour. Turn off the oven and let the cheesecake stand in the oven with the door ajar for 1 hour. Remove to a wire rack and cool to room temperature. (You may store in the refrigerator for 24 to 36 hours at this point and bring to room temperature before serving.)

To serve, remove the side of the pan. (You may remove the bottom of the pan, if desired, by dipping a spatula in hot water and running the spatula underneath to loosen.) Spread sour cream over the top and/or side of the cheesecake. Garnish with fresh dill weed, capers and smoked salmon "roses."

Note: *Any leftovers may be frozen.*

Belgian Endive with Roquefort, Walnuts and Cranberries

Serves 10 to 12

3	to 4 heads Belgian endive	1/2	cup coarsely chopped walnuts
4	ounces Roquefort cheese, lightly crumbled	1/2	cup (or more) Roquefort Dressing (below)
1/4	cup dried cranberries		

Trim the base from the endive with a diagonal cut and separate the leaves. Toss the cheese, cranberries and walnuts in a bowl, being careful to not break up the cheese too much. Stir in a small amount of the Roquefort dressing to bind together. Spoon a small amount of the cheese mixture onto each endive leaf. (You may make ahead up to this point and chill, covered, up to 3 hours before serving.) Garnish with watercress and drizzle with the remaining Roquefort dressing.

Note: *If endive is unavailable, use celery sticks.*

Roquefort Dressing

1/4	cup crumbled Roquefort cheese	1/2	teaspoon Worcestershire sauce
3/4	cup mayonnaise	1	tablespoon red wine vinegar
1/3	cup buttermilk	1/8	teaspoon cayenne pepper
•	Juice of 1 to 2 limes		

Melt the cheese in a saucepan, stirring constantly. Do not scorch. Remove from the heat to cool. Combine the cheese, mayonnaise, buttermilk, lime juice, Worcestershire sauce, vinegar and cayenne pepper in a bowl and mix well. You may add additional cheese, if desired. Chill, covered, in the refrigerator.

Note: *You may alternatively melt the cheese in the oven.*

East-West Dates

Stuff each of 2 dozen fresh or packaged dates with a whole water chestnut. Wrap each date with a slice of center-cut bacon and secure with a wooden pick. Place on a baking sheet and broil until the bacon is crisp. Turn and broil the other side until crisp. Drain and place in a chafing dish. Serve warm. You may assemble several days in advance and store in the refrigerator until ready to broil.

Artichoke Bites

Makes 4 dozen

1	(14-ounce) can artichoke hearts, drained	2	tablespoons lemon juice
1	cup seasoned bread crumbs	4	garlic cloves, pressed
2	eggs	2	tablespoons freshly grated Parmesan cheese
2	tablespoons olive oil		

Mash the artichoke hearts in a bowl. Add the bread crumbs, eggs, olive oil, lemon juice and garlic and mix well. Chill, covered, for 4 to 12 hours. Shape into small balls and roll in the cheese. Place on a baking sheet and bake at 400 degrees until light brown. Serve warm or at room temperature.

Note: *This recipe may be prepared ahead of time and frozen.*

Stuffed Mushrooms

Makes 12

12	mushroom caps	2	tablespoons vermouth
6	tablespoons butter, melted	1	teaspoon soy sauce
1	garlic clove, minced	1/2	cup fine cracker crumbs
3	tablespoons shredded Jack cheese		

Place the mushroom caps on a baking sheet and brush with 2 tablespoons of the butter to coat thoroughly. Combine the remaining 4 tablespoons butter, garlic and cheese in a bowl and stir to blend well. Add the vermouth, soy sauce and cracker crumbs and mix well. Stuff the mushroom caps with the mixture. Broil 6 inches from the heat source for 3 minutes. Serve warm.

Mushroom Tarts

Makes 3 dozen

36	slices white bread	1/4	teaspoon black pepper
5	tablespoons unsalted butter	1	teaspoon finely chopped
1/4	cup minced onion		fresh chives
8	ounces minced mushrooms	2	tablespoons finely chopped
2	tablespoons all-purpose flour		fresh parsley
1	cup half-and-half	1	teaspoon fresh lemon juice
1/2	teaspoon salt	3	tablespoons freshly grated
1/8	teaspoon cayenne pepper		Parmesan cheese

Cut each bread slice with a 3-inch round cookie cutter. Press the bread rounds over the bottom and up the side of 2-tablespoon muffin cups. Bake in batches at 400 degrees on the middle oven rack for 12 to 15 minutes or until golden brown. Remove to wire racks to cool. Reduce the oven temperature to 350 degrees.

Melt the butter in a skillet over medium-high heat. Add the onion and sauté for 3 minutes. Add the mushrooms and sauté for 15 minutes or until the liquid from the mushrooms evaporates. Remove the skillet from the heat. Sprinkle with the flour and stir until combined. Add the half-and-half and return the skillet to the heat. Cook until the mixture is very thick, stirring constantly. Remove the skillet from the heat and stir in the salt, cayenne pepper, black pepper, chives, parsley and lemon juice. Let stand until cool.

Place the bread cups on a baking sheet. Pour equal amounts of the mushroom mixture into the bread cups and sprinkle with the cheese. (You may make ahead up to this point and store, tightly wrapped, in the freezer.) Bake on the middle oven rack for 10 minutes or until the cheese is melted. If frozen, bake for 20 minutes or until heated through.

Olive Balls

Makes 50

25	(or more) large stuffed olives, drained	3	(2-ounce) packages finely ground pecans
8	ounces softened cream cheese	•	Seasoned salt to taste (optional)

Cover each olive with about 1/2 teaspoon cream cheese and roll in the pecans. Place on a tray and sprinkle with seasoned salt. Chill, covered, for 1 to 2 hours. (You may make ahead up to this point and store in the refrigerator for a week or longer.) Cut each olive ball into halves and serve.

Note: *There are usually more than twenty-five olives in a big jar so you might need more pecans and softened cream cheese if you want to use the whole jar.*

Bacon-Filled Cherry Tomatoes

Makes 2 to 3 dozen

1	pound bacon, crisp-cooked and crumbled	2	tablespoons chopped parsley
1/4	cup chopped green onions	1/2	cup mayonnaise
		24	to 36 cherry tomatoes

Combine the bacon, green onions, parsley and mayonnaise in a bowl and mix well. Cut a thin slice off the top of each tomato. Hollow out each tomato with a melon baller or sharp knife. Fill each tomato with the bacon mixture.

Note: *You may need to slice a small amount from the bottom of each tomato to make them stand upright.*

Cheese and Bacon Puffs

Serves 10

1	cup mayonnaise	2	to 3 teaspoons horseradish, drained
1	teaspoon Tabasco sauce	1/2	cup crumbled crisp-cooked bacon
1/2	cup (2 ounces) shredded sharp Cheddar cheese	1	loaf party rye bread

Combine the mayonnaise, Tabasco sauce, cheese, horseradish and bacon in a bowl and mix well. Spread on the bread slices and place on a baking sheet. Broil until golden brown.

Note: *This recipe can easily be doubled or tripled. Feel free to increase the amounts of bacon, cheese and horseradish to taste. Chop the bacon before cooking for more even browning.*

Olive and Cheese Tidbits

Makes 4 dozen

11/2	cups finely chopped green onions	1	cup good-quality mayonnaise
11/2	cups chopped black olives and green olives	3	cups (12 ounces) shredded sharp Cheddar cheese
1	teaspoon pepper	6	English muffins, split into halves

Combine the green onions, olives, pepper, mayonnaise and cheese in the order listed in a bowl and mix well. Spread thickly on each muffin half. Cut each muffin half into quarters and place on a baking sheet. Freeze until firm and store in a plastic freezer bag.

To serve, place the frozen muffin quarters on a baking sheet. Bake at 350 degrees for 10 to 15 minutes or until brown.

Note: *To serve as a luncheon entrée, add some crab meat to the cheese mixture and spread on the muffin halves before baking.*

DYSIE'S BACON APPETIZER

Arrange 1 pound of center-cut bacon slices in a baking pan lined with foil. Bake at 400 degrees until the bacon is partially cooked through. Remove from the oven and cover the bacon slices with 1/4 cup packed light brown sugar. Bake for 20 minutes or until the bacon is crisp and cooked through. Remove to paper towels to drain and cool. Cut the bacon slices into halves to serve. You may prepare 1 hour in advance.

Wine Pairings
Montes Pinot Noir
Belle Glos Pinot Noir

Palm Beach Cheese Puffs

Makes 3 dozen

1	small onion, finely chopped	3	dozen (1-inch) rounds white Pepperidge Farm original bread
1/4	cup (1 ounce) grated Parmesan cheese	•	Grated Parmesan cheese for sprinkling
1	cup mayonnaise (very cold)		
5	drops of Tabasco sauce		

Fold the onion, 1/4 cup cheese, the mayonnaise and Tabasco sauce together in a bowl; do not beat. Chill in the refrigerator until ready to use.

Fill a pastry bag fitted with a large nozzle with the cheese mixture. Pipe the cheese mixture high onto the bread rounds. Place on a baking sheet and sprinkle with Parmesan cheese. Broil for 3 to 5 minutes or until brown and toasted.

Note: *This recipe has been popular at cocktail parties in Palm Beach, Florida, since the 1950s.*

Asparagus Prosciutto Rolls

Serves 12

1/2	cup vegetable oil	18	slices prosciutto
2	tablespoons balsamic vinegar	5	ounces goat cheese
1	tablespoon Dijon mustard	36	(6-inch) asparagus spears, blanched
•	Salt and pepper to taste		

Whisk the oil, vinegar and Dijon mustard in a bowl until blended. Season with salt and pepper. Slice the prosciutto into halves lengthwise. Spread each slice with a thin layer of goat cheese and wrap around the asparagus spears. Drizzle with the vinaigrette.

Fresh Mozzarella and Olive Toasts with Basil and Vinaigrette

Serves 8

1 (10-ounce) jar black olive spread	• Thinly sliced fresh mozzarella cheese
• French baguette slices, toasted	• Vinaigrette (below)
	• Chopped fresh basil

Spread the black olive spread over the toasted baguette slices. Top each with a slice of cheese. Drizzle with Vinaigrette and sprinkle with basil.

Note: *You may process two or three medium jars of niçoise olives or kalamata olives, drained, with a splash of olive oil in a food processor until puréed and use instead of the black olive spread.*

Vinaigrette

1/4	cup chopped shallots	1/2	teaspoon salt
1/2	cup white wine vinegar	•	Freshly ground pepper to taste
1	cup extra-virgin olive oil		

Whisk the shallots, vinegar, olive oil, salt and pepper in a bowl until blended.

Oscar Night Party Ideas

Jazz up your wonderful Oscar Night Party menu with these decorative touches to create just the right atmosphere:

Use a gold, black, and white color scheme for your table settings.

Add elegance by using crystal vases, candlesticks, and Champagne glasses in your tablescapes.

Play music from movie soundtrack CDs to enhance the mood.

Miniature Oscars can be used in your table decorations, as seating place cards, or as party favors.

Hand out Oscar ballots for your guests to use in voting.

Chutney Fingers

Makes 64

8	ounces Monterey Jack cheese, shredded	1	(11-ounce) jar spicy or mild Major Grey chutney
1	pound bacon, crisp-cooked and crumbled	•	Butter to taste
		16	slices Pepperidge Farm thin white bread

Mix the cheese, bacon and chutney in a bowl and set aside. Spread butter on one side of each bread slice and brown in a skillet. Spread the chutney mixture on the unbuttered side of each bread slice, pressing down lightly. Cut the bread into four fingers or triangles per slice and place on a baking sheet. Freeze until firm. Place in a freezer container and store in the freezer until ready to use. Thaw the bread at room temperature for 15 to 20 minutes. Place on a baking sheet and broil for 2 to 3 minutes or until brown.

It's-a-Wrap "Appeteasers"

Makes 2 dozen

8	ounces cream cheese, softened	8	ounces thinly sliced deli ham
2	tablespoons Dijon mustard	3/4	cup (3 ounces) shredded Swiss cheese
1	tablespoon honey	1	large tomato, seeded and chopped
6	(8-inch) whole wheat flour tortillas	1	green bell pepper, chopped
1 1/2	cups thinly sliced iceberg lettuce	6	slices bacon, crisp-cooked and crumbled

Mix the cream cheese, Dijon mustard and honey in a small bowl. Spread 2 tablespoons on each tortilla to 1/4 inch from the edge. Cover each with 1/4 cup lettuce and press down lightly. Top each with two ham slices and cover with 2 tablespoons Swiss cheese. Sprinkle each tortilla with equal amounts of the tomato, bell pepper and bacon. Roll up tightly to enclose the filling. Cut each into four sections with a serrated knife and secure with a wooden pick.

Chutney

Chutneys are relishes of fruits preserved with sugar, vinegar, and spices. Chutneys are sweet, tart, and complex, full of flavor and chunky in texture. Fruits and vegetables, sometimes in combination, that make good chutneys include tomato, peach, cherry, fig, date, eggplant, plum, blueberry, cranberry, mango, onion, apple, carrot, pear, and jalapeño chile. Try chutney with roasted meats or poultry, hot or cold, on a hamburger, in an omelet, or with cheese on a cracker. Chutneys can be that little extra that makes the difference in a recipe.

Chicken Wraps with Tomatoes and Goat Cheese

Serves 8

3	large plum tomatoes, sliced	2	boneless skinless chicken breasts
1	tablespoon olive oil		(about 12 ounces)
•	Salt and pepper to taste	1	tablespoon olive oil
3/4	cup (5.3 ounces) softened	4	(8-inch) flour tortillas
	goat cheese	1½	cups shredded romaine
2	tablespoons minced chervil		

Place the tomato slices in a single layer on a foil-lined baking sheet. Drizzle with 1 tablespoon olive oil and sprinkle with salt and pepper. Bake at 300 degrees for 30 minutes or until the tomato slices shrivel slightly.

Combine the cheese and chervil in a bowl and mix until smooth. Cook the chicken in 1 tablespoon olive oil in a medium nonstick skillet over medium-high heat for 8 to 10 minutes or until cooked through, turning once. Remove to a cutting board and cool for 5 minutes. Cut into very thin slices. Microwave each tortilla for 10 seconds to soften. Place on a clean work surface and spread each tortilla with the cheese mixture. Top each with equal amounts of the lettuce, tomatoes and chicken. Roll up tightly to enclose the filling. Wrap each in plastic wrap and chill in the refrigerator. To serve, remove the plastic wrap from each roll-up and cut into 1-inch pieces.

Spicy Chicken Roll-Ups

Serves about 8

1	pound sliced bacon	1	(16-ounce) bottle Italian salad
1	package chicken breast tenders		dressing
6	ounces pickled jalapeño chile slices	1	(5-ounce) bottle Pickapeppa Sauce

Cut the bacon slices into halves. Cut the chicken into halves lengthwise. Place one chicken half on one bacon half. Place one jalapeño chile on top of the chicken. Roll the bacon around the chicken and jalapeño chile and secure with a wooden pick. Repeat with the remaining bacon, chicken and jalapeño chiles. Place the roll-ups in a single layer in a shallow dish. Mix the salad dressing and Pickapeppa Sauce together in a bowl and pour over the roll-ups. Marinate in the refrigerator for 1 hour. Drain the roll-ups, discarding the marinade. Place on a grill rack and grill until the chicken is cooked through.

Cranberry Cocktail Meatballs

Makes 125 meatballs

MEATBALLS
2	pounds ground beef
1	cup cornflake crumbs
1/2	cup chopped fresh parsley
2	eggs
1/3	cup ketchup
1/8	teaspoon Tabasco sauce
3	tablespoons minced onion
2	tablespoons soy sauce
1/4	teaspoon garlic powder
1/4	teaspoon freshly ground pepper

CRANBERRY GLAZE
1	(16-ounce) can jellied cranberry sauce
1	(12-ounce) bottle chili sauce
1	tablespoon brown sugar
1	tablespoon lemon juice

To prepare the meatballs, combine the ground beef, cornflake crumbs, parsley, eggs, ketchup, Tabasco sauce, onion, soy sauce, garlic powder and pepper in a bowl and mix well. Shape into small balls about 3/4 inch in diameter and place in a baking pan.

To prepare the glaze, combine the cranberry sauce, chili sauce, brown sugar and lemon juice in a saucepan and mix well. Cook over medium heat until smooth, stirring constantly.

To assemble, pour the glaze over the meatballs. Bake at 300 degrees for 30 to 45 minutes or until the meatballs are cooked through. Keep warm in the oven, a chafing dish or a slow cooker. Serve with wooden picks for spearing.

Note: You may prepare the meatballs ahead of time and freeze. When ready to serve, add the glaze to the meatballs and bake.

Tequila and Jalapeño Shrimp

Serves 8

2	pounds shrimp, grilled or boiled	1/3	cup fresh lime juice
1 1/2	tablespoons top-quality tequila	1/2	teaspoon coarse salt
		1/8	teaspoon white pepper
2	tablespoons chopped seeded jalapeño chiles	2	teaspoons olive oil
		1	small can pear tomatoes
1	tablespoon chopped fresh cilantro	•	Handful each of chopped olives and chopped celery (optional)

Peel and devein the shrimp. Combine the tequila, jalapeño chiles, cilantro, lime juice, salt, white pepper, olive oil, undrained tomatoes, olives and celery in a large bowl and mix well. Stir in the shrimp. Marinate in the refrigerator for at least 2 hours before serving. Serve in the marinade in a bowl that is placed in ice to keep cool.

Note: *This modified recipe from Central Market is good to serve for buffets, showers, or parties.*

Italian Tomato Tart Delight

Makes 24 pieces

1	(10-ounce) can refrigerator pizza dough	1	to 3 teaspoons Roasted Garlic (at right)
8	ounces cream cheese, softened	4	or 5 Italian plum tomatoes, sliced 1/4 inch thick
1	package fresh basil, finely chopped	2	tablespoons olive oil
1/2	tablespoon dried thyme	•	Salt and pepper to taste

Unroll the pizza dough and press over the bottom of a lightly greased 10×13-inch baking sheet. Bake at 425 degrees for 12 to 14 minutes or until light brown. Remove from the oven and reduce the oven temperature to 350 degrees. Mix the cream cheese, basil, thyme and Roasted Garlic in a bowl until blended. Spread evenly over the crust. Layer with the tomatoes and drizzle with the olive oil. Sprinkle with salt. Bake for 8 minutes. Sprinkle with pepper and cut into twenty-four pieces. Serve warm or at room temperature.

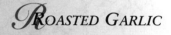

Roasted Garlic

Cut the top from one head of garlic. Place the garlic in foil and drizzle with olive oil. Wrap tightly in the foil. Bake at 350 degrees for 30 to 45 minutes or until tender. Remove from the oven to cool. Unwrap and squeeze each clove to release the garlic.

Mexican Clam Dip

Makes 2¹/₂ cups

12   ounces cream cheese, softened
³/₄ cup green chile salsa
1   (4-ounce) can diced green chiles
¹/₂ cup chopped fresh cilantro

3   (6-ounce) cans chopped clams, drained
•   Salt and pepper to taste

Beat the cream cheese in a large mixing bowl until smooth. Add the salsa, green chiles, cilantro and clams and mix well. Season to taste with salt and pepper. Remove to an ovenproof dish. Bake at 350 degrees for 35 minutes or until heated through and bubbly around the edges. Serve with corn chips or tortilla chips.

Note: *You may use mild, medium, or hot salsa to suit your taste. Tabasco sauce may also be added. Can be prepared one day in advance. Chill, covered, in the refrigerator.*

Crab Dip

Serves 6 to 8

12   ounces cream cheese, softened
2   tablespoons Worcestershire sauce
1   teaspoon lemon juice
2   tablespoons mayonnaise

1   cup chili sauce
8   to 16 ounces fresh crab meat, cooked, shells removed and flaked
¹/₄ cup chopped fresh parsley

Combine the cream cheese, Worcestershire sauce, lemon juice and mayonnaise in a bowl and mix well. Spread in a pie plate or shallow baking dish. Spread the chili sauce in a thin layer over the cream cheese mixture. Top with the crab meat and sprinkle with the parsley. Serve with crackers, bagel chips or thin pita bread.

Note: *You may use imitation crab meat.*

Crab Canoe

Makes 2 loaves

2	(6-ounce) cans crab meat, or 12 ounces fresh crab meat	12	ounces sharp Cheddar cheese, shredded
1	onion, finely chopped	2	loaves French bread
1	cup mayonnaise		

Drain the crab meat, reserving the liquid from one of the cans. Mix the crab meat, reserved liquid, onion, mayonnaise and cheese in a bowl. Chill, covered, in the refrigerator for 30 minutes.

Remove the center of each loaf to form the shape of a canoe, reserving the centers. Pull the reserved bread centers into bite-size pieces and place on a baking sheet. Bake at 350 degrees until toasted and brown. Remove from the oven and maintain the oven temperature.

Spoon the crab meat mixture into the hollowed out bread loaves and place on a baking sheet. Bake for 30 minutes or until heated through. Serve with the toasted bread centers.

Tejas Shrimp and Crab Salsa

Serves 10 to 12, or makes 6 cups

1	cup chopped avocado	1/2	to 3/4 cup Pico de Gallo (at right)
1	tablespoon lime juice		
2	cups cooked shrimp, chopped	1	(12-ounce) bottle cocktail sauce
2	cups lump crab meat		

Place the avocado in a bowl and sprinkle with the lime juice. Add the shrimp and crab meat and mix well. Stir in the Pico de Gallo and cocktail sauce. Serve in small, individual bowls with corn chips.

PICO DE GALLO

Chop 1 tomato, 1/2 onion and 1 jalapeño chile separately and place in a bowl. Add 1/2 cup cilantro, chopped, and 1 tablespoon lime juice and mix well.

Ceviche

Serves 8 to 10

12	ounces red snapper, cut into 1-inch pieces	2	tablespoons finely chopped jalapeño chiles
8	to 16 ounces small shrimp	1	tablespoon jalapeño chile juice
•	Juice of 6 limes		
3/4	cup finely chopped white onion	3/4	cup tomato juice
2	serrano chiles, finely chopped	2	tablespoons olive oil
2	tomatoes, finely chopped	2	tablespoons Worcestershire sauce
1/2	cup cilantro, finely chopped	2	tablespoons dried oregano
1	tablespoon chopped fresh garlic	•	Salt to taste
		1	avocado, chopped

Place the fish and shrimp in a glass container and cover with lime juice. Marinate in the refrigerator for 4 to 12 hours; drain.

Combine the onion, serrano chiles, tomatoes, cilantro, garlic, jalapeño chiles and jalapeño chile juice in a bowl and mix well. Stir in the tomato juice, olive oil, Worcestershire sauce, oregano and salt. Pour over the fish and shrimp mixture. Marinate in the refrigerator for 2 days. Stir in the avocado just before serving. Serve with chips.

Note: *You may store in the refrigerator for up to five days.*

Texas Shrimp Dip

Serves 10 to 12, or makes 3 cups

8 ounces cream cheese, softened	1 garlic clove, finely chopped or pressed
1/2 to 1 (10-ounce) can tomatoes with green chiles, drained	1 teaspoon Tabasco sauce (optional)
1/4 cup chopped cilantro	1 cup chopped boiled shrimp

Beat the cream cheese and 1/2 can tomatoes with green chiles in a mixing bowl until smooth. Add the cilantro and garlic and mix well. Add the remaining tomatoes with green chiles and Tabasco sauce for additional heat, if desired. Fold in the shrimp. Chill until ready to serve. Serve with corn chips.

Layered Shrimp Dip

Serves 8 to 10

CHILI SAUCE
1 cup ketchup
1 tablespoon horseradish
2 teaspoons lemon juice
1 teaspoon Worcestershire sauce
• Dash of Tabasco sauce

DIP
8 ounces cream cheese, softened
1 pound boiled shrimp, peeled and chopped
1 cup chopped green bell pepper
5 to 6 green onions, chopped
1 (4-ounce) can chopped olives, drained
8 to 16 ounces mozzarella cheese, shredded

To prepare the chili sauce, mix the ketchup, horseradish, lemon juice, Worcestershire sauce and Tabasco sauce in a bowl.

To prepare the dip, spread the cream cheese over the bottom of a 9- or 10-inch shallow serving dish. Layer the chili sauce, shrimp, bell pepper, green onions, olives and cheese in the order listed over the cream cheese layer. Serve with Doritos or your favorite chips.

Note: You may alternatively use bottled chili sauce and two cans of small shrimp.

Appetizer Pie

Serves 6 to 8

8 ounces cream cheese, softened
2 tablespoons milk
1/2 cup sour cream
1 package corned beef, chopped
2 tablespoons chopped green onions
2 tablespoons chopped green bell pepper
• Dash of pepper
• Chopped pecans

Beat the cream cheese, milk and sour cream in a mixing bowl until smooth. Stir in the corned beef, green onions, bell pepper and pepper. Spread in a microwave-safe pie plate or shallow serving dish. Sprinkle with pecans. Microwave on Low for 1 to 2 minutes or until warm. Garnish with green onion tops or chives. Serve with crackers.

Olé Chevrolet

Serves 15 to 20

2 pounds ground beef
8 ounces Velveeta cheese, cut into small cubes
8 ounces sharp Cheddar cheese, shredded
10 ounces mozzarella cheese, shredded
2 (14-ounce) cans tomatoes, drained
1 onion, chopped
2 (4-ounce) cans green chiles, drained and chopped
• Garlic powder to taste
• Tabasco sauce to taste

Brown the ground beef in a skillet, stirring until crumbly; drain. Combine the Velveeta cheese, Cheddar cheese and mozzarella cheese in a bowl and mix well. Layer one-third of the cheese mixture in a 3 1/2-quart baking dish. Layer one-half of the ground beef, tomatoes, onion and green chiles over the cheese layer. Sprinkle with garlic powder and Tabasco sauce. Continue to layer with one-half of the remaining cheese mixture, remaining ground beef, tomatoes, onion and green chiles. Sprinkle the top with the remaining cheese mixture. Bake at 350 degrees for 30 minutes. Serve hot with tortilla chips or cocktail crackers.

Note: *You may prepare this recipe one day ahead and store in the refrigerator. This recipe was named by a General Motors executive, who worked in the Chevrolet division for thirty years.*

Cranberry Jalapeño Relish

Makes about 2¹/₂ cups

1 cup dried cranberries	1 teaspoon minced garlic
¹/₂ cup orange juice	1 jalapeño chile, seeded and
¹/₄ cup fresh lime juice	finely chopped
¹/₂ cup chopped red onion	¹/₂ teaspoon cumin
¹/₂ cup chopped cilantro	¹/₂ teaspoon salt

Combine the cranberries, orange juice, lime juice, onion, cilantro, garlic, jalapeño chile, cumin and salt in a bowl and stir to mix well. Chill, covered, for 2 hours before serving. Serve over cream cheese with bagel chips or crackers.

Cheesy Artichoke Dip

Serves 6 to 8

2 (13-ounce) cans artichoke hearts	1 cup mayonnaise
1¹/₂ cups (6 ounces) shredded	2 garlic cloves
Parmesan cheese	¹/₈ teaspoon garlic salt
1 cup (4 ounces) shredded Monterey	¹/₈ teaspoon crushed pepper
Jack cheese	

Drain the artichoke hearts and squeeze out any excess liquid. Finely chop the artichoke hearts and place in a bowl. Add the Parmesan cheese, Monterey Jack cheese, mayonnaise, garlic, garlic salt and pepper and mix well. Spoon into a glass baking dish. Bake at 350 degrees for 30 minutes. Serve with Wheat Thins.

Artichoke Prosciutto Gratin

Serves 12

2 (14-ounce) cans artichoke hearts, drained and cut into quarters
12 thin slices prosciutto di Parma, cut into halves crosswise
1 cup heavy cream
1/2 cup crumbled Gorgonzola cheese
1/3 cup toasted pine nuts
1/3 cup grated Parmigiano cheese
2 teaspoons very thinly sliced fresh sage

Pat the artichoke quarters dry with paper towels. Wrap each artichoke quarter in a half slice of prosciutto and place in a single layer in a 9×13-inch glass baking dish. Pour the cream over the artichokes and sprinkle with Gorgonzola cheese, pine nuts, Parmigiano cheese and sage. Bake at 350 degrees for 25 minutes or until bubbly and the sauce thickens. Serve with warm, crusty ciabatta bread to soak up the sauce.

Rodeo Chili Cheese Dip

Serves 10 to 12

8 ounces cream cheese, softened
1 (8-ounce) can chili without beans
1 (4-ounce) can chopped green chiles, drained
3 tablespoons picante sauce
1/2 cup chopped pickled jalapeño chiles
1 1/2 cups (6 ounces) shredded Cheddar cheese

Layer the cream cheese, chili, green chiles, picante sauce, jalapeño chiles and Cheddar cheese in the order listed in a microwave-safe serving dish. Microwave on High until the cheese melts. Serve with tortilla chips.

Galveston Beach House Dip

Serves 8 to 10

8	ounces cream cheese, softened	1	(10-ounce) can tomatoes with green chiles, drained
1	(15-ounce) can black beans, drained	1	cup (4 ounces) shredded sharp Cheddar cheese

Spread the cream cheese in an 8- or 9-inch pie plate. Layer the black beans, tomatoes with green chiles and Cheddar cheese over the cream cheese layer. Bake at 350 degrees for 20 minutes. Serve with blue corn chips or yellow corn chips.

Mexican Corn Dip

Serves 10 to 12

2	(11-ounce) cans Mexicorn	8	to 10 ounces Cheddar cheese, shredded
1	(4-ounce) can chopped green chiles	1	jalapeño chile, chopped
1	(8-ounce) jar mayonnaise	•	Tony Chachere's Creole seasoning to taste
1	cup sour cream		

Combine the Mexicorn, green chiles, mayonnaise, sour cream, cheese, jalapeño chiles and Creole seasoning in a bowl and mix well. Chill, covered, for at least 8 hours before serving.

Note: *You may add an additional can of Mexicorn or additional Cheddar cheese, if desired.*

Gone in a Flash!

Combine 1 cup (4 ounces) shredded Cheddar cheese, 1 cup chopped pecans, 1/2 cup chopped green onions and 4 ounces softened cream cheese in a bowl and mix well. Shape into a small mold or a flattened ball. Chill, covered, for at least 2 hours. To serve, place on a serving plate and spoon 1/2 cup hot raspberry chipolte sauce over the top. Serve with crackers.

Swiss Cheese Dip

Serves 6

2	cups (8 ounces) shredded Swiss cheese	6	green onions, chopped
		1/4	to 1/2 cup mayonnaise

Mix the cheese and green onions in a bowl. Stir in enough of the mayonnaise to bind together. Chill, covered, in the refrigerator before serving, if desired. Serve with garlic bagel chips.

Onion Soufflé

Serves 6 to 8

2	cups chopped onions	2	cups (8 ounces) grated Parmesan cheese
8	ounces cream cheese, softened		
1/2	cup mayonnaise		

Combine the onions, cream cheese, mayonnaise and Parmesan cheese in a bowl and mix well. Spoon into a shallow pie plate and bake at 425 degrees for 20 minutes. Serve with corn chips.

Cheesy Onion Dip

Serves 6 to 8

2	cups (8 ounces) shredded extra-sharp Cheddar cheese	8	ounces cream cheese, softened
1	cup mayonnaise	3/4	cup finely chopped purple onion

Combine the Cheddar cheese, mayonnaise, cream cheese and onion in a bowl and mix well. Spread in a shallow baking dish and bake at 350 degrees for 20 to 25 minutes or until melted. Serve with specialty crackers such as Wheat Thins.

Goat Cheese Spread

Serves 8 to 10

3	or 4 Roma tomatoes, chopped	1	garlic clove, finely chopped
1	tablespoon chopped green onions	8	ounces goat cheese
1	tablespoon olive oil	2	tablespoons chopped fresh dill weed
2	tablespoons chopped cilantro		

Combine the tomatoes, green onions, olive oil, cilantro and garlic in a bowl and mix well. Chill, covered, in the refrigerator for 8 hours. Remove from the refrigerator and bring to room temperature.

Pat the goat cheese in an even layer in a microwave-safe quiche dish and sprinkle with the dill weed. Microwave on Low until warm. Spread the tomato mixture over the top. Serve with chips.

Maple-Flavored Pecans

Makes 4 cups

2	cups sugar	1	teaspoon maple flavoring
1/2	cup water	4	cups pecan halves (1 pound)
2	teaspoons ground cinnamon		

Bring the sugar and water to a boil in a saucepan. Boil for 4 to 5 minutes. Add the cinnamon and maple flavoring. Add the pecans and stir to coat well. Pour onto a baking sheet and separate the pecan halves. Let stand until cool. Store in a sealable plastic bag.

Note: *The recipe for this delicious snack is from The Nut House in Boerne, Texas. It is also good served over ice cream.*

Cosmopolitans

Serves 4

1	cup vodka	1/4	cup fresh lime juice
1/2	cup Triple Sec	•	Ice
1/2	cup cranberry juice cocktail		

Pour the vodka, Triple Sec, cranberry juice cocktail and lime juice into a pitcher. Pour half the mixture into a cocktail shaker and add ice. Shake well and pour through a strainer into martini glasses. Repeat with the remaining mixture.

CHILLING BEVERAGES

For an outdoor party, use a Chinese blue and white urn for a wine cooler. If the event is more casual, chill the drinks in a garden urn lined with a galvanized tub.

Big Easy Frozen Daiquiris

Serves 10 to 12

1	(46-ounce) can pineapple juice	2	tablespoons lemon juice
1/2	(46-ounce) can orange juice	1 1/2	cups light rum
2	cans of lemon-lime soda	2 1/2	cups to 3 cups cherry juice

Blend the pineapple juice, orange juice, lemon-lime soda, lemon juice and rum in a large freezer container. Freeze until slushy. Spoon into daiquiri glasses and add 2 ounces (1/4 cup) cherry juice to each glass.

Metropolitans

Serves 1 to 2

2	ounces citrus-flavored vodka
1/2	to 1 ounce Grand Marnier
1	ounce Rose's lime juice
4	to 6 ounces cranberry juice cocktail

Combine the vodka, Grand Marnier, lime juice and cranberry juice cocktail in a cocktail shaker. Add ice and shake to blend well. Pour into martini glasses and garnish each glass with a lemon or lime slice.

Champagne Punch

Serves 50

FRUIT ICE RING
- Orange juice
- Assorted fruit of choice

PUNCH
1   (12-ounce) can frozen lemonade concentrate, thawed

1   (12-ounce) can frozen orange juice concentrate, thawed
1   (46-ounce) can orange juice, chilled
1   (46-ounce) can pineapple juice, chilled
1   fifth Champagne, chilled

To *prepare the ice ring,* fill a ring mold with orange juice and fruit. Freeze for 8 to 10 hours or until firm. (You may make the ice ring the day before and freeze in layers so the fruit will not float to the top.)

To prepare the punch, combine the lemonade concentrate, orange juice concentrate, orange juice and pineapple juice in a punch bowl and stir to blend well. Add the Champagne and mix well. Unmold the ring mold by placing in a sink filled with hot water. When the ice ring is loosened enough to slide out, float in the punch.

Note: *You may substitute one-quart ginger ale for the Champagne to make a nonalcoholic punch.*

Hostess Tip

It is a nice touch to serve a signature drink when your guests arrive at the party. This is a great ice breaker and gets the conversation started and people acquainted.

Open House Punch

Serves 24

2 1/2 cups Southern Comfort
6 ounces fresh lemon juice
1 (6-ounce) can frozen orange juice concentrate, thawed

2 (6-ounce) cans frozen lemonade concentrate, thawed
• Several drops of red food coloring (optional)
1 liter lemon-lime soda

Combine the Southern Comfort, lemon juice, orange juice concentrate, lemonade concentrate and food coloring in a punch bowl and mix well. Add the soda slowly just before serving. Garnish with thin slices of oranges and lemons.

Pineapple Punch

Makes 6 quarts

64 ounces (2 quarts) pineapple juice
• Juice of 4 lemons
• Juice of 4 limes
• Juice of 4 oranges

1 cup sugar
2 cups (1 pint) sparkling water
32 ounces (1 quart) ginger ale
• Large block of ice

Combine the pineapple juice, lemon juice, lime juice, orange juice and sugar in a large bowl and mix well. Chill for 2 hours to allow the flavors to blend. Add the sparkling water and ginger ale. Pour over a large block of ice in a punch bowl. Garnish with fresh fruit and sprigs of fresh mint.

Note: *This punch tends to be sweet.*

Really Red Punch

Serves 60

1	(46-ounce) can pineapple juice	4	cups (1 quart) water
2	(3-ounce) packages cherry gelatin or strawberry gelatin	1	(20-ounce) can crushed pineapple
1	cup sugar	1	pint Hawaiian Punch concentrate
2	envelopes cherry drink mix or strawberry drink mix	4	quarts lemon-lime soda or ginger ale

Bring the pineapple juice nearly to a boil in a large saucepan; do not boil. Remove from the heat. Add the gelatin and stir until dissolved. Dissolve the sugar and drink mix in the water in a large pitcher. Stir in the pineapple and Hawaiian Punch concentrate. Add the pineapple juice mixture and stir to mix well. Pour into two freezer containers, dividing equally. Freeze until firm. Remove from the freezer 1 hour before serving.

To serve, mix one container of the punch with 2 quarts of the lemon-lime soda in a punch bowl. Replenish as needed by adding the remaining punch and lemon-lime soda.

Strawberry Slush

Serves 25 to 30

2	cups sugar	2	(10-ounce) containers frozen strawberries with juice, thawed
6	cups boiling water	1	(64-ounce) bottle lemon-lime soda or ginger ale
2 1/2	cups orange juice		
1/2	cup lemon juice		
4	cups unsweetened pineapple juice		

Dissolve the sugar in the boiling water in a large stockpot. Remove from the heat. Stir in the orange juice, lemon juice and pineapple juice. Add the strawberries and mix well. Pour into small plastic containers and freeze until firm. Remove from the freezer 1 hour before serving and place in a punch bowl. Add the lemon-lime soda and stir until slushy.

Stuart's Award-Winning Planter's Punch

Makes 1 gallon

1	quart orange juice	2	(1-liter) bottles white rum
1	quart pineapple juice	2	(1-liter) bottles dark rum
8	ounces grenadine		

Combine the orange juice, pineapple juice, grenadine, white rum and dark rum in a large pitcher and mix well. Serve over ice.

List for Stocking a Bar for a Cocktail Party

Serves 50

2	liters of vodka
1	small bottle of vermouth
1	liter each of rum, scotch, bourbon, tequila, Triple Sec and gin
1	bottle of Rose's lime juice
1	bottle of Worcestershire sauce
1	bottle of Tabasco sauce
2	gallons each of orange juice and cranberry juice
1	gallon each of grapefruit juice and tomato juice
10	bottles each of red and white wine
6	liters each of tonic water, seltzer, cola, diet cola, and club soda
2	cases of beer

GARNISHES
- Lemon and lime wedges, cherries, olives, cocktail onions, and celery sticks
- 100 pounds of ice (2 pounds per guest)

Note: *A 750-milliliter bottle of wine pours five glasses per bottle.*

TEXARITA MARGARITA

Place a double shot of tequila, a double shot of light beer (optional), 2 double shots of Texarita mix, a splash of Cointreau, the juice of 2 oranges, the juice of 1 lime and a pinch of salt in a shaker with ice. Shake well and serve over ice. For a party, combine 1 fifth of tequila, 1 quart of Texarita mix, juice of 5 oranges, 1 cup water and 1 teaspoon of salt in a pitcher with ice and stir to mix well. Serve over ice.

Brunch and Breads

Ballunar Liftoff Festival

The Ballunar Liftoff Festival, Inc., celebrated its fourteenth anniversary in 2006 on the grounds of the Johnson Space Center. This colorful celebration attracts thirty thousand spectators and is a tribute to human flight—from these simple, serene balloons to the high-tech, complicated world of space flight. Included in the one hundred balloons from all over the United States are these classic and beautifully colored shapes that float over our community. The Festival concludes with an evening Ballunar Glow, which is a wonderful sight to watch as these silent balloons glide above the Clear Lake area illuminated against the night sky.

Ballunar Breakfast

MIMOSA PUNCH, PAGE 67

RED GRAPE SALAD, PAGE 105

FESTIVE CRANBERRY SCONES, PAGE 73

MILLION-DOLLAR BANANA NUT BREAD, PAGE 70

PEAR BREAD, PAGE 72

LEEK AND GOAT CHEESE QUICHE, PAGE 56

Crepes Marquis

Serves 4

10	slices bacon	8	Crepes (below)
1/2	cup chopped onion	1	(8-ounce) can tomato sauce
1/2	cup chopped bell pepper	1/3	cup sour cream
3/4	cup sliced mushrooms		
2	cups (8 ounces) shredded Cheddar cheese		

Cook the bacon in a skillet until crisp. Drain the bacon, reserving 2 tablespoons of the drippings in the skillet. Crumble the bacon into small pieces. Sauté the onion and bell pepper in the reserved drippings until soft. Add the mushrooms and sauté for 2 to 3 minutes or until tender. Add the bacon and two-thirds of the cheese and mix well. Fill each crepe with the filling and roll up. Place in a baking dish. Blend the tomato sauce and sour cream in a bowl. Pour over the crepes and sprinkle with the remaining cheese. Bake at 350 degrees for 20 to 30 minutes or until bubbly.

Crepes

1 1/4	cups all-purpose flour	2	tablespoons butter, melted
3	eggs, beaten	1/4	teaspoon salt
1 1/2	cups milk		

Combine the flour, eggs, milk, butter and salt in a bowl and mix until smooth. Chill, covered, for 1 hour. Pour a thin layer of batter at a time in a hot nonstick skillet, tilting the pan to evenly coat the bottom. Cook until bubbles appear on the surface and the bottom is golden brown. Turn and cook until golden brown.

Note: *The crepes may be frozen.*

Bunch for Brunch

Serves 8 to 10

1/4	cup (1/2 stick) butter or margarine	1/4	teaspoon pepper
1/4	cup all-purpose flour	3	cups (12 ounces) shredded Cheddar cheese
1	cup cream	18	hard-cooked eggs
1	cup milk	1	pound sliced bacon, crisp-cooked and crumbled
1/4	teaspoon thyme	1/4	cup parsley, chopped
1/4	teaspoon marjoram	1	cup seasoned bread crumbs, buttered
1/4	teaspoon basil		
1/4	teaspoon salt		

Melt the butter in a saucepan. Add the flour and mix well. Stir in the cream and milk. Add the thyme, marjoram, basil, salt and pepper and mix well. Bring to a boil and cook until thickened, stirring constantly. Remove from the heat and stir in the cheese.

Cut the eggs with an egg slicer into thin slices. Layer the eggs, bacon, parsley and cheese sauce one-third at a time in a 9×13-inch glass baking dish. Sprinkle the top with the bread crumbs. Bake, uncovered, at 350 degrees for 30 minutes or until bubbly.

Note: *The eggs and bacon can be prepared a day ahead. The cheese sauce should be made the day of serving.*

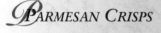

Parmesan Crisps

Drop 1/2 cup (2 ounces) grated Parmesan cheese by heaping tablespoonfuls 1/2 inch apart onto a silicone or parchment-lined baking sheet, lightly patting down the cheese. Bake at 400 degrees for 3 to 5 minutes or until golden brown and crisp. Let stand until cool.

South-of-the-Border Casserole

Serves 10

1 teaspoon unsalted butter, softened	1/2 teaspoon freshly ground pepper
11/2 pounds hot bulk pork sausage	1/2 cup chopped green onion tops
1 cup chopped yellow onion	2 (4-ounce) cans chopped green chiles, drained
1/2 cup chopped red bell pepper	1/4 cup chopped fresh cilantro
4 teaspoons minced garlic	11/2 cups (6 ounces) shredded Pepper Jack cheese
4 teaspoons chili powder	
10 eggs	11/2 cups (6 ounces) shredded medium Cheddar cheese
3 cups half-and-half	
• Tabasco sauce to taste	5 corn tortillas, cut into quarters
1/2 teaspoon salt	

Spread the butter in a 9×13-inch glass baking dish to coat. Brown the sausage in a large skillet over medium-high heat, stirring until crumbly. Add the yellow onion and bell pepper and sauté for 4 minutes. Add the garlic and chili powder and sauté for 1 minute. Remove from the heat.

Whisk the eggs, half-and-half, Tabasco sauce, salt and pepper in a large bowl until smooth. Combine the green onion tops, green chiles, cilantro, Pepper Jack cheese and Cheddar cheese in a bowl and toss to mix. Layer the sausage mixture, tortilla quarters and the cheese mixture one-third at a time in the prepared dish, ending with the cheese mixture. Pour the egg mixture over the layers. Chill, covered, in the refrigerator for 6 to 10 hours. Remove from the refrigerator and let stand at room temperature for 1 hour before baking. Bake at 350 degrees for 1 hour and 10 minutes to 1 hour and 15 minutes or until bubbly and golden brown. Remove from the oven and let stand for 10 minutes before serving. Serve with sour cream and picante sauce.

Spinach Frittata

Serves 4

4	eggs	2	tablespoons chopped fresh parsley
2	tablespoons milk	1/4	cup (1 ounce) shredded
1/4	cup thawed chopped frozen spinach		Swiss cheese
1/4	cup chopped Roma tomatoes	2	tablespoons chopped green onions
2	ounces sliced fresh mushrooms	1/2	teaspoon freshly ground pepper
4	slices crisp-cooked bacon, crumbled	1/4	teaspoon salt
5	fresh basil leaves, sliced	1/4	teaspoon minced fresh garlic

Beat the eggs in a large bowl. Add the milk, spinach, tomatoes, mushrooms, bacon, basil, parsley, cheese, green onions, pepper, salt and garlic and mix gently. Pour into a hot greased ovenproof skillet. Cook over medium-low heat until the eggs are almost set. Broil until brown on top and the eggs are set. Cut into wedges to serve.

Note: *You may use fresh spinach and/or substitute any cheese for the Swiss cheese. If you do not have an ovenproof skillet, cook the eggs on the stove top until set.*

Leek and Goat Cheese Quiche

Serves 6 to 8

2	leeks	2	egg yolks
2	tablespoons unsalted butter	3/4	cup milk
4	ounces goat cheese, crumbled	3/4	cup heavy cream
1	partially baked (10-inch) deep-dish	1/2	teaspoon salt
	pie shell	1/2	teaspoon ground white pepper
2	eggs	•	Pinch of grated nutmeg

Rinse the leeks. Trim the green portion from the leeks and discard. Cut the white part of the leeks into 1/2-inch pieces. (You should have about 2 cups.) Sauté the leeks in the butter in a skillet over medium heat for 5 to 7 minutes or until soft. Spread the leeks and goat cheese over the bottom of the pie shell. Whisk the eggs, egg yolks, milk, heavy cream, salt, white pepper and nutmeg in a medium bowl until blended. Pour over the prepared layer. Bake at 375 degrees for 35 to 40 minutes or until semi-firm in the center. Remove to a wire rack to cool.

Note: *The quiche cuts better if warm or at room temperature. Bake the night before and chill in the refrigerator. Heat the slices in the morning for breakfast.*

Cool Shrimp Quiche

Serves 6 to 8

2	tablespoons minced green onions	3	eggs
3	tablespoons butter	1	cup heavy whipping cream
4	ounces cooked fresh shrimp, peeled and chopped	1	tablespoon tomato paste
•	Salt and pepper to taste	1	partially baked (9-inch) pie shell
2	tablespoons white wine or vermouth	1/4	cup (2 ounces) shredded Swiss cheese

Sauté the green onions in the butter in a skillet until soft. Add the shrimp, salt and pepper and sauté for 3 minutes. Stir in the wine and bring to a boil. Remove from the heat.

Beat the eggs, cream and tomato paste in a mixing bowl until smooth. Season with salt and pepper and stir in the shrimp mixture. Pour into the pie shell and sprinkle with the cheese. Bake at 375 degrees for 30 minutes or until puffed. Remove to a wire rack to cool. Serve at room temperature.

Note: *This recipe may be frozen.*

Vegetable Strata

Serves 8

3	or 4 slices bread, cut into cubes	1/2	cup chopped onion
6	eggs	1	cup fresh baby spinach
2	cups milk	1/4	cup chopped green onions with tops
1	teaspoon salt		
1	teaspoon dry mustard	1	cup (4 ounces) shredded Cheddar cheese
1/2	cup chopped bell pepper		

Layer the bread cubes in a greased 9×13-inch glass baking dish. Beat the eggs, milk, salt and dry mustard together in a bowl. Microwave the bell pepper and onion in a microwave-safe dish on High for 2 to 3 minutes or until softened. Layer the cooked vegetables, spinach and green onions over the bread and sprinkle with the cheese. Pour the egg mixture over the prepared layers. Bake at 350 degrees for 45 minutes.

Note: *You may assemble this recipe the night before.*

Tomato, Basil and Cheese Tart

Serves 6

PÂTE BRISÉE

4 ounces bacon, crisp-cooked and crumbled

1 1/4 cups all-purpose flour

1/4 teaspoon salt

6 tablespoons cold unsalted butter, cut into very small pieces

2 tablespoons cold shortening

3 tablespoons ice cold water

TART

1 cup packed fresh basil leaves

1/2 cup plus 2 tablespoons whole-milk ricotta cheese

2 eggs, lightly beaten

1 cup (4 ounces) coarsely shredded mozzarella cheese

1/2 cup (2 ounces) freshly grated Parmesan cheese

1 teaspoon salt

• Pepper to taste

3 large ripe tomatoes, horizontally sliced 1/3 inch thick

• Olive oil for brushing

To *prepare the pâte brisée,* mix the bacon, flour and salt in a bowl. Cut in the butter and shortening until the mixture resembles cornmeal. Add the ice water and toss until incorporated. Shape the dough into a ball. Knead the dough lightly with the heel of your hand for a few seconds to distribute the shortening evenly and reshape into a ball. Flatten the ball into a disc and wrap in waxed paper. Chill in the refrigerator for 1 hour.

Roll the pastry dough into a circle 1/8 inch thick. Fit into a 9-inch tart pan with a removable fluted rim. Prick the shell lightly with a fork and chill for 30 minutes. Line the shell with foil and fill with uncooked rice or dried beans. Bake at 425 degrees in the lower third of the oven for 15 minutes. Remove the foil with the rice or beans carefully. Bake for 3 to 5 minutes longer or until pale golden brown. Cool in the pan on a wire rack. (You may prepare ahead up to this point.)

To prepare the tart, purée the basil leaves and ricotta cheese in a food processor or blender. Add the eggs and process until combined. Add the mozzarella cheese, Parmesan cheese, salt and pepper and process just until combined. Pat the tomatoes dry with a paper towel. Line the bottom of the pastry crust with the tomato end pieces. Spoon the cheese mixture over the tomatoes and spread evenly. Arrange the remaining tomato slices in a single layer over the cheese mixture, overlapping slightly. Brush the tomatoes with olive oil. Bake at 350 degrees for 40 to 50 minutes or until the cheese mixture is set. Remove to a wire rack and let stand for 10 minutes. Garnish with three sprigs of fresh basil. Serve hot or at room temperature.

Chilled Chicken Spaghetti

Serves 8

SPICY MAYONNAISE DRESSING

1/4	cup olive oil
1/4	cup white wine
1	tablespoon Dijon mustard
1/2	cup chopped green onions with tops
1/2	cup chopped celery
3	pimentos, chopped
1/2	cup mayonnaise
1	teaspoon Tabasco sauce
1	teaspoon salt
1/2	teaspoon black pepper
1/4	teaspoon paprika

CHICKEN SPAGHETTI

4	chicken breasts
1	onion, cut into quarters
2	ribs celery
1	teaspoon salt
6	ounces spaghetti or fettuccini
8	ounces mushrooms, sliced
1	tablespoon olive oil
1	tablespoon lemon juice
•	Paprika to taste

To prepare the dressing, combine the olive oil, wine, Dijon mustard, green onions, celery, pimentos, mayonnaise, Tabasco sauce, salt, black pepper and 1/4 teaspoon paprika in a bowl and mix well. Chill until ready to use.

To prepare the spaghetti, cook the chicken with the onion, celery and salt in water to cover in a saucepan for 45 minutes or until the chicken is cooked through. Drain the chicken, discarding the vegetables. Chop or shred the chicken, discarding the skin and bones. Chill the chicken in the refrigerator. Cook the spaghetti in a saucepan using the package directions until al dente; drain. Sauté the mushrooms in the olive oil in a skillet until soft and sprinkle with the lemon juice. Combine the chicken, spaghetti and sautéed mushrooms in a large bowl and toss to mix. Add the dressing to taste and toss to coat. Sprinkle with paprika. Chill, covered, in the refrigerator for 6 hours or longer before serving. Add the remaining dressing before serving, if needed. Serve with warm bread and fruit.

Sausage Bread

Serves 8

1	(13-ounce) package refrigerator pizza dough	•	Dash of cayenne pepper
1	pound regular or spicy bulk pork sausage	•	Dash of Worcestershire sauce
•	Dash of Italian herbs	2	tablespoons olive oil
1	tablespoon minced garlic	2	cups (8 ounces) shredded Cheddar and Monterey Jack cheese
		•	Egg whites (optional)

Unroll the dough and spread evenly on a baking sheet sprayed with nonstick cooking spray. Brown the sausage with the Italian herbs, garlic, cayenne pepper and Worcestershire sauce in the olive oil in a skillet, stirring until the sausage is crumbly; drain well. Spread evenly on the dough almost to the edges. Sprinkle evenly with the cheese. Roll up the dough lengthwise to enclose the filling and form into a "U" shape, sealing the edges. Brush with egg whites. Bake at 350 degrees for 20 minutes or until evenly brown. Let stand for about 10 minutes before cutting into slices.

Note: *You may substitute pepperoni, ham or bacon for the sausage. The bread can be made ahead of time and stored in a sealable plastic bag in the refrigerator until ready to serve. Microwave before serving.*

Sausage and Grits Casserole with a Kick

Serves 8

1	pound hot bulk pork sausage, turkey sausage or spicy pork	1/4	cup (1/2 stick) butter, melted
1	teaspoon Tabasco sauce	1	cup (4 ounces) shredded extra-sharp Cheddar cheese
1	garlic clove, minced	3	eggs, well beaten
1/2	teaspoon salt	1	(8-ounce) can mild green chiles, drained, seeded and chopped
1/4	teaspoon crushed red pepper		
1	cup uncooked quick-cooking grits		

Brown the sausage in a skillet, stirring until crumbly; drain. Pat the sausage dry with paper towels and place in a large bowl. Add the Tabasco sauce, garlic, salt and red pepper and mix well. Cook the grits using the package directions. Add to the sausage mixture and mix well. Add the butter, cheese, eggs and green chiles and mix well. Pour into a well buttered 9×13-inch baking dish. Bake, uncovered, at 350 degrees for 1 hour. Serve with fresh fruit and biscuits.

Shrimp and Cheese Grits

Serves 4

3 slices bacon	1/2 cup chopped green onions
1 pound medium shrimp, peeled and deveined	2 garlic cloves, minced
1/4 teaspoon pepper	1/2 cup low-sodium fat-free chicken broth
1/8 teaspoon salt	2 tablespoons fresh lemon juice
1/4 cup all-purpose flour	• Cheese Grits (below)
1 cup sliced mushrooms	

Cook the bacon in a large nonstick skillet until crisp. Remove the bacon to paper towels to drain. Crumble the bacon. Drain the skillet, reserving 1 tablespoon of the drippings in the skillet.

Sprinkle the shrimp with pepper and salt. Dredge the shrimp in the flour. Sauté the mushrooms in the reserved drippings for 5 minutes or until tender. Add the green onions and sauté for 2 minutes. Add the shrimp and garlic and sauté for 2 minutes or until the shrimp are light brown. Stir in the broth and lemon juice. Cook for 2 minutes, stirring to deglaze and loosen the brown bits from the bottom of the skillet. Spoon the shrimp over the hot cheese grits and top with the crumbled bacon. Serve with lemon wedges.

Cheese Grits

2 cups water	1/4 cup (1 ounce) grated Parmesan cheese
1 (14-ounce) can chicken broth	2 tablespoons butter
3/4 cup half-and-half	1/2 teaspoon hot red pepper sauce
3/4 teaspoon salt	1/4 teaspoon white pepper
1 cup uncooked quick-cooking grits	
3/4 cup (3 ounces) shredded Cheddar cheese	

Bring the water, chicken broth, half-and-half and salt to a boil in a medium saucepan. Whisk in the grits gradually. Reduce the heat and simmer for 10 minutes or until thickened, stirring occasionally. Add the Cheddar cheese, Parmesan cheese, butter, hot sauce and white pepper and mix well. Remove from the heat and keep warm.

Marinated Shrimp

Serves 8 to 10

1/4	cup red wine vinegar	2	tablespoons snipped fresh chives
2	teaspoons Dijon mustard	1	teaspoon Worcestershire sauce
2/3	cup olive oil	1	teaspoon fresh lemon juice
1	garlic clove, minced	•	Salt and pepper to taste
1	small onion, minced	2	pounds large shrimp, peeled and
1	green bell pepper, minced		deveined

Blend the vinegar and Dijon mustard in a large glass bowl. Add the olive oil in a fine stream, whisking constantly until blended. Add the garlic, onion, bell pepper, chives, Worcestershire sauce, lemon juice, salt and pepper and mix well.

Place the shrimp in a large saucepan of boiling salted water. Return to a boil and boil the shrimp for 1 minute; drain. Add the shrimp to the marinade and toss to coat. Marinate, covered, in the refrigerator for 12 to 24 hours. Remove the shrimp with a slotted spoon to a serving bowl and garnish with fresh Italian parsley and lemon slices.

Crawfish in Sherried Cream

Serves 4

1	pound cooked crawfish tails, cleaned	3	tablespoons all-purpose flour
		1	pint heavy cream
1/4	cup (1/2 stick) butter	1/4	cup dry sherry
1	bunch green onions, chopped	1	teaspoon lemon juice
1/2	cup chopped parsley	•	Tabasco sauce or cayenne pepper
1/2	cup (1 stick) butter		to taste

Sauté the crawfish in 1/4 cup butter in a skillet and set aside. Sauté the green onions and parsley in 1/2 cup butter in a skillet for 3 to 4 minutes. Blend in the flour to form a roux and cook for 2 to 3 minutes longer. Stir in the cream, sherry, lemon juice and Tabasco sauce gradually. Cook until the sauce thickens slightly, stirring constantly. Stir in the crawfish. Place in a chafing dish and serve warm on Melba toast, in pastry shells or over hot cooked rice.

Note: *This recipe may be prepared ahead of time.*

Apple Dumplings

Serves 12

2	(8-count) cans refrigerator crescent rolls	1	cup (2 sticks) butter
2	green apples, cored and chopped	1½	cups sugar
		1	teaspoon ground cinnamon
		1	can Mountain Dew

Unroll the crescent roll dough and separate into triangles. Place a small amount of the chopped apples at the wide end of each triangle and roll up to the small end. Arrange in a baking pan sprayed with nonstick cooking spray. Melt the butter in a saucepan. Add the sugar and cinnamon and mix well. Pour over the dumplings. Pour the Mountain Dew over the top. Bake at 350 degrees for 30 to 35 minutes or until golden brown. Serve with ice cream or whipped cream.

Cream Cheese Breakfast Roll

Serves 8 to 10

2	(8-count) cans refrigerator crescent rolls	1	egg yolk
16	ounces cream cheese, softened	1	teaspoon vanilla extract
1	cup granulated sugar	1	egg white, lightly beaten
1	egg	1	cup pecans, chopped
		•	Confectioners' sugar for sprinkling

Unroll one can of the crescent roll dough and press over the bottom of a 9×13-inch metal baking pan. Beat the cream cheese, granulated sugar, egg, egg yolk and vanilla in a mixing bowl until smooth. Pour in the prepared pan. Unroll the remaining can of crescent roll dough on a sheet of waxed paper and press into a 9×13-inch rectangle. Invert onto the cream cheese filling and remove the waxed paper. Brush the top lightly with the beaten egg white and sprinkle with the pecans. Bake at 350 degrees for 20 to 30 minutes or until golden brown. Sprinkle with confectioners' sugar.

Note: *You must use a metal baking pan for this recipe.*

Baking Pans

When baking, the type of pan you use can make a difference. If the recipe specifies a metal pan, a shiny one is best. If you use a dark metal, glass, or nonstick pan, the baked goods may become too brown. It is recommended that you reduce your baking temperature by twenty-five degrees when using glass or dark metal pans.

Danish Almond Puff Pastries

Makes 24 to 32 pieces

1/2 cup (1 stick) margarine, softened	1 cup all-purpose flour
1 cup all-purpose flour	3 eggs
2 tablespoons cold water	2 cups sifted confectioners' sugar
1 cup water	1 tablespoon margarine
1/2 cup (1 stick) margarine, softened	2 tablespoons milk
1 tablespoon almond extract	1 teaspoon vanilla extract

Cut 1/2 cup margarine into 1 cup flour in a bowl until the mixture resembles coarse cornmeal. Add 2 tablespoons cold water and stir until blended. Divide the dough into two equal portions and shape each into a ball. Grease your hands with the margarine wrapper and press each ball into a 3×12-inch oblong shape on an ungreased baking sheet. Bring 1 cup water and 1/2 cup margarine to a boil in a saucepan. Remove from the heat and stir in the almond extract and 1 cup flour. Add the eggs one at a time, beating well after each addition. Spread over the dough. Bake at 375 degrees for 30 to 35 minutes or until golden brown. Remove from the oven and cool for 5 minutes. Beat the confectioners' sugar and 1 tablespoon margarine in a mixing bowl. Add the milk and 1 teaspoon vanilla and beat until smooth. Spread over the pastries. Cut each pastry into small pieces.

French Toast Casserole

Serves 4 to 6

8 eggs	• Sliced sourdough bread or ciabbata bread
1 1/2 cups milk	
2 teaspoons vanilla extract	1/2 cup (1 stick) butter
1 tablespoon brown sugar	1/2 cup packed brown sugar
	1/4 cup real maple syrup

Blend the eggs, milk, vanilla and 1 tablespoon brown sugar in a bowl. Pour one-half of the batter into a 9×13-inch pan. Layer the bread slices in two layers in the prepared pan. Pour the remaining batter over the bread. (You may prepare ahead up to this point and chill in the refrigerator for 1 hour.) Melt the butter with 1/2 cup brown sugar and maple syrup in a small saucepan. Pour the butter mixture into a second 9×13-inch baking pan. Place the soaked bread in the prepared pan and pour any remaining batter over the top. Bake at 350 degrees for 30 to 35 minutes or until puffy.

Puffy Pancake with Banana-Berry Compote

Serves 4

4	eggs	2	bananas, sliced
1	cup milk	1	pint strawberries, sliced
1	cup all-purpose flour	1	tablespoon granulated sugar
2	tablespoons granulated sugar	1	tablespoon fresh lemon juice
1/4	teaspoon salt	•	Confectioners' sugar
2	tablespoons margarine or butter		for sprinkling

Heat an ovenproof 10-inch skillet in a 425-degree oven until very hot. Process the eggs, milk, flour, granulated sugar and salt at medium speed in a blender until smooth. Remove the skillet from the oven and maintain the oven temperature. Place the margarine in the hot skillet and swirl until melted. Add the batter. Bake for 15 minutes or until puffy and golden. Combine the bananas, strawberries, sugar and lemon juice in a bowl and toss to mix. Spoon over the pancake and sprinkle with confectioners' sugar. Cut into wedges to serve.

Amaretto Hot Fruit Compote

Serves 12 to 14

1	(16-ounce) can peach halves, drained	1	(16-ounce) can pear halves, drained
1	(15-ounce) can pineapple chunks, drained	2	bananas, sliced
		1	teaspoon lemon juice
1	(17-ounce) can apricot halves, drained	12	soft coconut macaroons, crumbled
1	(16-ounce) can pitted dark sweet cherries, drained	1	(2-ounce) package sliced almonds, toasted
		1/4	cup (1/2 stick) butter
		1/2	cup amaretto

Combine the canned fruits in a large bowl and toss to mix. Toss the bananas gently in the lemon juice in a bowl. Add to the fruit mixture and toss to mix. Layer one-half of the fruit mixture and one-half of the macaroon crumbs in a 2 1/2-quart baking dish. Sprinkle with 3 tablespoons of the toasted almonds and dot with 2 tablespoons of the butter. Repeat the layers with the remaining ingredients, reserving some of the almonds for topping. Pour the amaretto evenly over the layers. Bake at 350 degrees for 30 minutes. Sprinkle with the reserved almonds. Stir before serving.

Fruit Salad with Spiced Yogurt Sauce

Serves 4

1	cantaloupe	1 1/2 cups	vanilla yogurt
2	oranges	1/2 cup	crème fraîche or yogurt
8	ounces fresh blueberries	1/2 teaspoon	ground cinnamon
3	cups seedless green grapes	1/4 teaspoon	ground nutmeg
1	tablespoon sugar	1/4 teaspoon	ground ginger

Cut the cantaloupe into halves and remove the seeds. Cut the cantaloupe into bite-size pieces. Peel the orange and separate into sections. Cut each section into halves. Combine the cantaloupe, orange sections, blueberries, grapes and sugar in a serving bowl and toss to mix. Whisk the yogurt, crème fraîche, cinnamon, nutmeg and ginger in a medium bowl until blended. Spoon over the fruit salad.

Note: *You can find information on crème fraîche on page 226 of* Settings on the Dock of the Bay.

Pineapple Mint Tea

Serves 20 to 25

1	family-size regular tea bag	3 1/4	cups water
3	or 4 mint tea bags	2 1/2	cups pineapple juice
4	cups boiling water	1	(6-ounce) can frozen lemonade
1	cup sugar		concentrate, thawed

Steep the tea bags in the boiling water in a large pitcher. Discard the tea bags. Add the sugar to the hot tea and stir until dissolved. Stir in 3 1/4 cups water, pineapple juice and lemonade concentrate. Serve over ice.

Note: *This recipe can easily be doubled.*

Mimosa Punch

Serves 50

ICE RING		PUNCH	
2	or 3 large cans pineapple slices	5	quarts cold freshly squeezed
1	large bottle maraschino		orange juice with no pulp
	cherries without stems	5	bottles chilled Brut
1	cup ginger ale		Champagne
1	cup cold water	1/2	to 1 quart ginger ale
1	medium can pineapple juice		

To *prepare the ice ring,* drain the pineapple slices and cherries, reserving the juices separately. Pour 1/4 cup of the ginger ale and 1/4 cup of the cold water in the bottom of a bundt pan or your favorite mold. Layer a single layer of pineapple slices side by side in the pan, placing a cherry in each pineapple hole. Continue layering the pineapple slices and cherries until all of the pineapple slices are used, placing each layer in the middle of the two slices under it. Fill in spaces with additional cherries. Mix the reserved pineapple juice and can of pineapple juice with enough of the reserved cherry juice to turn the juice red. Pour into the mold. Add enough of the remaining cold water and ginger ale to reach within 1/2 inch of the top of the mold. Add enough of the remaining cold water to reach the top. Freeze for 6 to 8 hours.

To prepare the punch, carefully pour the orange juice and Champagne into a punch bowl. Pour in 1/2 quart of the ginger ale. Add the remaining ginger ale to taste. Unmold the ice ring and float in the punch. Ladle into punch cups.

Note: *This punch has been served at the Assistance League® of the Bay Area Holiday Coffee since our organization was an auxiliary. It is always popular and is welcomed at brunches, showers, or for any other mid-morning entertaining. For a smaller group, reduce the amounts to 1 quart orange juice, 1 bottle of Champagne and 1/2 to 1 cup ginger ale. Serve in stemmed glasses and garnish each with an orange section and pineapple section speared on a cocktail pick.*

ORANGE DELIGHT

Process one 6-ounce can orange juice concentrate, 1 cup milk, 1 cup water, 1/4 cup sugar, 1 teaspoon vanilla extract and 10 to 12 ice cubes in a blender for 30 seconds or until smooth. Serve immediately. This tastes like the commercial drink "Orange Julius."

Spiced Apricot Tea Muffins

Makes about 3 dozen

2	cups all-purpose flour	1/2	teaspoon ground cinnamon
1	teaspoon baking soda	6	tablespoons butter or margarine, melted
1/2	teaspoon salt		
6	ounces dried apricots, minced	1	cup water
1	cup sugar	1	egg, beaten
1/2	teaspoon ground cloves	1	cup chopped pecans or walnuts, or a combination
1/4	teaspoon ground nutmeg		

Sift the flour, baking soda and salt together. Cook the apricots, sugar, cloves, nutmeg, cinnamon, butter and water in a saucepan for 5 minutes. Remove from the heat to cool thoroughly. Add the egg and mix well. Add the flour mixture and mix well. Stir in the pecans. Pour into greased tea muffin cups. Bake at 350 degrees for 10 to 15 minutes.

Cinnamon Dunkins

Makes 2 dozen

1 1/2	cups all-purpose flour	1/2	teaspoon vanilla extract
1 1/2	teaspoons baking powder	1/2	cup milk
1/2	teaspoon salt	1/2	cup sugar
1/2	teaspoon ground nutmeg	1	teaspoon ground cinnamon
1/3	cup shortening	1/2	teaspoon ground nutmeg
1/2	cup sugar	1/2	cup (1 stick) butter or margarine, melted
1	egg		

Mix the flour, baking powder, salt and 1/2 teaspoon nutmeg in a mixing bowl. Cream the shortening, 1/2 cup sugar, the egg and vanilla in a mixing bowl until smooth. Add to the flour mixture with the milk and beat until smooth. Fill twenty-four lightly greased miniature muffin cups two-thirds full. Bake at 350 degrees for 10 to 15 minutes or until golden brown. Mix 1/2 cup sugar, the cinnamon and 1/2 teaspoon nutmeg together in a small bowl. Dip the warm muffins into the melted butter and then into the sugar mixture to coat thoroughly.

Raspberry Almond Muffins

Makes 1 dozen

1/2 cup granulated sugar	1 teaspoon lemon juice
1/2 cup packed brown sugar	2 cups all-purpose flour
2 1/2 tablespoons almond paste	1/2 teaspoon baking powder
1/4 cup (1/2 stick) butter, softened	1/2 teaspoon baking soda
2 eggs	1/4 teaspoon salt
1/2 cup buttermilk	2 cups fresh raspberries
1 teaspoon vanilla extract	2 tablespoons granulated sugar

Pulse 1/2 cup granulated sugar, brown sugar and almond paste in a food processor until blended. Add the butter and pulse four or five times. Add the eggs one at a time, pulsing twice after each addition. Add the buttermilk, vanilla and lemon juice and pulse until blended. Whisk the flour, baking powder and salt together in a large bowl. Make a well in the center and add the batter. Stir just until moistened. Fold in the raspberries gently. Let stand for 5 minutes. Spoon into twelve muffin cups coated with nonstick cooking spray. Sprinkle with 2 tablespoons granulated sugar. Bake at 375 degrees for 22 minutes.

Old-Fashioned Banana Bread

Makes 1 loaf

1 1/2 cups all-purpose flour	3 eggs
1 teaspoon baking soda	1 1/2 cups mashed bananas
1 teaspoon salt	1/2 cup buttermilk
1/2 cup shortening	1 teaspoon vanilla extract
1 1/2 cups sugar	1 cup chopped pecans

Mix the flour, baking soda and salt together. Beat the shortening and sugar in a mixing bowl until light and fluffy. Add the eggs and bananas and beat well. Add the flour mixture alternately with the buttermilk, beating well after each addition. Add the vanilla and pecans and mix well. Pour into a 5×9-inch loaf pan and bake at 325 degrees for 1 hour.

Note: *For muffins, bake in twelve muffin cups until golden brown.*

Million-Dollar Banana Nut Bread

Makes 2 loaves

BREAD

3	cups all-purpose flour
1/2	teaspoon baking powder
1/2	teaspoon baking soda
1/2	teaspoon salt
3/4	cup (1 1/2 sticks) butter, softened
8	ounces cream cheese, softened
2	cups sugar
2	eggs
1 1/2	cups mashed ripe bananas
1	cup chopped pecans, toasted
1/2	teaspoon vanilla extract
1/2	teaspoon rum flavoring

ORANGE GLAZE

3	tablespoons orange juice
1	teaspoon grated orange zest
1	cup confectioners' sugar

To prepare the bread, mix the flour, baking powder, baking soda and salt together. Beat the butter and cream cheese at medium speed in a mixing bowl until creamy. Add the sugar gradually, beating until light and fluffy. Add the eggs one at time, beating just until blended after each addition. Add the flour mixture gradually, beating at low speed just until blended. Stir in the bananas, pecans, vanilla and rum flavoring. Spoon into two greased and floured 4×8-inch loaf pans. Bake at 350 degrees for 1 1/4 hours or until a wooden pick inserted in the center comes out clean and the sides pull away from the pan. Cover with foil during the last 15 minutes to prevent overbrowning, if necessary. Cool the loaves in the pan on wire racks for 10 minutes. Remove from the pans and cool on wire racks for 30 minutes.

To prepare the glaze, combine the orange juice, orange zest and confectioners' sugar in a bowl and mix until smooth. Drizzle over the warm loaves.

Note: *This recipe may be frozen.*

BANANAS

The perfect bananas to use in this recipe should be very speckled and almost black. A 6-ounce banana will yield approximately 1/3 cup mashed banana. To hasten ripening a banana, place in a paper bag with a bruised apple. Once ripe, chill or freeze the unpeeled banana in a sealable plastic freezer bag. Thaw before mashing.

Cranberry Macadamia Nut Loaves

Makes 3 small loaves

1	pound walnut halves or pecan halves	1/2	teaspoon baking powder
8	ounces macadamia nuts	1/2	teaspoon salt
1	pound dried cranberries	3/4	cup sugar
3/4	cup all-purpose flour	3	eggs, beaten
		1/2	teaspoon vanilla extract

Toss the walnut halves, macadamia nuts and cranberries together in a large bowl. Sift the flour, baking powder and salt together. Add to the nut mixture and toss to coat. Combine the sugar, eggs and vanilla in a bowl and mix well. Add to the dry ingredients and mix well. Divide the batter evenly among three greased and floured 3×7-inch loaf pans, packing well to prevent air pockets. Bake at 325 degrees for 50 minutes or until a wooden pick inserted in the center comes out clean. Cool slightly in the pans. Loosen the edges from the side of the pans and remove to wire racks to cool completely. Wrap in plastic wrap and heavy foil.

Note: *These loaves are perfect for holiday hostess gifts and are wonderful for afternoon tea. This recipe works well with unchopped nuts and may be frozen for up to three months.*

Luscious Lemon Bread

Makes 1 loaf

1 1/4	cups all-purpose flour	1/2	cup milk
1	teaspoon baking powder	1/2	cup finely chopped walnuts
1/4	teaspoon salt	•	Grated zest of 1 lemon
1/2	cup (1 stick) margarine, softened	1/4	cup sugar
1	cup sugar	•	Juice of 1 lemon
2	eggs, lightly beaten		

Sift the flour, baking powder and salt together. Cream the margarine and 1 cup sugar in a mixing bowl until light and fluffy. Beat in the eggs. Add the flour mixture alternately with the milk, beating well after each addition. Stir in the walnuts and lemon zest. Pour into a greased 5×9-inch loaf pan. Bake at 350 degrees for 45 to 60 minutes or until the loaf tests done.

Mix 1/4 cup sugar and lemon juice in a bowl. Remove the bread from the oven and pierce the top with a skewer to form small holes. Pour the lemon mixture over the top of the hot bread. Cool in the pan. Loosen the edges from the sides of the pan before removing.

Pear Bread

Makes 1 loaf

2	cups all-purpose flour	1	cup sugar
1/2	teaspoon salt	2	eggs
1/2	teaspoon baking soda	1/4	cup buttermilk
1	teaspoon baking powder	1	cup coarsely chopped peeled pears
•	Pinch of ground nutmeg	1	teaspoon vanilla extract
1/2	cup (1 stick) butter, softened	1/2	cup walnuts, chopped

Mix the flour, salt, baking soda, baking powder and nutmeg together. Cream the butter in a mixing bowl. Beat in the sugar gradually. Add the eggs one at a time, beating well after each addition. Add the flour mixture alternately with the buttermilk, beating well after each addition. Stir in the pears, vanilla and walnuts. Pour into a greased 4×8-inch loaf pan. Bake at 350 degrees for 1 hour. Cool before slicing. Serve plain or with cream cheese.

Note: *This recipe may be frozen.*

"Pumped-Up" Pumpkin Bread

Makes 2 loaves

3	cups sugar	4	eggs
3 1/2	cups all-purpose flour	2	cups canned pumpkin
2	teaspoons baking soda	1	cup vegetable oil
1/2	teaspoon salt	1/2	cup water
2	teaspoons ground nutmeg	1/2	cup rum or water
2	teaspoons ground allspice	1	cup chopped pecans
2	teaspoons ground cloves	1	cup raisins
2	teaspoons ground cinnamon		

Mix the sugar, flour, baking soda, salt, nutmeg, allspice, cloves and cinnamon in a large bowl. Combine the eggs, pumpkin, oil, water and rum in a large bowl and mix well. Add to the flour mixture and stir until well mixed. Fold in the pecans and raisins. Pour into two 5×9-inch loaf pans sprayed with nonstick baking spray. Bake at 325 degrees for 1 hour or until the loaves test done.

Note: *The key to this recipe is to use very fresh spices. You may bake in six 3×5-inch loaf pans for 45 to 50 minutes or until the loaves test done.*

Festive Cranberry Scones

Makes 8 large scones or 24 miniature scones

3	cups all-purpose flour	1	egg
1/3	cup sugar	1 1/2	teaspoons vanilla extract
2	teaspoons baking powder	1	cup (6 ounces) white
1/2	teaspoon salt		chocolate chips
1/4	cup (1/2 stick) unsalted butter	1	cup toasted walnuts
1/2	cup whipping cream	1	cup chopped dried cranberries

Mix the flour, sugar, baking powder and salt in a large bowl. Cut in the butter until the mixture resembles coarse crumbs. Whisk the cream, egg and vanilla in a bowl. Add to the flour mixture and knead until combined. (You may process in a food processor until blended up to this point and then stir in the remaining ingredients.) Knead in the white chocolate chips, walnuts and cranberries. Place the dough in a large scone pan or miniature scone pan. Bake at 375 degrees for 15 to 20 minutes or until the scones test done.

Note: *You may shape the dough into a 9-inch circle in the center of an ungreased baking sheet and cut into eight wedges before baking. The dough may be prepared a day ahead and stored in the refrigerator.*

Sun-Dried Tomato and Basil Miniature Scones

Makes 20 to 24 miniature scones

2	cups buttermilk baking mix	1/2	cup oil-pack sun-dried tomatoes,
1/4	cup (1 ounce) shredded		drained and chopped
	Romano cheese	2/3	cup reduced-fat (2%) milk
1 1/2	teaspoons dried basil	1/4	cup chopped green onions

Combine the baking mix, cheese and basil in a medium bowl. Stir in the sun-dried tomatoes, milk and green onions until moistened. Do not overmix. Drop by teaspoonfuls onto a greased baking sheet. Bake at 450 degrees for 8 to 10 minutes or until golden brown. Let stand for 5 minutes before removing from the baking sheet. Serve immediately.

Note: *This recipe may be frozen.*

Cinnamon Bread

Makes 2 loaves

1	envelope dry yeast	5	cups all-purpose flour
1/2	cup warm water	1	cup sugar
1 3/4	cups lukewarm water or milk	1 1/2	tablespoons ground cinnamon
1/2	cup sugar	•	Melted butter
1	tablespoon salt	•	Cinnamon-sugar to taste
2	tablespoons shortening	•	Butter

Dissolve the yeast in 1/2 cup warm water in a large bowl. Add 1 3/4 cups lukewarm water, 1/2 cup sugar, the salt and shortening and stir to mix well. Add the flour gradually, stirring to form a soft dough. Place the dough on a floured board and knead until smooth and elastic. Place in a greased bowl, turning to coat the surface. Let rise in a warm place for 2 hours or until doubled in bulk.

Mix 1 cup sugar and 1 1/2 tablespoons cinnamon together in a bowl. Place the dough on a floured board and knead again. Divide the dough into two equal portions. Roll each portion into a rectangle and dot with a few drops of water. Spread each rectangle with 1/2 cup of the cinnamon-sugar. Roll up to enclose the filling and place in two greased 5×9-inch loaf pans. Let rise until doubled in bulk. Spread melted butter over the top of each loaf and sprinkle with cinnamon-sugar to taste. Bake at 375 degrees for 35 to 40 minutes or until the loaves test done. Remove from the pans and cool on wire racks.

To serve, cut the bread into slices and spread with butter. Place on a baking sheet and broil until golden brown.

Note: *You may prepare the dough in a bread machine following the manufacturer's directions.*

Dill Bread

Makes 2 loaves

1	cake of yeast	3/4	teaspoon salt
1/4	cup warm water	1/4	teaspoon baking soda
1	tablespoon butter	2	teaspoons dill seeds
1	cup cottage cheese	1	tablespoon finely chopped onion
1	egg	21/4	to 21/2 cups all-purpose flour, sifted
2	tablespoons sugar		

Dissolve the yeast in the warm water. Melt the butter and cottage cheese in a small saucepan, stirring frequently; do not boil. Combine with the egg, sugar, salt, baking soda, dill seeds, onion and yeast mixture in a large bowl and mix well. Add 21/4 cups of the flour and mix to form a soft dough. Knead in enough of the remaining flour on a lightly floured surface until satiny smooth and elastic. Place in a greased bowl, turning to coat the surface. Let rise in a warm place for 1 hour or until doubled in bulk. Punch the dough down. Divide the dough into two equal portions and shape each into a ball. Cover and let rise for 10 minutes. Shape into loaves and place in two greased 5×9-inch loaf pans. Let rise for 45 minutes or until doubled in bulk. Bake at 325 degrees for 50 to 60 minutes or until the loaves test done, covering with foil during the last 20 minutes to prevent overbrowning.

Texas Panhandle Bread

Makes 1 loaf

1	cup milk	2	eggs
1/2	cup (1 stick) butter	1/2	cup sugar
1	envelope dry or fast-rising yeast	1/2	teaspoon salt
1/4	cup warm water (100 to 110 degrees)	3	cups all-purpose flour
		6	tablespoons butter

Scald the milk with 1/2 cup butter in a saucepan; cool. Dissolve the yeast in the water. Beat the eggs in a mixing bowl until light and fluffy. Add the sugar and salt and beat well. Stir in the milk mixture. Beat in 11/2 cups of the flour until smooth. Stir in the yeast mixture. Let rise, uncovered, for 1 hour. Add the remaining 11/2 cups flour and mix well. Cover with a damp cloth and chill for 8 to 10 hours. Let stand at room temperature for 2 hours. Melt 6 tablespoons butter in a bundt pan, turning to coat the sides. Place the dough in the prepared pan and let rise for 30 minutes. Bake at 350 degrees for 30 minutes or until a wooden pick inserted in the center comes out clean. Cool in the pan for 10 minutes. Invert onto a wire rack to cool completely.

Focaccia

Serves 8

1 cup warm water (105 to 115 degrees)	1 teaspoon dried oregano
1 envelope dry yeast	1 teaspoon basil
1 tablespoon honey	1 tablespoon salt
1 cup all-purpose flour or bread flour	1/2 cup (2 ounces) grated Parmesan cheese
3 tablespoons dry milk	2 1/2 to 3 1/2 cups all-purpose flour
2 tablespoons olive oil	1/4 cup olive oil
	1 tablespoon chopped garlic

Combine the water, yeast, honey, 1 cup flour and dry milk in a mixing bowl and beat until smooth. Cover and let stand for 20 minutes or until the mixture is bubbly. Add 2 tablespoons olive oil, the oregano, basil, salt, Parmesan cheese and 2 1/2 cups of the flour and mix well. Add enough of the remaining 1 cup flour to form a stiff dough. Place on a floured surface and knead until smooth and elastic. Place in a greased bowl, turning to coat the surface. Cover loosely and let rise until doubled in bulk.

Preheat the oven to 450 degrees. Combine 1/4 cup olive oil and garlic in a bowl and mix well. Flatten the dough on a lightly floured surface until 1/2 inch thick. Brush with the olive oil mixture and place on a pizza pan or baking sheet. Reduce the oven temperature to 400 degrees. Bake for 15 to 20 minutes or until golden brown on the bottom and top.

Note: *This recipe may be frozen.*

Soups Salads Sandwiches

Williamses' Home

There is no better way to celebrate in true American style than with a tailgate picnic. This 1938 completely restored Bantam makes this party extra special.

Pictured here at the Williamses' home, under the shade of Chinese Tallows, this truck is a former Best-of-Show winner at the National Austin Bantam Club Meet.

Appreciating the uniqueness of this vehicle are Butler Longhorn Cattle, a breed developed at the Butler Ranch just south of the Clear Lake area.

Cattle Guard Tailgate
Williamses' Ranch

A Variety of Beer and Wine Coolers
(Iced down in a favorite galvanized tub or bucket)

It's-a-Wrap "Appeteasers," page 30
Seashell Pasta with Salmon and Dill, page 139
Pico Sandwiches, page 114

Beef Vegetable Soup, Italian Style, page 84

Garlic Green Beans with
Toasted Bread Crumbs, page 120
Cherry Tomato Caper Salad, page 110

Pecan Cake Squares, page 210
Fudgy Chocolate Cookies, page 222
White Chocolate with Raspberry Bars,
(See Settings on the Dock of the Bay, *page 220)*

Seafood Bisque

Serves 6

1	onion, finely chopped
2	tablespoons olive oil
1	(14-ounce) can artichoke hearts
2	cups chicken broth
1/2	cup white wine
1	pound mixed uncooked shellfish (shrimp, scallops and crab meat)
1	cup heavy cream
2	tablespoons fresh parsley, chopped
1	teaspoon salt
1/2	teaspoon ground nutmeg
1/4	teaspoon white pepper

Sauté the onion in the olive oil in a large skillet over medium-high heat for 5 minutes or until softened. Add the artichokes, broth and wine. Bring to a boil and reduce the heat to low. Simmer, covered, for 5 to 7 minutes. Process in a food processor or blender until smooth and pour into a large saucepan. Remove the shells from the shellfish. Stir the shellfish into the soup. Add the cream, parsley, salt, nutmeg and white pepper. Bring just to a simmer over medium heat. Reduce the heat to low. Simmer, uncovered, very gently for 10 minutes. Do not boil. Add additional broth if the soup is too thick. Ladle into soup bowls and garnish with additional fresh parsley.

Elegant Crab Bisque

Serves 6 to 8

1	pound crab meat
1	tablespoon minced garlic
1/4	cup (1/2 stick) butter
3	tablespoons all-purpose flour
2	cups heavy cream
1	cup milk
1	(8-ounce) bottle clam juice
1/4	cup brandy
•	Salt to taste
1/2	teaspoon white pepper

Remove the shells from the crab meat and flake. Sauté the garlic in the butter in a large saucepan over medium heat for 30 seconds. Stir in the flour until blended. Add the cream, milk and clam juice gradually, stirring constantly. Cook until thickened, stirring constantly. Stir in the crab meat, brandy, salt and white pepper and bring to a boil. Ladle into soup bowls and garnish with shaved Parmesan cheese and chives.

Cheesy Chicken Chowder

Serves 7

Wine Pairing
Rioja

2 slices bacon	2¹/4 cups frozen whole kernel corn
1 pound boneless skinless chicken breasts, cut into bite-size pieces	¹/2 cup all-purpose flour
1 cup chopped onion	2 cups half-and-half
1 cup chopped red bell pepper	1 cup (4 ounces) shredded Cheddar cheese
2 garlic cloves, minced	¹/2 teaspoon salt
4¹/2 cups chicken broth	¹/4 teaspoon pepper
1³/4 cups chopped red potatoes	

Cook the bacon in a Dutch oven over medium-high heat until the bacon is crisp. Remove the bacon to paper towels to drain, reserving the bacon drippings in the Dutch oven. Crumble the bacon and set aside. Sauté the chicken, onion, bell pepper and garlic in the reserved bacon drippings for 5 minutes. Add the broth and potatoes and bring to a boil. Cover and reduce the heat. Simmer for 20 minutes or until the potatoes are tender. Stir in the corn. Place the flour in a medium bowl and whisk in the half-and-half gradually until blended. Stir into the chowder. Cook over medium heat for 15 minutes or until thickened, stirring frequently. Remove from the heat. Stir in the cheese, salt and pepper. Top with the crumbled bacon and ladle into soup bowls.

Note: *This recipe may be prepared ahead of time.*

Corn Chowder with Sausage

Serves 6 to 8

1	(16-ounce) package smoked sausage	1	(2-pound) package frozen O'Brien potatoes
2	bunches scallions, chopped		
•	Vegetable oil or butter for sautéing	1	teaspoon Tony Chachere's Creole Seasoning
2	(14-ounce) cans vegetable broth	•	Salt and pepper to taste
1	(15-ounce) can cream-style corn	1/2	cup heavy cream

Slice and quarter each link of smoked sausage. Sauté the scallions and sausage in a small amount of oil in a large saucepan. Add the broth, corn and potatoes. Bring to a boil and reduce the heat. Simmer for 30 minutes. Add the Creole Seasoning, salt and pepper. Stir in the cream. Ladle into soup bowls. Serve with a salad and bread.

Note: *This recipe may be doubled.*

Poblano Corn Chowder with Shrimp

Serves 6 as a main course and 12 as a soup course

2	tablespoons butter, softened	2	(14-ounce) cans low-salt chicken broth
2	tablespoons all-purpose flour		
1	cup chopped celery	1	cup whipping cream
1	onion, coarsely chopped	2	teaspoons sugar
2	large poblano chiles, seeded and chopped	1	pound uncooked shrimp, peeled, deveined and coarsely chopped
2	tablespoons butter, softened	1/4	cup chopped fresh cilantro
1	(15-ounce) can cream-style corn	•	Salt and pepper to taste
1	(16-ounce) package frozen whole kernel corn, thawed	2	tablespoons chopped fresh cilantro

Mix 2 tablespoons butter and flour in a small bowl until blended. Process the celery and onion in a food processor until finely chopped. Sauté the celery, onion, and chiles in 2 tablespoons butter in a large stockpot over medium-high heat for 6 minutes or until soft. Add the cream-style corn, whole kernel corn, broth, cream and sugar and mix well. Bring to a boil and reduce the heat. Whisk in the flour mixture. Simmer for 15 minutes to blend the flavors. Add the shrimp and 1/4 cup cilantro. Simmer for 5 minutes or until the shrimp turns pink. Season with salt and pepper. Ladle into soup bowls and sprinkle with 2 tablespoons cilantro.

Beef Vegetable Soup, Italian Style

Serves 14 to 16

1	(2¹/2- to 4-pound) chuck rump roast	3	ribs of celery with leaves, chopped
2	to 3 (14-ounce) cans beef broth	2	or 3 carrots, peeled and coarsely chopped
1	(14-ounce) can crushed tomatoes	1	large onion, cut into quarters
1	(10-ounce) can tomatoes with green chiles	1	or 2 potatoes, peeled and chopped
1	to 2 (15-ounce) cans tomato sauce	5	tablespoons minced garlic
3	(14-ounce) cans diced tomatoes with basil, garlic and oregano, or Italian-style tomatoes	¹/4	cup salt
		3	to 5 tablespoons pepper
		8	ounces acini di pepe or tiny pasta, cooked and drained (optional)

Place the roast in a large stockpot and cover with 2 inches of cold water. Add the broth, crushed tomatoes, tomatoes with green chiles, tomato sauce, diced tomatoes, celery, carrots, onion, potatoes, garlic, salt and pepper. Bring to a rolling boil over high heat, removing any foam that may form on the top. Reduce the heat and gently boil for 45 minutes. Reduce the heat and simmer for 2¹/2 to 3 hours, stirring occasionally. Adjust the seasonings to taste. Remove the cooked roast and cut into bite-size pieces or shred. Return to the stockpot. Cook over low heat for 15 minutes. Stir in the cooked pasta. Ladle into soup bowls and garnish with freshly grated Parmesan cheese. Serve with corn bread.

Note: *This recipe makes a large quantity of soup. Plan on freezing any remaining soup or sharing with friends. Adjust the recipe as needed by adding more or less crushed tomatoes or vegetables. Add any leftover cooked vegetables, a package of frozen yellow whole kernel corn, or okra. You may substitute 1 large package of frozen mixed vegetables for the celery, carrots and potatoes. You may omit the can of tomatoes with green chiles or add an additional can for a spicier flavor.*

Tamale Soup

Serves 10

1	onion, chopped	1	(15-ounce) can tomatoes, chopped
1	green bell pepper, chopped	1	teaspoon cumin
1	pound ground beef	•	Salt, black pepper and red pepper
2	(16-ounce) cans whole kernel corn		to taste
2	(15-ounce) cans ranch-style beans	2	(15-ounce) cans tamales
1	(10-ounce) can tomatoes with green chiles, chopped		

Sauté the onion and bell pepper in a nonstick skillet until soft. Add the ground beef and cook until brown, stirring until crumbly. Add the corn, beans, undrained tomatoes with green chiles, undrained tomatoes, cumin, salt, black pepper and red pepper. Simmer for 45 minutes. Cut the tamales into 1-inch pieces and add to the soup. Simmer for 15 minutes. Ladle into soup bowls.

Note: *This recipe may be frozen.*

Chicken Tortilla Soup

Serves 12

4	chicken breasts, cooked	1	jalapeño chile, seeded and chopped
1	garlic clove, minced	2	teaspoons cumin
1	large onion, chopped	2	teaspoons salt
1	teaspoon olive oil	1/2	cup cilantro, chopped
2	large boxes fat-free chicken broth	5	corn tortillas, sliced
2	(10-ounce) cans tomatoes with green chiles	1/2	cup (2 ounces) shredded Monterey Jack cheese
		3	avocados, sliced

Chop the chicken, discarding the skin and bones. Sauté the garlic and onion in the olive oil in a large stockpot. Add the chicken broth, tomatoes with green chiles, chicken, jalapeño chile, cumin and salt. Cook for 1 hour. Add the cilantro and cook for 10 minutes. Ladle over the sliced tortillas in soup bowls. Sprinkle with the cheese and top with the avocados.

Oyster and Artichoke Soup

Serves 6

1	large onion, chopped	2	dozen oysters, chopped
4	shallots, chopped	2	large cans artichoke hearts,
1/2	cup (1 stick) butter		drained and chopped
2	garlic cloves, finely chopped	1	cup oyster liquid
	or pressed	1	(10-ounce) can cream of
1	bay leaf		mushroom soup
2	tablespoons chopped parsley		

Sauté the onion and shallots in the butter in a large saucepan until translucent. Add the garlic, bay leaf and parsley and sauté for 2 to 3 minutes. Add the oysters and sauté for 3 minutes. Add the artichokes and sauté for 3 minutes. Add the oyster liquid and soup and simmer for 20 minutes. Discard the bay leaf. Ladle into soup bowls.

Note: *This soup is best when prepared one to two hours before serving. Reheat before serving.*

Black Bean Soup with Cognac

Serves 4

2	cups drained canned black beans	•	Vegetable oil
4	small tomatoes, peeled, seeded	1/4	teaspoon oregano
	and chopped	•	Salt and pepper to taste
1/4	cup chopped onion	1/4	cup cognac
1	small garlic clove, mashed	11/3	cups chicken stock

Purée the beans, tomatoes, onion and garlic in a blender. Heat oil in a sauté pan over medium heat. Add the bean mixture, oregano, salt, pepper and cognac. Reduce the heat and cook for 15 minutes. Add the stock, stirring constantly. Cook until the soup is creamy, stirring constantly. Ladle into soup bowls.

Cool and Creamy Avocado Soup

Makes 8 cups

3 avocados, cut into quarters
1/2 cup fresh cilantro, coarsely chopped
1/4 cup coarsely chopped onion
1/4 cup coarsely chopped green onions
1/4 cup fresh parsley, coarsely chopped
3 tablespoons lime juice
1 teaspoon chili powder
1 teaspoon salt
1/4 teaspoon pepper
1/4 teaspoon cumin
1/4 teaspoon Tabasco sauce, or to taste
1 (32-ounce) can chicken broth
2 cups sour cream or light sour cream

Process the avocado in a blender or food processor until smooth, stopping to scrape the side. Add the cilantro, onion, green onions, parsley, lime juice, chili powder, salt, pepper, cumin and hot sauce and process until smooth, stopping to scrape down the side once or twice. Pour into a large bowl. Stir in the broth and sour cream. Cover and chill for 3 hours. Ladle into soup bowls.

Cold Peach Soup

Serves 6 to 8

5 large ripe peaches, peeled and cut into quarters
1/4 cup sugar or Splenda
1 cup sour cream or fat-free sour cream
1/4 cup fresh lemon juice
1/4 cup sweet sherry
2 tablespoons thawed orange juice concentrate

Purée the peaches with the sugar in a blender. Add the sour cream and mix well. Add the lemon juice, sherry and orange juice concentrate and blend until smooth. Pour into a serving bowl. Chill, covered, in the refrigerator. Ladle into soup bowls and garnish with a small sliver of peach.

Creamy Cauliflower Soup

Serves 6

5 cups chopped cauliflower (1 head)	1/4 teaspoon pepper
1/2 cup chopped onion	1 bay leaf
1/4 cup (1/2 stick) butter or olive oil	1 cup (4 ounces) shredded Cheddar cheese
2 cups chicken broth	1 1/2 cups half-and-half or fat-free half-and-half
1/2 teaspoon marjoram	
1/2 teaspoon fines herbes	
1/4 teaspoon salt	

Sauté the cauliflower and onion in the butter in a saucepan until tender. Add the broth, marjoram, fines herbes, salt, pepper and bay leaf and mix well. Cook until of the desired consistency, stirring frequently. Discard the bay leaf. Purée the mixture in a blender and return to the saucepan. Stir in the cheese. Cook over low heat until the cheese melts, stirring frequently. Stir in the half-and-half. Cook just until heated through. Do not boil. Ladle into soup bowls.

Note: *This recipe may be doubled.*

Cheese Soup

Serves 8

1/3 cup finely chopped carrots	4 cups milk
1/3 cup finely chopped celery	4 cups chicken broth
1 cup finely chopped green onions	1 (15-ounce) jar Cheez Whiz
2 cups water	• Salt and pepper to taste
1 white onion, finely chopped	• Dash of Tabasco sauce
1/2 cup (1 stick) butter	1 tablespoon prepared mustard
1/2 cup all-purpose flour	

Process the carrots, celery and green onions in a food processor. Combine with the water in a saucepan and bring to a boil over high heat. Boil for 5 minutes and remove from the heat. Sauté the onion in the butter in a large stockpot over medium heat for 1 minute. Blend in the flour. Bring the milk and broth to a boil in a large saucepan. Whisk into the flour mixture. Stir in the Cheez Whiz, salt, pepper and Tabasco sauce. Stir in the mustard and undrained cooked vegetables. Bring to a boil and remove from the heat. Ladle into soup bowls.

Note: *This recipe may be frozen.*

Stilton Soup

Serves 4 to 6

1 large onion, chopped	1³/4 cups milk
2 garlic cloves, chopped	6 ounces Stilton cheese, crumbled
2 ribs celery, finely sliced	3 ounces whipping cream
1/4 cup (1/2 stick) butter	1/4 teaspoon pepper
1/4 cup all-purpose flour	1/4 teaspoon ground nutmeg
2¹/2 cups chicken stock	

Sauté the onion, garlic and celery in the butter in a saucepan for 5 minutes. Stir in the flour. Add the stock and milk gradually, stirring constantly. Bring to a boil and reduce the heat. Simmer for 15 minutes. Add the cheese and cream. Cook for 1 minute, stirring constantly. Stir in the pepper and nutmeg and remove from the heat. Ladle into soup bowls and garnish with chopped celery leaves.

Note: *This is an old Scottish family recipe.*

A Really Good Gazpacho

Serves 8 to 10

1 cup finely chopped peeled tomatoes	2 tablespoons olive oil
1/2 cup finely chopped seeded bell pepper	1 teaspoon salt
1/2 cup finely chopped celery	1/2 teaspoon pepper
1/2 cup finely chopped seeded cucumber	1 tablespoon Worcestershire sauce
1/2 cup finely chopped green onions	3 cups vegetable juice cocktail
1/4 cup finely chopped fresh cilantro	2/3 cup frozen corn kernels
1 garlic clove, pressed	1 cup sour cream
2 tablespoons white wine vinegar	1 garlic clove, pressed
	1 avocado, sliced

Combine the tomatoes, bell pepper, celery, cucumber, green onions, cilantro, 1 garlic clove, vinegar, olive oil, salt, pepper, Worcestershire sauce, vegetable juice cocktail and corn in a large bowl and mix well. Process one-third of the mixture in a blender and return to the remaining mixture. Chill, covered, in the refrigerator for 8 to 10 hours. Mix the sour cream and 1 garlic clove in a small bowl. Ladle the soup into serving bowls and top each with a dollop of the sour cream mixture and one or two avocado slices.

Famous Barr's French Onion Soup

Makes 2 quarts

5	pounds onions, peeled	3	quarts canned beef broth or beef consommé
1/2	cup (1 stick) butter	•	Kitchen Bouquet
1 1/2	teaspoons ground pepper	2	teaspoons salt, or to taste
2	tablespoons paprika	1	loaf French bread, sliced
1	bay leaf	12	ounces Swiss Cheese
3/4	cup all-purpose flour		
1	cup white wine (optional)		

Cut the onions into slices 1/8 inch thick. Sauté the onions in the melted butter in a large stockpot over low heat for 1 1/2 hours. Season with the pepper, paprika and bay leaf. Stir in the flour and sauté over low heat for 10 minutes. Stir in the wine and broth and simmer for 2 hours. Add enough Kitchen Bouquet to adjust the color to a rich brown. Stir in the salt. Chill, covered, in the refrigerator for 8 to 10 hours. Reheat the soup to serving temperature and discard the bay leaf. Ladle 1 cup of soup into ovenproof soup bowls. Top each serving with a slice of French bread and 1 1/2 ounces of Swiss cheese. Broil for 5 minutes or until brown.

Note: *This recipe may be frozen.*

Roasted Red Pepper Soup

Serves 6 to 12

6	large red bell peppers	•	Salt and pepper to taste
1	cup marinara sauce	•	Puff pastry or crescent roll dough
4	cups heavy whipping cream	4	eggs, beaten
1	cup (4 ounces) grated Parmigiano cheese		

Remove the seeds from the bell peppers and grill until charred. Process the bell peppers with 2 to 3 tablespoons of the marinara sauce for 30 seconds in a food processor. Bring the cream to a light boil in a saucepan and reduce the heat. Add the remaining marinara sauce, cheese and bell pepper mixture. Season with salt and pepper. Heat over medium heat for 3 to 5 minutes. Pour into ovenproof soup bowls. Cover the top and side of the bowl with pastry and brush with the beaten eggs. Bake at 350 degrees for 15 to 20 minutes or until golden brown.

Note: *You may prepare without the pastry and garnish with sour cream.*

Spicy Tomato Soup

Serves 6 to 8

2	(10-ounce) cans tomato soup	1	lemon, cut into quarters
2	(10-ounce) cans beef consommé	1/4	teaspoon grated nutmeg
1/3	cup sliced onion	1	cup water
6	black peppercorns	1/2	cup sherry
1/2	teaspoon chef's salt or seasoning salt	1	tablespoon chopped parsley

Combine the soup, consommé, onion, peppercorns, salt, lemon quarters, nutmeg and water in a saucepan and mix well. Bring to a boil and reduce the heat. Simmer, covered, for 25 minutes. Strain the soup, discarding the solids. (You may prepare a day or so ahead up to this point.) Return the soup to the saucepan. Add the sherry and cook until heated through. Do not boil. Ladle into soup bowls and sprinkle with the parsley.

Note: *Serve in demitasse cups for a special ladies' luncheon.*

Cold Zucchini Soup

Serves 8

4	zucchini, cut into quarters and sliced	1/4	teaspoon white pepper
1	(48-ounce) can chicken broth	16	ounces cream cheese, softened
1	bunch green onions, chopped	1	tablespoon chopped fresh dill weed, or 1 teaspoon dried dill weed
1	teaspoon salt	1	cup sour cream

Combine the zucchini, broth, green onions, salt and white pepper in a saucepan and mix well. Cook for 20 minutes over medium-high heat, stirring frequently. Remove from the heat and let stand for 10 minutes. Add the cream cheese and dill weed and stir until the cream cheese melts. Process in small batches in a blender or food processor until smooth. Chill, covered, for 8 hours or longer. Stir in the sour cream just before serving. Ladle into soup bowls and garnish with chopped chives or paprika.

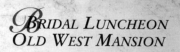

Entertaining Chicken Salad
Serves 6 to 8

3	pounds chicken breasts	1	teaspoon salt
1	large onion, cut into quarters	1/2	teaspoon white pepper
2	carrots, cut into quarters	1/2	to 3/4 teaspoon cayenne pepper
3	ribs celery with tops	1	cup finely chopped celery (optional)
3	bay leaves		
1	tablespoon salt	1	cup chopped apple (optional)
3	peppercorns	8	ounces slivered almonds, toasted (optional)
1/2	cup apple cider vinegar		
1 3/4	to 2 cups mayonnaise	8	ounces chopped pecans, lightly toasted (optional)
1 1/4	cups half-and-half		
3/4	teaspoon lemon juice		

Place the chicken in a large saucepan and add enough water to cover by 2 inches. Place the onion, carrots, celery, bay leaves, salt and peppercorns in a porous boiling bag and place in the saucepan with the chicken. Bring to a boil over high heat. Reduce the heat to medium and simmer until the chicken is cooked through. Remove from the heat and cool the chicken in the broth mixture for 2 hours. Drain the chicken, discarding the solids. Cut the chicken into 1-inch pieces, discarding the skin and bones. Place the chicken in a bowl. (You may prepare a day ahead up to this point.)

Sprinkle the vinegar over the chicken. Combine 1 1/2 cups of the mayonnaise and the half-and-half in a large bowl and mix well. Stir in the lemon juice, salt, white pepper and cayenne pepper. Add the celery, apple, almonds and pecans and stir to coat. Fold in the chicken and adjust the seasonings to taste. Stir in the remaining mayonnaise to reach the desired consistency. Serve on lettuce leaves or use as a filling for finger sandwiches for entertaining.

Note: *This recipe may be doubled for entertaining.*

Fried Chicken Salad by the Bay

Serves 6 to 8

HONEY RASPBERRY DRESSING

3	tablespoons balsamic vinegar
1	tablespoon rice vinegar
1	tablespoon raspberry liqueur or wine
2	tablespoons Creole mustard
3	tablespoons honey, or more to taste
1/2	teaspoon salt
1	teaspoon freshly ground pepper
3/4	cup olive oil

SALAD

1	red apple, chopped
1	green apple, chopped
•	Juice of 1/2 lemon
1	package romaine, torn into bite-size pieces
1	package mixed salad greens
1	bunch green onions, chopped
1	cup toasted pecan pieces
12	fried chicken strips, cut into bite-size pieces
1	pound blue cheese, crumbled
•	Blueberries or raspberries

To *prepare the dressing,* blend the balsamic vinegar, rice vinegar, raspberry liqueur, Creole mustard, honey, salt and pepper in a bowl. Whisk in the olive oil until blended.

To prepare the salad, toss the red apple and green apple with the lemon juice in a bowl. Toss the romaine and salad greens together and divide among individual salad plates. Scatter equal amounts of the apples, green onions and pecans over the salad greens. Arrange the chicken pieces over the top. Sprinkle with the cheese and blueberries and drizzle with the dressing.

Chicken Salad with Fruit

Serves 16

7 1/2	cups shredded cooked chicken
2 1/4	cups finely chopped celery
2 1/4	cups chopped red and green apples
2 1/4	cups chopped red and green seedless grapes
1	cup mayonnaise
1	cup vanilla yogurt
1/2	teaspoon curry powder
1	teaspoon dill weed
3/4	teaspoon salt
2	cups slivered almonds

Combine the chicken, celery, apples and grapes in a bowl and toss to mix. Mix the mayonnaise, yogurt, curry powder, dill weed and salt in a bowl until blended. Add to the chicken mixture and toss to mix. Sprinkle with the almonds just before serving.

Pork Tenderloin Salad

Serves 6 to 8

CURRIED CITRUS VINAIGRETTE
3   tablespoons fresh lime juice
1   tablespoon fresh orange juice
1   tablespoon Dijon mustard
1   teaspoon curry powder, toasted
1/2   teaspoon salt
•   Pepper to taste
1/2   cup olive oil

ROASTED PORK
2   teaspoons salt
1/2   teaspoon pepper
1   teaspoon cumin
1   teaspoon chili powder
1   teaspoon ground cinnamon

2   pork tenderloins
    (2 1/4 to 2 1/2 pounds total)
2   tablespoons olive oil
1   cup packed dark brown sugar
2   tablespoons finely chopped garlic
1   tablespoon Tabasco sauce

SALAD
3   Navel oranges
5   ounces baby spinach, trimmed
4   cups Napa cabbage, thinly sliced
    (about 1 medium head)
1/2   cup golden raisins
2   avocados, sliced

To prepare the vinaigrette, whisk the lime juice, orange juice, Dijon mustard, curry powder, salt and pepper in a bowl until blended. Add the olive oil in a fine stream, whisking until emulsified.

To prepare the pork, mix the salt, pepper, cumin, chili power and cinnamon together. Coat the pork with the spice rub. Heat the olive oil in a 12-inch heavy ovenproof skillet over medium-high heat until it just begins to smoke. Add the pork and cook for 4 minutes or until brown, turning frequently. Remove from the heat. Mix the brown sugar, garlic and Tabasco sauce together and pat on top of each tenderloin. Insert a meat thermometer into the center of each tenderloin. Roast at 350 degrees on the middle oven rack for 20 minutes or until the meat thermometers register 140 degrees. Remove from the oven and let stand at room temperature. The temperature will rise to about 155 degrees. (The pork may be prepared ahead of time.)

To prepare the salad, peel the oranges including the white pith. Cut the oranges crosswise into slices 1/4 inch thick. Combine the spinach, cabbage and raisins in a large bowl. Add about 1/4 cup of the vinaigrette and toss to coat.

To assemble the salad, cut the pork at a 45-degree angle into slices 1/2 inch thick. Line a platter with the dressed salad and arrange slices of the pork, oranges and avocados on top. Drizzle the remaining vinaigrette over the avocados and oranges. Pour any pan juices from the skillet over the pork.

Cracker Crisp Salad

Serves 4

1	garlic clove, chopped	4	tomatoes, chopped
3/4	teaspoon salt	1	(6-ounce) can salmon, tuna
1/2	cup mayonnaise		or chicken
1/4	teaspoon Worcestershire	1	cup small cheese crackers
	sauce	6	radishes, sliced
1	tablespoon red wine vinegar	1	small bunch green
4	cups crisp salad greens		onions, chopped

Mix the garlic, salt, mayonnaise, Worcestershire sauce and vinegar in a bowl. Chill, covered, in the refrigerator. Combine the salad greens, tomatoes, salmon and crackers in a bowl. Add the dressing and toss to coat. Top with the radishes and green onions and serve.

Bay Oaks Country Club Tex-a-Cali Salad

CHEF'S RECIPE

Serves 6

2	cups mayonnaise	•	Juice of 1 lemon
1/4	cup lemon juice	2	heads romaine, torn into
1/2	cup white wine		bite-size pieces
1/2	cup capers	2	heads iceberg lettuce, torn
1/4	cup chopped parsley		into bite-size pieces
•	Salt and pepper to taste	2	pounds fresh jumbo lump
3	avocados, cut into halves		crab meat (pasteurized)

Mix the mayonnaise, 1/4 cup lemon juice and the wine in a bowl until smooth. Fold in the capers, parsley, salt and pepper. Cut each avocado half lengthwise into five strips and coat with the juice of 1 lemon. Toss the romaine, iceberg lettuce and mayonnaise mixture in a bowl to coat. Place the salad greens in the center of each salad plate. Arrange the avocado slices in a pinwheel over the salad greens. Top each with the crab meat. Garnish each with a twisted lemon slice.

Greek Pasta Salad with Shrimp

Serves 4 to 6

3	quarts water		1	tablespoon snipped fresh mint, or 1/2 teaspoon dried mint, crushed
1	teaspoon salt (optional)			
1	tablespoon olive oil (optional)		1/4	teaspoon pepper
4	ounces bow tie pasta		•	Lettuce leaves (optional)
1	cucumber, quartered lengthwise, seeded and cut into slices 1/2 inch thick		1	pound shrimp, boiled and peeled
1/4	cup chopped red onion		1	cup (4 ounces) crumbled feta cheese
1/4	cup sliced pitted black olives		5	cherry tomatoes, cut into halves
1/4	cup olive oil			
1/4	cup lemon juice			
1	tablespoon snipped fresh oregano, or 1 teaspoon dried oregano, crushed			

Bring the water to a boil in a stockpot over high heat. Add the salt and 1 tablespoon olive oil to help keep the pasta separate. Add the pasta a small amount at a time so the water does not stop boiling. Reduce the heat slightly and cook, uncovered, until al dente. Rinse with cold water and drain. Combine the cooked pasta, cucumber, red onion and olives in a large bowl and toss lightly to mix. Combine 1/4 cup olive oil, the lemon juice, oregano, mint and pepper in a screw-top jar. Screw on the lid and shake well. Pour over the pasta mixture and toss to coat. Chill, covered, for 4 to 24 hours.

To serve, spoon the pasta onto lettuce-lined serving plates. Place equal amounts of the shrimp and feta cheese on top of each and top with the tomatoes.

Wine Paring
St. Supery Sauvignon Blanc

Shrimp Pasta Salad

Serves 4

8 ounces uncooked medium macaroni shells	2 teaspoons chopped parsley
1 tablespoon vegetable oil	1 cup diagonally sliced celery
2 tablespoons lemon juice	1/4 cup chopped green bell pepper
1/2 cup sour cream	4 green onions with tops, sliced
1/2 cup mayonnaise	1 pound shrimp
3 tablespoons prepared mustard	3 tablespoons bottled French vinaigrette
3/4 teaspoon salt	1 broccoli crown, cut into small florets
1/2 teaspoon Tabasco sauce	

Cook the macaroni using the package directions; drain. Rinse with cold water and drain. Add the oil and lemon juice and toss to coat. Chill, covered, in the refrigerator.

Combine the sour cream, mayonnaise, mustard, salt, Tabasco sauce and parsley in a bowl and mix well. Add the mayonnaise mixture, celery, bell pepper and green onions to the chilled macaroni mixture. Chill, covered, in the refrigerator.

Boil the shrimp in water to cover in a saucepan for 3 to 5 minutes or until the shrimp turn pink. Drain and peel the shrimp. Toss the shrimp with the vinaigrette in a bowl. Cover and chill for 30 minutes before serving. Cook the broccoli in a small amount of water in a saucepan until tender-crisp; drain. Place the broccoli in ice water to stop the cooking process and drain.

To serve, add the broccoli and shrimp to the macaroni mixture and toss to mix. Place in a serving bowl and garnish with salad greens.

Sakowitz Shrimp Salad

Serves 6

1 1/2	pounds shrimp, cooked and peeled
3/4	cup chopped celery
1	cup mayonnaise
•	Juice of 1/2 lemon
•	Salt to taste
1	hard-cooked egg, grated
2	green onions, chopped
1/4	cup chopped, drained, cooked spinach
1	garlic clove, minced
1	tablespoon Worcestershire sauce
1	cup mayonnaise
1	tablespoon Creole mustard
1	tablespoon lemon juice
•	Dash of Tabasco sauce
1/3	ounce anchovy paste (optional)

Combine the shrimp, celery, mayonnaise, lemon juice and salt in a bowl and mix well. Cover and chill in the refrigerator. Mix the remaining ingredients in a bowl. Cover and chill in the refrigerator. Place a mound of the shrimp salad on lettuce-lined serving plates. Top each serving with two dollops of the sauce.

Taco Salad with a Twist

Serves 8

2	cups macaroni, cooked
1	pound ground round
1	envelope taco seasoning mix
1/2	cup spicy ranch or Catalina salad dressing
1/2	head lettuce, shredded
1	pint cherry tomatoes, cut into halves
1/2	cup chopped green onions
1/2	cup chopped green bell pepper
1	cup (4 ounces) shredded sharp Cheddar cheese
1	small can sliced black olives, drained
1	(11-ounce) can Mexicorn, drained
1	(15-ounce) can black beans, rinsed and drained

Rinse the macaroni with cold water and drain. Chill for at least 1 hour. Brown the ground round in a skillet, stirring until crumbly; drain. Stir in the taco seasoning mix and salad dressing. Let stand until cool. Combine the macaroni, ground round mixture and remaining ingredients in a large bowl and toss to mix. Serve immediately.

Asian Soba Noodle Salad with Orange Vinaigrette

Serves 12

ORANGE VINAIGRETTE

- 5 tablespoons frozen orange juice concentrate, thawed
- 3/4 cup olive oil
- 1 garlic clove, minced
- 2 teaspoons sugar
- 1 teaspoon fresh lemon juice
- 1/2 teaspoon Dijon mustard

SALAD

- • Salt to taste
- 8 ounces soba noodles or spaghetti

- 1 1/2 teaspoons Asian sesame oil
- 3 tablespoons sesame seeds
- 2 (5-ounce) packages mixed baby salad greens
- 1 red bell pepper, julienned
- 1 3/4 cups julienned carrots
- 1 cup snow peas
- 2 tablespoons pickled ginger
- 3/4 cup chopped green onion tops
- 1/3 cup fresh cilantro, chopped
- 1/3 cup fresh mint, chopped

To *prepare the vinaigrette,* process the orange juice concentrate, olive oil, garlic, sugar, lemon juice and Dijon mustard in a blender until well blended.

To prepare the salad, bring salted water to a boil in a large stockpot. Break the noodles into four pieces and add to the water, stirring well. Cook for 6 to 7 minutes or until al dente. Drain and rinse with cool water. Toss the noodles with sesame oil in a bowl to coat. Sauté the sesame seeds in a small sauté pan over medium heat for 2 minutes or until light brown. Combine the salad greens, bell pepper, carrots, snow peas, ginger, toasted sesame seeds, green onion tops, cilantro and mint in a large salad bowl and toss to mix. Add the noodles and toss to mix. Drizzle with the vinaigrette and toss to coat. Garnish with a sprig of fresh mint.

SOBA NOODLES

Soba noodles come to us from Japan where many times the word soba is used when referring to noodles in general. They are made from buckwheat flour and resemble a thick, dark brown-grayish version of spaghetti. Served in both hot and cold dishes, they are almost always eaten with chopsticks. These versatile noodles lend themselves to many additions, including wasabi, ginger, and greens such as kale. Soba noodles are also used in stir-fry dishes. For cooking, add a few noodles at a time to boiling water, gently stirring the water until it returns to a boil. Cook the noodles for approximately 8 to 10 minutes and drain. Rinse the noodles with cold water to stop the cooking process. Soba noodles may be stored in the unopened package in a cool, dry place for six to eight months.

Finger Caesar Salad

Serves 8 to 10

HOMEMADE CROUTONS

1/2 to 1 loaf good-quality Italian
    bread or French bread
1/4 cup (1/2 stick) unsalted
    butter, melted
1/4 cup olive oil
• Garlic salt to taste

CAESAR SALAD DRESSING

4 anchovy fillets, rinsed and drained
3 garlic cloves, pressed
2 tablespoons extra-virgin olive oil
1 teaspoon Worcestershire sauce
1 teaspoon Dijon mustard

1/2 teaspoon hot red pepper sauce
11/3 cups mayonnaise
2 tablespoons freshly grated
    Parmesan cheese
2 tablespoons (or more) fresh
    lemon juice
• Salt and pepper to taste

SALAD

1 pound thickly sliced bacon,
    crisp-cooked
• Large romaine leaves
• Freshly grated Parmesan cheese

To *prepare the croutons,* cut the bread into strips 6 inches long and place on a baking sheet. Drizzle with the butter and olive oil. Sprinkle with garlic salt. Bake at 375 degrees for 15 to 20 minutes or until toasted, turning every 5 minutes.

To prepare the dressing, blend the anchovy fillets, garlic, olive oil, Worcestershire sauce, Dijon mustard and hot sauce in a food processor until smooth. Pour into a small bowl. Whisk in the mayonnaise, Parmesan cheese and 2 tablespoons lemon juice. Season with salt and pepper. Whisk in additional lemon juice, if needed, to reach the desired consistency.

To prepare the salad, layer one bacon slice on each lettuce leaf and top with one crouton strip. Drizzle with the dressing and sprinkle with Parmesan cheese. Roll up lengthwise and eat with your fingers.

Avocado Winter Salad

Serves 6

- 1/4 cup sugar
- 1 teaspoon salt
- 1 teaspoon paprika
- 1 teaspoon dry mustard
- 1/4 teaspoon seasoned pepper
- 1/4 cup fresh lemon juice
- 1 teaspoon celery seeds
- 1 tablespoon chopped onion
- 1 large, or 2 medium garlic cloves, minced
- 3/4 cup extra-virgin olive oil
- 2 tablespoons honey
- 1 head romaine, torn into pieces
- 2 oranges, peeled and sectioned
- 1 grapefruit, peeled and sectioned
- • Garlic salt to taste
- • Salt and pepper to taste
- 1 red onion, thinly sliced and separated into rings
- 1 ripe avocado, sliced into wedges
- 1/4 cup walnuts, lightly toasted and chopped

Process the sugar, 1 teaspoon salt, the paprika, dry mustard, seasoned pepper, lemon juice, celery seeds, onion, garlic, olive oil and honey in a blender until smooth. Combine the romaine, oranges and grapefruit in a salad bowl and toss to mix. Sprinkle with garlic salt, salt and pepper. Add the dressing just before serving and toss to coat. Arrange the onion rings and avocado wedges on top of the salad. Sprinkle with the walnuts.

Spinach, Goat Cheese and Bacon Salad with Orange-Pecan Dressing

Serves 6

- 8 cups fresh spinach
- 1/3 cup crumbled goat cheese
- 1/2 small red onion, thinly sliced
- 6 slices bacon, cooked and crumbled
- 1 orange, sectioned with pith removed
- 1/4 cup pecans, lightly toasted
- 2 teaspoons red wine vinegar
- 1/8 teaspoon cayenne pepper
- 1/2 cup olive oil

Layer the spinach, goat cheese, onion and bacon in a salad bowl. Chill in the refrigerator until ready to serve. Process the orange, pecans, vinegar and cayenne pepper in a blender or food processor until incorporated. Add the olive oil in a fine stream, processing until emulsified. Pour over the salad and toss to coat.

Jicama and Romaine Salad with Cumin Dressing

Serves 2

3   tablespoons olive oil
1   tablespoon red wine vinegar
1   teaspoon cumin
•   Salt and pepper to taste
1/2   small head romaine
1 1/2   cups matchstick-size strips peeled jicama

4   thin red onion slices, separated into rings
8   to 10 brine-cured olives, such as kalamata olives
3   tablespoons pine nuts, toasted

Whisk the olive oil, vinegar and cumin in a small bowl until blended. Season with salt and pepper. Cover and let stand at room temperature. (The dressing may be prepared up to 4 hours in advance.) Arrange the lettuce leaves on a serving platter. Arrange the jicama, onion rings and olives in the order listed over the lettuce. Sprinkle with the pine nuts. Drizzle the dressing evenly over the salad and serve.

Leek and Bell Pepper Salad

Serves 2

1   large leek
1   small yellow or red bell pepper, cut into thin strips
2   tablespoons olive oil
1   cup torn leaf lettuce or Bibb lettuce
1   tablespoon olive oil

1/2   teaspoon soy sauce
1   tablespoon fruit-flavored vinegar, such as raspberry vinegar or apple cider vinegar
1/4   teaspoon crushed dried thyme
•   Salt and freshly ground white pepper to taste

Trim off the stem end and the green portion of the leek and discard. Cut the white portion into halves and rinse with cold water, if necessary. Cut into half circles 1/4 inch thick. Sauté the leek and bell pepper in 2 tablespoons olive oil in a skillet over low heat for 10 to 15 minutes or until tender. Remove from the heat and cool until warm. Toss the lettuce and sautéed vegetables in a salad bowl to mix. Whisk 1 tablespoon olive oil, the soy sauce, vinegar and thyme in a small bowl. Season with salt and white pepper. Pour over the salad and toss to coat.

Note: *This recipe may be doubled or tripled.*

Gorgonzola and Walnut Salad with Walnut Vinaigrette

Serves 6 to 8

1 tablespoon Dijon mustard	1 head romaine, torn into bite-size pieces
3 tablespoons white wine vinegar	
1 tablespoon fresh lemon juice	8 ounces Gorgonzola cheese or blue cheese, crumbled
1/2 cup walnut oil or vegetable oil	
1/4 teaspoon salt	1 cup chopped walnuts, toasted
	1 red Delicious apple

Combine the Dijon mustard, vinegar, lemon juice, walnut oil and salt in a jar with a tight-fitting lid and mix well. Seal the jar and shake to mix well. (The vinaigrette may be prepared in advance.) Combine the romaine, cheese and walnuts in a salad bowl and toss to mix. Slice the unpeeled apple and add to the salad. Add just enough of the vinaigrette to coat the lettuce. Serve immediately.

Mandarin Salad

Serves 10

3/4 cup vegetable oil	1/2 cup plus 1 tablespoon sugar
1/3 cup honey	1 head iceberg lettuce, torn
1/4 cup red wine vinegar	2 heads romaine, torn
2 tablespoons poppy seeds	2 cups chopped celery
1 tablespoon minced onion	4 whole green onions, chopped
1 tablespoon Dijon mustard	3 (11-ounce) cans mandarin oranges, drained
1/2 teaspoon salt	
1 1/2 cups sliced almonds	

Process the oil, honey, vinegar, poppy seeds, onion, Dijon mustard and salt in a blender at low speed until blended. Cover and chill in the refrigerator. Stir well before serving.

Cook the almonds and sugar in a small saucepan until the almonds are coated and the sugar is dissolved, stirring constantly. Remove from the heat to cool. Separate and store in an airtight container. Mix the iceberg lettuce, romaine, celery and green onions in a large bowl. Add the almonds and oranges just before serving. Add the desired amount of dressing and toss to coat.

Raspberry Vinaigrette Salad

Serves 8

•	Red leaf lettuce, torn	1	tablespoon sour cream
•	Green leaf lettuce, torn	1	tablespoon poppy seeds
•	Bibb lettuce, torn	1	tablespoon Dijon mustard
1/2	cup vegetable oil	3/4	cup chopped red onion
2	tablespoons raspberry vinegar	1	cup caramelized walnuts
1	tablespoon lemon juice	1	pint fresh raspberries or strawberries

Place the lettuce in a large salad bowl. Cover and chill. Combine the oil, raspberry vinegar, lemon juice, sour cream, poppy seeds and Dijon mustard in a jar with a tight-fitting lid. Seal the jar and shake to mix well. Chill in the refrigerator. To serve, add the onion and walnuts to the lettuce mixture. Drizzle with the vinaigrette and toss to coat. Divide among salad plates and sprinkle with equal amount of the raspberries.

Spinach and Berries Salad

Serves 8 to 10

1/2	cup olive oil	1	pound baby spinach leaves, trimmed and torn
1/4	cup red wine vinegar	1	pound baby butterhead lettuce, torn
1/4	cup sugar		
2	garlic cloves, crushed	1	bunch green onions, chopped
1/4	teaspoon each salt and pepper	1/2	pint fresh strawberries, sliced
1/4	teaspoon onion powder	1/2	pint fresh raspberries
1/4	teaspoon dry mustard	1/2	pint fresh blueberries
1	cup slivered almonds, toasted		

Combine the olive oil, vinegar, sugar, garlic, salt, pepper, onion powder and dry mustard in a jar with a tight-fitting lid and shake to mix well. Chill until ready to serve. Toss the almonds, spinach, lettuce, green onions, strawberries, raspberries and blueberries in a large salad bowl. Add the vinaigrette just before serving and toss to coat.

Warm Spinach Salad

Serves 4 to 6

1/3 cup ketchup	1 package fresh baby spinach
1/2 cup vinegar	3 hard-cooked eggs, sliced
1/2 cup vegetable oil	6 slices bacon, crisp-cooked
3 tablespoons Worcestershire sauce	and crumbled
1 cup sugar	1/2 red onion, thinly sliced
1 teaspoon salt	6 tablespoons grated Romano cheese

Cook the ketchup, vinegar, oil, Worcestershire sauce, sugar and salt in a saucepan over medium heat until blended and warm. Arrange the spinach, eggs, bacon and onion on individual salad plates. Pour the warm dressing over the salad and sprinkle with the Romano cheese.

Cranberry Salad with Pecans and Pineapple

Serves 8 to 10

8 ounces cream cheese, softened	1 (8-ounce) can crushed pineapple, drained
2 tablespoons mayonnaise	1/2 cup chopped pecans
2 tablespoons granulated sugar	1 cup heavy whipping cream
1 (16-ounce) can whole cranberry sauce	1/2 cup confectioners' sugar
	1 teaspoon vanilla extract

Beat the cream cheese, mayonnaise and sugar in a mixing bowl until blended. Add the cranberry sauce, pineapple and pecans and beat at low speed until well mixed. Whip the whipping cream in a mixing bowl until soft peaks form. Beat in the confectioners' sugar and vanilla. Fold into the cranberry mixture. Spoon into a loaf pan and freeze until firm. (You may make in advance up to 6 months to this point.) Thaw for 30 minutes before serving. Invert the mold onto a platter and place a hot towel over the top of the pan. Let stand until the salad releases to the platter. Cut into slices. Serve immediately or return to the freezer.

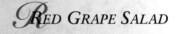

Red Grape Salad

Beat 8 ounces softened cream cheese, 1/4 cup milk and 3 tablespoons sugar in a mixing bowl until smooth. Stir in 2 pounds red seedless grapes and 1 cup chopped pecans. Chill in the refrigerator for up to 24 hours. Serve on lettuce leaves or a bed of mixed salad greens.

Fresh Avocado Salad

Serves 4 to 6

1	garlic clove, minced	4	small tomatoes, sliced
•	Salt to taste	1	small red onion, chopped
2	tablespoons red wine vinegar	1	green bell pepper, seeded
1	tablespoon olive oil		and chopped
4	drops of Tabasco sauce	1	fresh or canned jalapeño chile,
1	ripe avocado, chopped		finely chopped

Mash the garlic with the salt in a small bowl. Add the vinegar, olive oil and Tabasco sauce and mix well. Combine the avocado, tomatoes, onion, bell pepper and jalapeño chile in a bowl. Pour the dressing over the salad and toss to mix. Serve chilled or at room temperature.

Sunflower Broccoli Salad

Serves 12

•	Florets from 2 stalks of fresh broccoli	1	cup mayonnaise or mayonnaise-type salad dressing
8	ounces sharp Cheddar cheese, shredded	1/3	cup minus 1 tablespoon sugar, or equivalent amount of sugar substitute
1	red onion, minced		
1	cup sunflower seeds	1/4	cup raspberry wine vinegar or red wine vinegar

Cut the broccoli florets into bite-size pieces and place in a large bowl. Add the cheese, onion and sunflower seeds and toss to mix. Blend the mayonnaise, sugar and vinegar in a small bowl. Pour over the broccoli mixture and toss to coat. Cover and chill for at least 1 hour before serving. Serve slightly cool.

Note: *You may store the salad in the refrigerator for two to three days.*

Napa Cabbage Salad

Serves 8 to 10

1	large head Napa cabbage, finely chopped	1/2	cup sugar
5	green onions, chopped	2	packages ramen noodles
1/2	cup vegetable oil	1/4	cup (1/2 stick) butter
1/2	cup white vinegar	1	small package slivered almonds
2 1/2	teaspoons soy sauce	1/4	cup sesame seeds

Combine the cabbage and green onions in a large bowl and toss to mix. Chill, covered, in the refrigerator. Combine the oil, vinegar, soy sauce and sugar in a jar with a tight-fitting lid. Seal the jar and shake to mix well. Chill, covered, in the refrigerator. Crush the noodles, reserving the seasoning packets for another use. Melt the butter in a skillet and add the almonds, noodles and sesame seeds. Cook until brown and crunchy, stirring constantly. Remove to paper towels to drain. Add the almond mixture to the cabbage mixture and toss to mix. Shake the dressing well. Pour over the salad and toss to coat.

Margarita Coleslaw

Serves 12 to 14

12	cups shredded cabbage	1/4	cup rice vinegar
1	Granny Smith apple, chopped	1/4	cup vegetable oil
1	red apple, chopped	2	tablespoons honey
1	cup dried cranberries	1	teaspoon celery seeds
3/4	cup margarita mix, thawed		

Combine the cabbage, apples and cranberries in a large bowl and toss to mix. Combine the margarita mix, vinegar, oil, honey and celery seeds in a jar with a tight-fitting lid. Seal the jar and shake to mix well. Pour over the cabbage mixture and toss to coat.

Note: *You may prepare ahead and store in the refrigerator. For color, use a mixture of red and green cabbage.*

Corn Salad with Cilantro Dressing

Serves 10

2   bunches cilantro, stems removed (2 cups)
1/3 cup vegetable oil
1/3 cup white wine vinegar
3   tablespoons fresh lime juice
1   tablespoon honey
1/2 jalapeño chile, chopped
1/2 onion, chopped

1/2 teaspoon salt
1/4 teaspoon pepper
1   (16-ounce) package whole kernel yellow corn, thawed
1   red bell pepper, chopped
1   green bell pepper, chopped
1   small onion, chopped

Process the cilantro, oil, vinegar, lime juice, honey, jalapeño chile, 1/2 onion, the salt and pepper in a blender or food processor until blended. Combine the corn, bell peppers and 1 onion in a large bowl and stir to mix. Add the dressing and stir to coat. Chill, covered, for 4 to 8 hours. Drain before serving.

Pacific Rim Pasta Salad

Serves 6

3   packages chicken-flavored ramen noodles
1/2 cup mayonnaise
3   tablespoons soy sauce
1   tablespoon lemon juice

1/3 cup chopped carrots
1/3 cup chopped celery
1/3 cup chopped green onions
1/3 cup chopped red bell pepper

Crush the ramen noodles. Bring the seasonings from the noodles and water to a boil in a large saucepan. Add the noodles and cook for 3 minutes; drain. Let the noodles stand until cool.

Combine the mayonnaise, soy sauce and lemon juice in a bowl and mix well. Combine the cooled noodles, carrots, celery, green onions and bell pepper in a bowl and toss to mix. Add the mayonnaise mixture and toss to coat. Spoon into a serving bowl and garnish with fresh parsley.

Note: *You may chill the salad before serving to allow the flavors to blend.*

Spinach Fusilli Salad

Serves 8 to 10

12	ounces feta cheese	1	cup pitted kalamata olives
1	pound spinach fusilli, cooked al dente and drained	3	cups thinly sliced spinach
1/4	cup chopped red onion	1/2	cup virgin olive oil
3/4	cup sun-dried tomatoes, drained and chopped	3	tablespoons red wine vinegar
		1	garlic clove, crushed
		•	Salt and pepper to taste

Crumble the cheese over the cooked pasta in a large bowl. Add the onion, sun-dried tomatoes, olives and spinach and toss to mix. Combine the olive oil, vinegar, garlic, salt and pepper in a bowl and blend well. Pour over the pasta mixture and toss to coat.

Orzo and Artichoke Salad

Serves 8 to 10

1 1/2	cups uncooked orzo	•	Pepper to taste
•	Salt to taste	1/2	cup extra light olive oil
1/4	cup extra light olive oil	2	tablespoons minced fresh basil, or 1 teaspoon dried basil
1	(9-ounce) package frozen artichoke hearts, thawed	2	ounces prosciutto, minced
1/2	cup chicken broth	4	ounces Parmesan cheese, grated
1	egg yolk	1	tablespoon fresh lemon juice
2	tablespoons wine vinegar	1/4	cup minced fresh parsley
1	teaspoon Dijon mustard	4	scallions, minced

Boil the orzo in salted water in a saucepan for 7 to 8 minutes or until al dente. Drain in a sieve and rinse under cold water. Drain and toss with 1/4 cup olive oil. Cut the artichoke hearts into halves and simmer in the broth in a saucepan for 6 minutes or until tender; drain. Stir in the orzo. Whisk the egg yolk, vinegar, Dijon mustard, salt and pepper in a small bowl. Add 1/2 cup olive oil in a fine stream, whisking constantly. Whisk in the basil and pour over the orzo mixture. Stir in the prosciutto, cheese, lemon juice, parsley and scallions and chill.

Note: *Make sure you use extra light olive oil in this recipe to prevent an oily taste. If you are concerned about using a raw egg yolk, use the yolk from an egg pasteurized in the shell, which is sold at some specialty food stores, or use an equivalent amount of pasteurized egg substitute.*

Cherry Tomato Caper Salad

Serves 8

1/4 cup drained small capers	1/2 teaspoon pepper
3 tablespoons balsamic vinegar	32 large cherry tomatoes
1 teaspoon sugar	1 package spring mix salad greens
6 tablespoons olive oil	6 fresh basil leaves, chopped
1/2 teaspoon salt	

Mix the capers, vinegar, sugar, olive oil, salt and pepper in a bowl. Chill, covered, in the refrigerator. Cut the cherry tomatoes into slices and add to the dressing 1 hour before serving, stirring every 15 minutes. Divide the salad greens among eight salad plates. Spoon equal amounts of the tomato mixture over the salad greens and drizzle the remaining dressing over the top. Sprinkle with the basil.

Note: *You may add pine nuts and crumbled goat cheese, if desired.*

Marinated Vegetable Salad

Serves 12 to 15

1/2 cup vinegar	1 (11-ounce) can Shoe Peg corn, drained
1/2 cup vegetable oil	
1/2 cup sugar	1 small jar chopped pimento, drained
1 teaspoon salt	
1 teaspoon pepper	2 bunches green onions, sliced
1 (15-ounce) can green peas, drained	1 cup chopped green bell pepper (optional)
1 (15-ounce) can French-style green beans, drained	
	1 cup chopped celery

Bring the vinegar, oil, sugar, salt and pepper to a boil in a saucepan. Remove from the heat to cool. Combine the peas, green beans, corn, pimento, green onions, bell pepper and celery in a bowl and stir to mix. Add the marinade and stir to mix. Marinate, covered, in the refrigerator for 8 to 10 hours.

Plentiful "Ps" Salad

Serves 10 to 12

2	cups uncooked rotini	4	ounces fresh mushrooms
4	cups fresh black-eyed peas or drained canned black-eyed peas	1	(2-ounce) jar pimento, drained
1	red bell pepper, chopped	2	tablespoons chopped fresh parsley
1	green bell pepper, chopped	•	Italian salad dressing
1	purple onion, chopped	1/2	teaspoon salt
4	slices provolone cheese, chopped	1/4	teaspoon pepper
4	slices pepperoni or salami, chopped	2	tablespoons freshly grated Parmesan cheese

Cook the pasta using the package directions until al dente; drain. Combine the pasta, peas, bell peppers, onion, provolone cheese, pepperoni, mushrooms, pimento and parsley in a large bowl. Stir in enough salad dressing to coat. Sprinkle with the salt and pepper. Chill, covered, for 2 hours before serving. Sprinkle with the Parmesan cheese just before serving and toss lightly. Garnish with additional chopped fresh parsley.

Note: *You may use any pasta suitable for salads. Cauliflower, broccoli, carrots, or celery may also be added.*

GAIDO'S ROMANO CHEESE DRESSING

CHEF'S RECIPE

Process 1 egg, 1 garlic clove, minced, 1/2 cup (2 ounces) grated Romano cheese, 1/2 teaspoon red pepper, 1/2 teaspoon salt and 5 teaspoons white vinegar in a blender until smooth. Chill, covered, until ready to serve.

Note: *If you are concerned about using raw eggs, use eggs pasteurized in their shells, which are sold at some specialty food stores, or use an equivalent amount of pasteurized egg substitute.*

Tomato and Black Olive Salad with Feta Cheese

Serves 8

2 pints cherry tomatoes, cut into halves

1/2 cup pitted black olives, cut into halves

1 1/2 cups crumbled feta cheese with tomato and basil

3/4 cup olive oil

1/2 cup plus 2 tablespoons red wine vinegar

1 teaspoon dried whole oregano

1 teaspoon dried whole thyme

1 teaspoon minced garlic

• Salt and pepper to taste

Toss the tomatoes, olives and cheese in a salad bowl to mix. Combine the olive oil, vinegar, oregano, thyme, garlic, salt and pepper in a jar with a tight-fitting lid and shake vigorously to mix. Pour over the tomato mixture and chill for at least 4 hours before serving.

Chutney Chicken Salad Tea Sandwiches

Makes 16 sandwiches

1 pound boneless skinless chicken breasts

• Salt and freshly ground pepper to taste

1/2 cup finely chopped celery

3 tablespoons finely chopped red onion

1/4 cup finely chopped flat-leaf parsley

1 cup walnuts, toasted and chopped

1/3 cup mayonnaise

1 tablespoon fresh lemon juice

3 tablespoons Major Grey mango chutney

16 slices very thin white bread

1/4 cup (1/2 stick) butter, softened

Bring the chicken to a boil in salted water in a large saucepan and reduce the heat. Simmer for 15 to 20 minutes or until cooked through. Drain the chicken and cool for 10 minutes. Cut the chicken into thin strips and finely chop. Season with salt and pepper. Combine the chicken, celery, onion, parsley and walnuts in a bowl and toss to mix. Mix the mayonnaise, lemon juice and chutney in a bowl. Add to the chicken mixture and mix well. Adjust the seasonings to taste. Spread about 1/4 cup of the chicken salad evenly on half the bread slices. Spread butter on the remaining bread slices and place buttered side down on top of the chicken salad layer. Trim the crusts from the bread. Cut each sandwich diagonally into halves to form triangles. Cover the sandwiches with damp paper towels and wrap tightly with plastic wrap. Chill for up to 1 hour before serving.

Pulled Pork Sandwiches

Makes 12 to 14 sandwiches

1	onion, sliced	1/3	cup sugar
1	(4- to 5-pound) bone-in pork sirloin roast	1	bay leaf
		•	Salt and pepper to taste
2	cups undrained diced tomatoes	•	Garlic salt to taste
1/2	cup vinegar	3	drops of Tabasco sauce
1/4	cup barbecue sauce	•	Sandwich buns
1/2	cup Worcestershire sauce	•	Coleslaw (below)

Place the onion in the bottom of a slow cooker. Add the pork and enough water to cover by 1 to 2 inches. Cover and cook on Low for 8 hours; drain. Remove the pork and onion from the slow cooker. Shred the pork, discarding any fat. Cut the onion into bite-sized pieces. Return the pork and onion to the slow cooker. Add the tomatoes, vinegar, barbecue sauce, Worcestershire sauce, sugar, bay leaf, salt, pepper, garlic salt and Tabasco sauce and stir to mix well. Cook on Low for 2 hours, stirring occasionally. Remove the bay leaf. Serve on sandwich buns with Coleslaw.

Note: *Since slow cookers vary in size, the amount of water used will vary. This recipe may be frozen or chilled and reheated later in the day.*

Coleslaw

1/2	cup mayonnaise	3/4	teaspoons sugar
1/4	cup sour cream	1/2	teaspoon salt
2	tablespoons prepared mustard	1/2	teaspoon pepper
1	tablespoon cider vinegar	2	pounds green cabbage, thinly sliced

Whisk the mayonnaise, sour cream, mustard, vinegar, sugar, salt and pepper in a large bowl. Add the cabbage and toss to coat. Let stand for 30 minutes, stirring occasionally.

Wine Pairing
Rosemount
"Hill of Gold" Shiraz

Rich Boy Sandwiches
(Po' Boy's Rich Cousin)

Serves 6

6	individual loaves French bread or crusty rolls	2	tomatoes, thinly sliced
•	Mayonnaise to taste	6	slices Swiss cheese
•	Prepared mustard to taste	•	Slivered lettuce
1¹/₂	pounds assorted thinly sliced deli meat, such as ham, turkey, beef, pastrami and bologna	•	Thinly sliced red onion
		•	Thinly sliced dill pickles
		6	tablespoons Italian salad dressing
		18	dashes of Tabasco sauce

Cut each bread loaf in half and remove some of the inside of the bread. Spread the cut sides of the bread with mayonnaise and mustard. Layer the bread with deli meat, tomatoes, cheese, lettuce, onion and pickles. Drizzle each with 1 tablespoon of the salad dressing. Sprinkle each with three dashes of Tabasco sauce. Cover each with foil and bake at 350 degrees for 20 minutes or until heated through.

Pico Sandwiches

Serves a variable amount

•	Deli-style honey ham	•	Pico de Gallo (page 35)
•	Deli-cut provolone cheese	•	Jewish rye bread
•	Mayonnaise		

Layer one or two slices of ham and one slice of cheese on one slice of bread. Spread another slice of bread with mayonnaise and Pico de Gallo. Place on top of the cheese to form a sandwich.

Note: *This makes a very good and unusual sandwich. You may use as much or as little as you like.*

Side Dishes

Kemah Boardwalk

Tourists have discovered the Kemah Waterfront with its unique getaway destination, The Kemah Boardwalk. Visitors to the once-quiet Kemah boating and fishing community are captivated by this fourteen-acre waterfront multiplex, boasting themed dining and family attractions. The Kemah Boardwalk entertains guests with a boardwalk promenade, miniature train ride encircling the complex, and a family-oriented amusement park. The unusual selection of rides includes the C. P. Huntington, a gas powered train, and a thirty-six-foot classic carousel. A focal point of the park is the sixty-five-foot Century Ferris Wheel with gondola-style seating. As you enjoy the carnival music and bright lights of the ride, your climb to the top of the ferris wheel will be rewarded with spectacular views of the Clear Creek Channel, Galveston Bay, and the Boardwalk plaza.

Boardwalk South of the Border Picnic

OVERBOARD MARGARITAS,
(*See* Settings on the Dock of the Bay, *page 35*)

TEXAS SHRIMP DIP, PAGE 37
MEXICAN CLAM DIP, PAGE 34

TACO SALAD WITH A TWIST, PAGE 98

CORN SALAD WITH CILANTRO DRESSING, PAGE 108
MARGARITA COLESLAW, PAGE 107

PRALINES À LA MICROWAVE, PAGE 226
TEXAS CHOCOLATE CAKE, PAGE 203

Marinated Asparagus

Serves 6 to 8

2	pounds fresh asparagus		1/2	cup balsamic vinegar
1/4	cup olive oil		4	garlic cloves, minced
1	tablespoon sugar		1	teaspoon red pepper flakes

Snap off the tough ends of the asparagus. Cook the asparagus in boiling water to cover in a saucepan for 3 minutes; drain. Plunge the asparagus into ice water to stop the cooking process; drain. Arrange in a 9×13-inch dish. Whisk the olive oil, sugar, balsamic vinegar, garlic and red pepper flakes in a bowl until blended. Pour over the asparagus. Marinate, covered, in the refrigerator for 8 hours. Drain before serving.

Charro Beans

Serves 12

2	pounds dried pinto beans		6	to 8 tomatoes, chopped
1	bulb of garlic, chopped		1	bunch cilantro, stems removed
12	cups water		•	Jalapeño chile to taste
1	pound bacon, cut into cubes		•	Seasoned salt or Creole seasoning
6	onions, chopped			to taste

Sort and rinse the beans. Bring the garlic and water to a boil in a large stockpot. Add the beans and cook for 2 to 3 hours or until almost tender. Sauté the bacon in a skillet until almost cooked through but not crispy. Add the onions, tomatoes and cilantro leaves to the skillet and cook until the onions are tender. Add to the beans and cook for 30 minutes. Stir in the jalapeño chile and seasoned salt.

Note: *Do not soak the beans before cooking. This recipe may be frozen.*

Garlic Green Beans with Toasted Bread Crumbs

Serves 8

2 to 4 slices French bread, torn into pieces

1 tablespoon unsalted butter

1/4 teaspoon salt

• Freshly ground black pepper to taste

2 tablespoons grated Parmesan cheese

4 garlic cloves, minced (about 2 tablespoons)

1/4 teaspoon salt

2 tablespoons unsalted butter

2 teaspoons all-purpose flour

1/8 teaspoon red pepper flakes

1 teaspoon minced fresh thyme leaves

1 1/2 pounds fresh green beans, trimmed

1 cup chicken broth

1 tablespoon fresh lemon juice

• Salt to taste

Process the bread in a food processor to form fine crumbs. Brown the crumbs in 1 tablespoon melted butter in a large nonstick skillet, stirring frequently. Spoon into a bowl and stir in 1/4 teaspoon salt and black pepper. Stir in the Parmesan cheese. (You may prepare in advance up to this point.)

Sauté the garlic and 1/4 teaspoon salt in 2 tablespoons melted butter in a skillet over medium heat for 3 to 5 minutes or until the garlic is golden brown. Stir in the flour, red pepper flakes and thyme. Add the green beans and toss to coat. Stir in the broth and cook, covered, over medium heat until the green beans are tender-crisp. Uncover and cook until the green beans are tender and the sauce is thickened, stirring occasionally. Remove from the heat and add the lemon juice. Adjust the seasonings to taste. Spoon into a serving dish and sprinkle with the bread crumbs.

Note: *This recipe may be frozen.*

Marinated Green Beans with Feta Cheese

Serves 8 to 10

2	pounds fresh green beans	2	tablespoons red wine vinegar
1	teaspoon salt	1	tablespoon fresh oregano, finely
2	garlic cloves, minced		chopped
1/4	cup olive oil	1/2	teaspoon salt
1	cup kalamata olives, sliced	1/4	teaspoon pepper
2	tomatoes, seeded and chopped	6	ounces feta cheese, crumbled

Cook the green beans in boiling water seasoned with 1 teaspoon salt for 6 to 8 minutes or until tender-crisp. Drain and plunge into ice water to stop the cooking process. Place in a shallow serving dish.

Sauté the garlic in the olive oil over medium heat for 1 minute and remove from the heat. Stir in the olives, tomatoes, vinegar, oregano, 1/2 teaspoon salt and the pepper. Pour over the green beans and toss to coat. Marinate, covered, in the refrigerator for 2 to 10 hours. Sprinkle with the feta cheese just before serving.

Green Bean Bundles

Serves 8 to 10

4	(15-ounce) cans whole green beans	1 1/2	cups packed brown sugar
•	Bacon slices, cut into halves	1	tablespoon hickory smoke salt
1 1/2	cups (3 sticks) margarine		

Place several whole green beans in the middle of a bacon half. Wrap the bacon around the green beans to form a bundle and secure with a wooden pick. Place in a baking dish. Continue with the remaining green beans and bacon. Melt the margarine in a skillet and stir in the brown sugar and salt. Drizzle over the green bean bundles. Bake at 350 degrees for 30 to 35 minutes or until the bacon is cooked through.

Broccoli-Corn Casserole

Serves 8

2	(10-ounce) packages frozen chopped broccoli
2	tablespoons chopped onion
1/2	cup (1 stick) butter
2	cups herb-seasoned stuffing mix

2	(15-ounce) cans cream-style corn
2	eggs, well beaten
•	Salt and pepper to taste
3	slices bacon, cut into small pieces

Cook the broccoli using the package directions; drain. Sauté the onion in the butter in a skillet until translucent. Combine the sautéed onion and stuffing mix in a large bowl and mix well. Add the broccoli, corn, eggs, salt and pepper and mix well. Spoon into a 2-quart baking dish. Sprinkle the uncooked bacon over the top. Bake at 350 degrees for 30 minutes.

Red Cabbage

Serves 8

1	(3-pound) head red cabbage
4	slices bacon, chopped
1	tablespoon sugar
1	apple, peeled and chopped
1	onion, chopped

4	whole cloves
1/4	cup wine vinegar
1	cup dry red wine
•	Salt to taste
1/2	cup red currant jelly

Rinse the cabbage and remove the core. Cut the cabbage into quarters. Remove the tough outer leaves of the cabbage and discard. Shred the remaining cabbage.

Cook the bacon in an enameled or stainless steel pan until crisp. Remove the bacon to paper towels to drain, reserving the drippings in the pan. Add the sugar to the reserved bacon drippings and sauté until golden brown. Add the apple and onion. Cover and braise over low heat for 5 minutes. Stir in the cabbage, cloves and vinegar. Cover and braise for 10 minutes or until the cabbage turns a purplish blue. Add the wine and bacon. Cover and simmer slowly for 2 hours or until tender, adding additional wine or water if needed. Season with salt and stir in the red currant jelly.

Note: *This dish is best prepared the day before serving in order for the flavors to develop.*

Spanish Indian Baked Corn

Serves 8

4	ounces bacon, chopped into 1/2-inch pieces
1/3	cup chopped onion
1/3	cup chopped celery
1/3	cup chopped green bell pepper
1/2	cup (1 stick) butter
1/4	cup milk
1	(13-ounce) can whole kernel corn, drained
1	(13-ounce) can cream-style corn
2	tablespoons chopped jalapeño chile (optional)
2	tablespoons chopped pimento (optional)
1	tablespoon sugar
1	teaspoon salt
2	cups crumbled corn bread
2	tablespoons butter, melted

Cook the bacon in a large skillet over medium heat until crisp. Add the onion, celery and bell pepper. Sauté for 2 minutes over low heat and set aside.

Melt 1/2 cup butter in a medium saucepan. Add the milk, whole kernel corn, cream-style corn, jalapeño chile, pimento, sugar and salt. Cook over low heat until heated through. Add the bacon mixture and 1 cup of the corn bread. Cook until heated through, stirring frequently. Spoon into an 8×8-inch baking pan. Moisten the remaining corn bread crumbs with 2 tablespoons butter and sprinkle over the top of the corn mixture. Bake at 350 degrees for 20 to 25 minutes or until the crumbs are light brown.

Note: *This is a great side dish to serve at Thanksgiving.*

Frosted Cauliflower

Serves 6 to 8

1	head cauliflower
1	teaspoon salt
2	tablespoons water
1/2	cup mayonnaise
1	teaspoon finely chopped onion
1	teaspoon prepared mustard
1/2	cup (2 ounces) shredded Cheddar cheese

Remove the tough outer leaves and trim the base of the cauliflower; rinse well. Combine the salt and water in a 1 1/2-quart microwave-safe dish. Add the cauliflower and cover. Microwave on High for 8 to 9 minutes or until tender-crisp. Combine the mayonnaise, onion and mustard in a bowl and mix well. Spoon over the cauliflower and sprinkle with the cheese. Microwave at 60 percent power for 1 1/2 to 2 minutes or until the cheese melts.

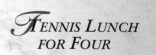

Okra Confit

Serves 5

3	cups (1/3-inch) sliced okra (about 1 pound)	2	sprigs of thyme
1	Roma tomato, cut into half-moon slices	2	to 4 tablespoons extra-virgin olive oil
3	or 4 garlic cloves, coarsely chopped	•	Salt and ground pepper to taste

Place the okra, tomato, garlic and thyme in a 10×15-inch baking pan. Drizzle with the olive oil and stir to coat. (To serve the confit over pasta, use 1/4 cup olive oil.) Season with salt and pepper. Bake at 275 degrees for 35 to 45 minutes or until tender.

Note: *If you prefer the vegetables on the crunchy side, reduce the baking time.*

1015 Onion Surprise Casserole

Serves 6 to 8

3	1015 super sweet onions, chopped	2	eggs
1/4	cup (1/2 stick) butter	3/4	cup light cream or half-and-half
2	cups (8 ounces) shredded Swiss cheese	1	teaspoon salt
1	cup crushed saltine crackers	1/8	teaspoon pepper
		2	tablespoons butter

Sauté the onions in 1/4 cup melted butter in a large skillet until tender. Layer one-half of the onions in a 1 1/2-quart baking dish. Sprinkle with 1 cup of the cheese and 1/2 cup of the cracker crumbs. Continue layering with the remaining onions and remaining cheese.

Beat the eggs, cream, salt and pepper in a mixing bowl until smooth. Pour evenly over the layers. Sauté the remaining cracker crumbs in 2 tablespoons melted butter in a skillet until light brown. Sprinkle over the layers. Bake at 350 degrees for 25 minutes.

Note: *Great served with roast beef or ham.*

Baked Mashed Potatoes Supreme

Serves 12

8	slices center-cut bacon	1	cup (or less) milk
8	red new potatoes	1	cup sour cream
1/2	teaspoon pepper	5	green onions, chopped
1/2	teaspoon Tony Chachere's Creole Seasoning	11/2	cups (6 ounces) shredded Cheddar cheese
6	tablespoons butter		

Cook the bacon in a skillet until crisp; drain. Cool the bacon and crumble. Scrub the potatoes. Boil the unpeeled potatoes in water to cover in a saucepan for 30 minutes or until tender; drain. Add the pepper, Creole Seasoning and butter. Beat with a hand mixer until the potatoes are mashed. Add the milk gradually, beating constantly until of the desired consistency. Add 1/2 cup sour cream, one-half of the green onions and one-half of the bacon and mix well.

Spoon the potato mixture into a 9×13-inch baking dish. Cover the top with the remaining 1/2 cup sour cream, the cheese and remaining bacon. Bake at 300 degrees for 20 minutes or until the cheese melts. Remove from the oven and sprinkle with the remaining green onions.

Note: *This recipe is great to take to potluck dinners and goes with everything.*

HORSERADISH ROASTED POTATOES

Peel a 1-inch strip around the center of each of 2 pounds of small new potatoes and place in a large bowl. (If larger potatoes are used, cut into quarters.) Add 1/4 cup (1/2 stick) melted butter, 2 tablespoons horseradish, 1/2 teaspoon salt and 1/2 teaspoon pepper and toss gently to coat. Place in a lightly greased roasting pan. Bake at 425 degrees for 45 minutes or until tender.

Potato Casserole with Onion and Garlic

Serves 10 to 12

4	1015 onions or other sweet onions, thinly sliced	8	russet potatoes, peeled and sliced
1/4	cup (1/2 stick) butter	•	Salt and pepper to taste
4	small garlic cloves, crushed	1	(10-ounce) can beef bouillon
2	tablespoons Worcestershire sauce		

Cook the onions in the butter in a skillet for 20 to 25 minutes or until tender. Add the garlic and Worcestershire sauce and stir to mix well. Place one-half of the potatoes in a large baking dish and sprinkle with salt and pepper. Continue layering with one-half of the onions, the remaining potatoes and the remaining onions. Pour the beef bouillon over the layers. (You may prepare 1 to 2 hours ahead at this point and store, covered, in the refrigerator until ready to bake.) Bake, covered, at 350 degrees for 1 hour or until the potatoes are tender.

Potatoes with a French Twist

Serves 6 to 8

6	Yukon gold potatoes, chopped	1/4	teaspoon grated nutmeg
•	Salt to taste	3/4	cup half-and-half
6	tablespoons butter	3	eggs, beaten
1	teaspoon salt	1 1/2	cups sour cream
1/4	teaspoon pepper	•	Paprika to taste

Boil the potatoes in salted water to cover in a saucepan until tender. Drain and shake dry. Place the potatoes in a bowl and add the butter, 1 teaspoon salt, the pepper, nutmeg, half-and-half and eggs. Beat until light and fluffy. Spoon into a soufflé dish and cover the top with the sour cream. Sprinkle with paprika. (You may prepare ahead up to this point and store, covered, in the refrigerator until ready to bake.) Bake at 350 degrees for 20 to 30 minutes or until heated through.

Mediterranean Spinach and Rice

Serves 6

3 tablespoons extra-virgin olive oil	1 red bell pepper, julienned (optional)
4 garlic cloves, chopped	3 cups cooked white rice
• Salt and pepper to taste	1 cup crumbled feta cheese
1/2 cup golden raisins	
2 pounds fresh spinach, rinsed and patted dry	

Heat the olive oil in a large wok. Add the garlic and sauté until golden brown. Add the salt, pepper and raisins and sauté for 1 minute. Add the spinach and sauté until just wilted. Add the bell pepper, rice and cheese and toss until heated through.

Note: *This recipe won the Grand Prize in the Oldways Rice and Raisins Recipe Contest.*

Spinach Bread Pudding

Serves 6

1 (10-ounce) package frozen chopped spinach	1/4 teaspoon salt
3/4 cup chopped onion	1/4 teaspoon coarsely ground pepper
2 tablespoons olive oil	1 cup (4 ounces) shredded Monterey Jack cheese
1 garlic clove, minced	4 cups (3/4-inch pieces) French bread
1 tablespoon rosemary	1/2 cup (2 ounces) grated Parmesan cheese
6 eggs	
1 cup milk	

Thaw the spinach and squeeze dry. Sauté the onion in the hot olive oil in a skillet until soft. Add the garlic and rosemary and sauté until the garlic is golden brown. Beat the eggs, milk, salt and pepper in a large mixing bowl. Stir in the spinach, onion mixture, Monterey Jack cheese and bread. Let stand until the bread soaks up the liquid. Pour into a 9×13-inch ceramic or glass baking dish. Sprinkle with the Parmesan cheese. Bake at 375 degrees for 20 to 25 minutes or until brown, puffy and a knife inserted in the center comes out clean. Let stand for 5 minutes before serving.

Calabacitas

Serves 4 to 6

2	tablespoons butter	1	cup frozen whole kernel corn
1	tablespoon olive oil	1	cup chicken stock
4	cups calabacitas (yellow squash and zucchini), chopped	•	Salt and pepper to taste
2	garlic cloves, minced	1/2	cup (2 ounces) shredded Monterey Jack cheese
1	white onion, chopped	1/2	cup chopped tomatoes
6	scallions, finely chopped	2	tablespoons chopped fresh cilantro
1	(4-ounce) can chopped green chiles		

Melt the butter in the olive oil in a large sauté pan over medium-high heat. Add the calabacitas, garlic and onion and sauté for 5 minutes. Add the scallions and sauté for 1 minute. Add the green chiles, corn and stock. Simmer for 20 minutes or until the calabacitas are tender, but not soft. Season with salt and pepper. Add the cheese, tomatoes and cilantro and simmer for 5 minutes. Spoon into a serving dish and garnish with additional chopped cilantro and cheese.

Squash Casserole

Serves 4 to 6

2	pounds yellow squash, sliced	2	tablespoons brown sugar
2	eggs	1	teaspoon salt
1/2	onion, chopped	2	slices bread, torn
6	tablespoons butter or margarine	1	cup (4 ounces) shredded Cheddar cheese
1/2	cup (scant) milk		

Cook the squash in water to cover in a saucepan until tender; drain and mash. Beat the eggs in a large bowl until light. Add the squash, onion, butter, milk, brown sugar and salt and mix well. Layer the bread, squash mixture and cheese one-half at a time in a buttered round baking dish. (You may prepare ahead up to this point and store, covered, in the refrigerator until ready to bake.) Bake at 350 degrees for 45 minutes.

Note: *This recipe may be doubled.*

Corn-Zucchini Boats with Pepper Jack Cheese

Serves 4

4	ears of corn, unhusked	1	cup (4 ounces) coarsely shredded Monterey Jack cheese with peppers
2	tablespoons olive oil		
1	zucchini, cut into 1/3-inch pieces		
•	Salt to taste	2	tablespoons finely crushed corn tortilla chips
3/4	cup finely chopped red onion		

Pull a lengthwise strip of corn husk about 1 1/2 inches wide from each ear of corn to expose a strip of kernels; discard the corn husk strip. Carefully peel back the remaining husks, keeping them attached to the stem ends and snap the ears from the stem ends. Discard the silk from the husks. Tear a thin strip from a tender inner piece of each husk and use to tie the loose end of each husk to form a boat. Cut the corn from the ears and discard the cobs.

Heat the olive oil in a large heavy skillet over medium-high heat until hot but not smoking. Add the zucchini and sauté for 2 to 3 minutes or until light brown and just tender. Remove the zucchini with a slotted spoon to a bowl and season with salt. Add the corn, onion and salt to the drippings in the skillet. Sauté over medium-high heat for 4 minutes. Cover and cook over low heat for 2 to 3 minutes or until the corn is tender-crisp. Add the corn mixture to the zucchini and let stand until cool. Stir in the cheese and spoon into the prepared corn husk boats. (You may prepare a day ahead up to this point and store, covered, in the refrigerator.) Arrange on a baking sheet and sprinkle the filling with the crushed tortilla chips. Bake at 375 degrees on the upper oven rack for 15 to 20 minutes or until the cheese is melted and the filling is heated through.

Note: *This is a great side dish to serve with grilled steak. You may also bake the filling in a baking dish instead of placing in the corn husk boats.*

Sweet Potato and Pineapple Casserole

Serves 4 to 6

2	eggs	1/2	teaspoon ground nutmeg
3/4	cup milk	1	(16-ounce) can pineapple
3/4	cup sugar		chunks, drained
1	(28-ounce) can sweet potatoes, drained and mashed	3/4	cup graham cracker crumbs
		1/2	cup pecans, finely chopped
6	tablespoons butter or margarine, melted	1/4	cup whole pecans
		6	tablespoons butter or
1/2	teaspoon ground cinnamon		margarine, melted

Beat the eggs in a large mixing bowl or food processor. Add the milk, sugar, sweet potatoes, 6 tablespoons butter, cinnamon and nutmeg and mix well. Pour into an 8×8-inch glass baking dish sprayed with nonstick cooking spray. Drop the pineapple chunks evenly over the top, pushing down the pineapple to cover. Bake at 350 degrees for 35 minutes. Remove from the oven to cool slightly, maintaining the oven temperature. Combine the graham cracker crumbs, finely chopped pecans, whole pecans and 6 tablespoons butter in a bowl and mix well. Separate the whole pecans from the mixture and set aside. Coat the top of the sweet potato mixture with the crushed pecan mixture. Line the edges with the reserved whole pecans. Bake for 10 minutes. Garnish the center with a thin slice of pineapple just before serving.

Tomatoes Rockefeller

Serves 6

1	(10-ounce) package frozen spinach, cooked and drained	2	tablespoons freshly grated Parmesan cheese
1/3	cup herb-seasoned stuffing mix, crushed	1/4	teaspoon pepper
		•	Dash of garlic salt
3	green onions, minced	6	thick tomato slices
1	egg, beaten	2	tablespoons freshly grated
3	tablespoons butter, melted		Romano cheese
1	teaspoon Tabasco sauce		

Combine the spinach, stuffing mix, green onions, egg, butter, Tabasco sauce, Parmesan cheese, pepper and garlic salt in a bowl and mix well. Place the tomato slices in a single layer in a buttered baking dish. Top each with the spinach mixture and sprinkle with the Romano cheese. Bake at 350 degrees for 20 to 30 minutes or until heated through.

Grilled Marinated Vegetable Kabobs

Makes 16 kabobs

VEGETABLE MARINADE

3	tablespoons vegetable oil
1	teaspoon chili powder
1/2	teaspoon paprika
1/4	teaspoon cumin
1/8	teaspoon ground red pepper
3	tablespoons fresh lime juice
2	tablespoons chopped fresh cilantro
2	tablespoons tomato paste
1 1/2	teaspoons honey
2	garlic cloves, minced
2	tablespoons water

VEGETABLE KABOBS

2	red bell peppers, cut into 1 1/2-inch pieces
2	green bell peppers, cut into 1 1/2-inch pieces
2	yellow bell peppers, cut into 1 1/2-inch pieces
2	large yellow squash, cut into 1 1/2-inch pieces
2	large zucchini, cut into 1 1/2-inch pieces
4	yellow onions, cut into 1 1/2-inch pieces

To *prepare the marinade,* combine the oil, chili powder, paprika, cumin, red pepper, lime juice, cilantro, tomato paste, honey, garlic and water in a medium bowl and stir until smooth.

To prepare the kabobs, thread the vegetables onto metal skewers. (You can make single vegetable skewers or use an assortment of vegetables on each skewer.) Lightly brush each skewer with the marinade. Place on a grill rack and grill 4 to 6 inches from the hot coals for 5 minutes per side or until brown and lightly charred and tender. Serve with the remaining marinade.

Note: *You may alternatively place the kabobs on a rack in a broiler pan and broil.*

Pan-Roasted Winter Vegetables

Serves 6 to 8

- Salt to taste
- 8 ounces rutabagas, peeled and cut into pieces
- 8 ounces carrots, peeled and cut into pieces
- 8 ounces parsnips, peeled and cut into pieces
- 8 ounces Brussels sprouts, trimmed
- 8 ounces sweet potatoes, peeled and cut into pieces
- 1 1/2 tablespoons unsalted butter
- 1 tablespoon extra-virgin olive oil
- 2 teaspoons chopped fresh thyme
- 2 teaspoons chopped fresh sage
- 1/8 teaspoon freshly ground nutmeg
- Salt and pepper to taste
- 1/2 cup marsala

Fill a large stockpot three-fourths full of salted water and bring to a boil. Add the rutabagas, carrots and parsnips and simmer for 4 minutes or until the vegetables give slightly when pierced with a fork; drain well. Place the boiled vegetables with the Brussels sprouts and sweet potatoes in a large roasting pan.

Melt the butter in a small saucepan over low heat. Add the olive oil, thyme, sage and nutmeg and stir to mix well. Drizzle over the vegetables and toss to coat evenly. Season with salt and pepper. Pour the wine in the bottom of the pan and cover tightly with foil. Roast at 450 degrees for 40 minutes. Remove the foil and toss the vegetables to coat. Continue to roast, uncovered, for 20 to 30 minutes or until the wine evaporates and the vegetables can be easily pierced with a knife.

GLAZED CARROTS

Peel 2 pounds of carrots and cut diagonally into slices. Cook, covered, in a small amount of boiling water for 12 minutes or until just tender; drain. Heat 3 tablespoons butter or margarine, 2 tablespoons sugar and 1/4 cup apricot jam in a saucepan until smooth, stirring frequently. Add the carrots and season with salt to taste. Cook for 3 minutes or until glazed, stirring gently.

Grits and Greens Casserole

Serves 16

2	cups whipping cream or half-and-half	2	cups chicken broth
6	cups chicken broth	1	cup (2 sticks) butter
2	cups uncooked quick-cooking grits	2¹/₂	cups (10 ounces) grated Parmesan cheese
•	Milk	¹/₂	teaspoon pepper
1	large package frozen collard greens, mustard greens or spinach	1	cup crumbled crisp-cooked bacon

Bring the cream and 6 cups broth to a boil in a large saucepan. Stir in the grits. Cook over medium heat until the grits return to a boil. Cover and reduce the heat. Simmer using the package directions until thickened, stirring frequently to prevent burning and adding milk if needed to make the consistency of slightly runny oatmeal. Cook the collard greens with 2 cups broth in a large saucepan for 10 minutes or until tender. Drain the collard greens in a colander, squeezing out any remaining liquid. Combine the butter, cheese and pepper with the hot cooked grits and stir until the butter is melted. Stir in the collard greens. Spoon into a greased 9×13-inch baking dish. Sprinkle with additional Parmesan cheese and the crumbled bacon. Serve at room temperature or bake at 350 degrees until brown on top.

Note: *You may use one 10-ounce can of broth with roasted garlic for part of the 8 cups of broth.*

Rice Pilaf

Serves 8

¹/₂	cup (1 stick) butter	1	small can mushrooms (optional)
1	yellow or red onion, finely chopped	•	Few drops of Worcestershire sauce
1	cup uncooked quick-cooking rice	1	(10-ounce) can beef broth
•	Salt and pepper to taste	1	can water
•	Garlic salt to taste	•	Finely chopped parsley to taste

Melt the butter in a cast-iron skillet. Add the onion, uncooked rice, salt, pepper, garlic salt, mushrooms and Worcestershire sauce. Carefully add the broth and water. Sprinkle with enough chopped parsley to cover the top. Bake at 350 degrees for 1 hour.

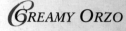

Creamy Orzo

Melt 3 tablespoons unsalted butter in a heavy skillet over medium-high heat. Add 1½ cups uncooked orzo and sauté for 2 minutes. Stir in 3 cups chicken stock or canned chicken broth. Bring to a boil and reduce the heat. Simmer for 20 minutes or until the orzo is tender and the liquid is absorbed. Stir in ½ cup (2 ounces) grated Parmesan cheese and 6 tablespoons chopped fresh basil, or 1½ teaspoons dried basil. Season with salt and pepper to taste.

Roasted Red Pepper Risotto

Serves 6 to 8

½ cup minced onion
3 tablespoons olive oil
1½ cups uncooked arborio rice
5 cups hot chicken stock
1 teaspoon salt
• Freshly ground pepper to taste

1 cup (4 ounces) freshly grated Parmesan cheese
½ cup (1 stick) cold unsalted butter
1 cup roasted red peppers, puréed

Cook the onion in hot olive oil in a saucepan for 2 minutes or until softened but not brown. Add the uncooked rice and cook for 1 to 2 minutes, stirring constantly to coat well. Add ½ cup of the stock and cook until most of the liquid is absorbed, stirring constantly. Repeat with the remaining stock ½ cup at a time until all of the liquid is incorporated. Add salt and pepper and continue to cook until the liquid is absorbed and the rice is tender but still slightly firm, stirring constantly. Add the cheese, butter and puréed roasted peppers and stir to mix. Cook until most of the liquid has been reduced and the rice is creamy yet slightly firm. Garnish with additional Parmesan cheese and roasted pepper strips.

Note: *See Roasting Peppers in the sidebar on page 189 in* Settings on the Dock of the Bay.

Seafood Entrées

Christmas Boat Parade

This holiday season Boat Parade started in 1961 with just six boats and has grown to more than one hundred beautifully decorated boats of all description. Its original home was Lakewood Yacht Club, but as it grew in popularity the launch site was moved to South Shore Harbor Marina. As darkness falls, the parade winds its way across Clear Lake, through the Kemah/Seabrook Channel, and briefly out into Galveston Bay before returning to the Marina. The event culminates with a spectacular fireworks display over Clear Lake. The Boat Parade is a much anticipated event along Clear Lake and a wonderful reason to celebrate the holiday season with good food and good friends.

Boat Parade

CEVICHE, PAGE 36
GOAT CHEESE SPREAD, PAGE 43
ASPARAGUS PROSCIUTTO ROLLS, PAGE 28

COLD BOILED SHRIMP WITH TEXAS RÉMOULADE, PAGE 154

WILD RICE SALAD,
(*See* Settings on the Dock of the Bay, *page 88*)

MARINATED GREEN BEANS WITH FETA CHEESE, PAGE 121

GRASSHOPPER MOUSSE IN CHOCOLATE SHELLS, PAGE 219
TOFFEE CRUNCH, PAGE 227

WINE PAIRING
BOLLINI PINOT GRIGIO

Salmon Fillet with Mustard Dill Sauce

Serves 6

MUSTARD DILL SAUCE
1/2 cup whole grain mustard
3/4 cup heavy cream
1/4 cup olive oil
1/2 cup chopped fresh dill weed
• Pepper to taste

SALMON
3 pounds salmon fillets
• Soy sauce
• Salt and pepper to taste

To *prepare the sauce,* combine the whole grain mustard, cream, olive oil, dill weed and pepper in a bowl and mix well. Chill, covered, in the refrigerator until ready to serve. Bring the sauce to room temperature and whisk before serving. (You may prepare up to 1 day in advance.)

To prepare the salmon, rinse the salmon and pat dry. Arrange skin side down in a foil-lined 10×15-inch baking pan. Rub thoroughly with soy sauce. Season with salt and pepper. Broil for 12 to 15 minutes or until cooked through and the salmon flakes easily. Remove the salmon to a platter and garnish with sprigs of fresh dill weed. Serve the salmon warm or at room temperature with the mustard dill sauce.

Seashell Pasta with Salmon and Dill

Serves 2

1 (8-ounce) salmon fillet, 3/4 inch thick
• Olive oil
• Salt and pepper to taste
4 ounces uncooked small pasta shells

1/2 cup finely chopped red onion
1/2 cup finely chopped celery
1/3 cup mayonnaise
3 tablespoons chopped fresh dill weed
1 tablespoon Dijon mustard

Brush both sides of the salmon with olive oil and season with salt and pepper. Place on a rack in a broiler pan and broil for 3 minutes per side or until just cooked through. Cool slightly.

Cook the pasta in boiling salted water in a stockpot until al dente; drain. Rinse the pasta with cold water and drain again. Combine the pasta, onion and celery in a large bowl. Remove the skin from the salmon. Tear the salmon into bite-size pieces and add to the pasta mixture. Whisk the mayonnaise, dill weed and Dijon mustard in a small bowl until blended. Add to the pasta mixture and toss gently to coat. Chill, covered, for up to 6 hours.

Note: *You may use smoked salmon or canned salmon.*

CHEF ROLAND KYBURZ

Born and raised in Switzerland, Chef Kyburz entered the Professional Chef's School in Aarau, Switzerland, at the age of fifteen. Having completed his student practice, he continued to refine his culinary skills with various positions in five-star hotels and restaurants throughout Switzerland. His desire to develop on an international level brought him to experiences in several ethnic cuisines with positions in locales such as Israel, Great Britain, Germany, and Puerto Rico.

In 1982, Chef Kyburz came to America, as Houston's Whitehall Hotel's Executive Sous-Chef and subsequently was promoted to Executive Chef. Then, in 1985, he accepted the enormous job of Executive Chef of the sprawling Houstonian Hotel and Conference Center, Fitness Center, and Phoenix Spa. ➤

South Shore Harbour Pistachio-Crusted Salmon with Mango Relish and Citrus Lime Butter Sauce

CHEF'S RECIPE

Serves a variable amount

CITRUS LIME BUTTER SAUCE
- 1/4 cup chopped onion
- 1/2 teaspoon finely sliced lemon grass
- 2 garlic cloves, chopped
- 1 tablespoon butter
- 1/2 cup dry white wine
- 2 tablespoons lime juice
- 1/2 teaspoon lemon pepper
- 1 cup (2 sticks) unsalted butter, cut into cubes

SALMON
- 1 (5- to 6-ounce) salmon fillet per person
- • Lemon juice
- • Salt and pepper to taste
- • Melted butter for brushing
- • Finely chopped pistachios
- • White wine
- • Mango Relish (page 141)

To *prepare the sauce,* sauté the onion, lemon grass and garlic in 1 tablespoon butter in a small pan until the onion is translucent. Add the wine, lime juice and lemon pepper and cook until the liquid is reduced to one-fourth. Remove from the heat. Whip in 1 cup butter one cube at a time until the butter is blended into the sauce; strain and serve.

To prepare the salmon, marinate the salmon in a small amount of lemon juice, salt and pepper. (The salmon does not have to be seasoned too much, since it has its own nice flavor.) Brush the salmon with melted butter and dip in pistachios to coat. Place in a baking pan with some white wine. Bake at 350 degrees until the flesh is firm and flakes easily. Serve over rice pilaf or tossed baby greens with the Citrus Lime Butter Sauce and Mango Relish.

Mango Relish

1   cup (¹/4-inch) cubed mango
2   tablespoons finely chopped red onion

1   tablespoon fresh lime juice
1   tablespoon finely chopped cilantro

Combine the mango, onion, lime juice and cilantro in a bowl and toss to mix. Chill, covered, until ready to serve or chill over ice.

South Shore Harbour Plantain-Crusted Snapper

CHEF'S RECIPE

Serves 4

4   unripe plantains
4   (6-ounce) snapper fillets or other fish fillets
•   Salt and pepper to taste
¹/2   cup (4 ounces) olive oil

•   Mango Relish (above)
•   Citrus Lime Butter Sauce (page 140)
•   Hot steamed rice

Cut the plantains into thin slices. Cook in a nonstick skillet until crisp. Process in a food processor until finely ground. Season the fish with salt and pepper and coat in the ground plantains. Sauté in the olive oil in a skillet for 4 minutes or until light brown and the fish flakes easily. Serve the fish over steamed rice with mashed sweet potatoes. Top the fish with Mango Relish and Citrus Lime Butter Sauce.

During the next eight years, he completely revamped the food operation and developed a well-deserved reputation for a successful in-house catering and special events operation. Prior to coming to South Shore Harbour Resort in 2001, he was the Executive Chef of the Intercontinental Hotel Central Park South in New York.

Among his distinguished accomplishments Chef Kyburz was honored in 1991 in his native Switzerland at the "le Chefs de Chefs" Conference for his renowned service to numerous heads of state from around the world.

Chef Kyburz is the Executive Chef for South Shore Harbour Resort and Conference Center.

Mark's Grilled Copper River Salmon with Summer Vegetables and Spicy Herbed Butter

CHEF'S RECIPE

Serves 4

MARK'S RESTAURANT

Mark's Restaurant is located in a 1920 renovated church and was voted Houston's Most Romantic Restaurant. Owner and chef, Mark Cox began cooking as a young man in West Virginia. At eighteen, he attended the Culinary Institute of America in upstate New York. Mark apprenticed at the Greenbriar in West Virginia and then moved to the Four Seasons Hotel in Washington, D.C. ➤

SUMMER VEGETABLES

1   yellow squash, cut lengthwise into 1/4-inch slices
1   zucchini, cut lengthwise into 1/4-inch slices
1   red bell pepper, steamed and cut into 1/4-inch slices
1   lemon, cut into 6 wedges
•   Extra-virgin olive oil for drizzling
•   Salt and freshly ground pepper to taste
•   Spicy Herbed Butter (page 143)

SALMON

4   (5-ounce) center-cut Copper River salmon fillets, skin on (about 1 inch thick)
2   tablespoons olive oil
•   Kosher salt and freshly ground pepper to taste

To *prepare the vegetables,* drizzle the vegetables and lemon wedges with the olive oil. Season with salt and pepper. Place on a grill rack and brush with Spicy Herbed Butter. Grill for 3 to 4 minutes per side or until brown and tender.

To prepare the salmon, brush the salmon lightly with the olive oil. Season with kosher salt and pepper. Place the salmon skin side up at an angle on a grill rack. Grill for 3 minutes or until the salmon has distinctive grill marks. Reposition the salmon with a spatula about 45 degrees with the skin side up to make cross-hatched grill marks. Grill for 3 minutes and turn the salmon over. Continue grilling the salmon for 2 to 3 minutes for pink inside, 5 minutes for medium or 7 minutes for well done, brushing with Spicy Herbed Butter. Remove the salmon from the grill to a serving platter. (If the skin comes loose during grilling, you may remove or discard before serving.) Place the vegetables on the platter with the salmon. Squeeze some of the grilled lemon wedges over the top and serve with Spicy Herbed Butter.

Spicy Herbed Butter

2 cups (4 sticks) unsalted
   butter, softened
3 garlic cloves, finely chopped
1 red jalapeño chile, seeded
   and coarsely chopped

1/4 cup coarsely chopped Italian
     parsley leaves
3   tablespoons chopped chives
•   Juice of 1 lemon
•   Salt and freshly
     ground pepper

Combine the butter, garlic, jalapeño chile, parsley, chives, lemon juice, salt and pepper in a food processor and process until smooth. Place in a small container and store, covered, in the refrigerator.

Southern Salmon

Serves 4

1 1/2 pounds fresh salmon, rinsed
       and patted dry
2   cups milk
•   Salt and cayenne pepper
       to taste

6 to 8 garlic cloves, chopped
6 to 8 sprigs of fresh dill weed
1 lemon, cut into halves
2 tablespoons butter

Place the salmon in a large dish and pour the milk over the top. Marinate, covered, in the refrigerator for 1 hour or longer. Drain the salmon, discarding the milk. Rub the salmon all over with salt and cayenne pepper. Place the salmon on a large sheet of baking parchment and then place on a large sheet of heavy-duty foil. Sprinkle the salmon with the garlic and dill weed. Squeeze the juice from the lemon halves over the salmon, taking care to remove the lemon seeds. Cut the butter into tiny pieces and place over the top of the salmon. Fold the baking parchment over the salmon to seal. Fold the foil tightly around the baking parchment, folding the seams twice. Place in a baking pan and bake at 350 degrees for 1 hour.

He relocated to Texas and by the age of twenty-five he became the Executive Chef of Brennans. He later joined Tony Valone to open Anthony's where he stayed until opening his own restaurant.

Just one of the awards he has received is the Fine Dining Hall of Fame in the National Restaurant News in May 2006. His restaurant was also recognized by the Zagat Houston Restaurant Survey 2001–2006 as the #1 Food Spot in Houston.

Portofino Fillets

Serves 4 to 6

3/4 cup Italian salad dressing	1 tablespoon chopped parsley
1 tablespoon minced garlic	1 tablespoon chopped sweet basil
1/2 cup olive oil	6 (6- to 8-ounce) red snapper, trout
1 tablespoon lemon juice	or flounder fillets
1 tablespoon dry sherry	

Combine the salad dressing, garlic, olive oil, lemon juice, sherry, parsley and basil in a bowl and mix well. Store, covered, in the refrigerator. (You may prepare ahead up to this point.)

Place the fish on a rack in a broiler pan. Broil until the fish flakes easily and turns white. Place the fish in a greased baking dish. Stir the sauce and spoon over the fish. Broil for 3 to 5 minutes longer.

Red Snapper Veracruz

Serves 6

1/2 cup sliced mushrooms	1/2 teaspoon salt
2 tablespoons butter	1/2 teaspoon pepper
1 onion, chopped	3 tablespoons chili sauce
1 green bell pepper, chopped	6 drops of Tabasco sauce
1 garlic clove, minced	1 tablespoon chopped parsley
1 tomato, chopped	2 tablespoons capers
1/4 cup (1/2 stick) butter	1/2 cup peeled small shrimp
2 tablespoons lemon juice	1/4 cup white wine
1/2 teaspoon thyme	6 red snapper fillets

Sauté the mushrooms in 2 tablespoons butter in a small skillet until soft; set aside. Sauté the onion, bell pepper, garlic and tomato in 1/4 cup butter in a skillet until the onion is translucent. Add the lemon juice, thyme, salt, pepper, chili sauce, Tabasco sauce, parsley and capers and simmer for 5 minutes. Add the sautéed mushrooms, shrimp and wine and mix well. Place the fish in a baking dish. Spoon the sauce over the fish. Bake at 400 degrees for 15 minutes or until the fish flakes easily.

San Francisco-Style Cioppino

Serves 4

1/4	cup olive oil		2	tablespoons chopped fresh basil
1	large onion, chopped		12	cracked crab claws and legs (preferably fresh or defrosted frozen)
4	large garlic cloves, chopped			
1/4	teaspoon crushed hot pepper flakes		1	pound white fish, cut into 1 1/2-inch squares
3	ribs celery, chopped		12	to 14 clams, scrubbed
2	carrots, chopped		12	to 14 mussels, scrubbed and beards removed
1	teaspoon chopped fresh rosemary, or 1/8 teaspoon dried rosemary			
1	cup dry red wine		4	round loaves sourdough or Italian bread
1	(25-ounce) jar marinara sauce			
1 1/2	cups water		3	tablespoons chopped fresh parsley
1	tablespoon chopped fresh oregano, or 1 teaspoon dried oregano			

Heat the olive oil in a large nonreactive saucepan with a lid. Add the onion and sauté until soft. Add the garlic and hot pepper flakes and cook for 1 minute. Stir in the celery, carrots and rosemary. Cook for 3 to 4 minutes. Add the wine, marinara sauce, water, oregano and basil. Cook, uncovered, for 8 to 10 minutes over medium heat until the liquid is reduced slightly. Add the crab and fish. Cover and cook for 3 to 4 minutes. Add the clams and mussels and cook for 5 minutes or until the shells open and the claws are bright red. Cut off the tops and remove the centers of the bread to form bowls. Ladle the stew into the bread bowls and sprinkle with the parsley.

Note: *You may use the bread tops to make garlic bread.*

Tilapia Parmesan

Serves 4 to 6

1	cup Hellman's mayonnaise		4	to 6 tilapia fillets
1	cup (4 ounces) shredded Parmigiano-Reggiaino		•	Seasoned salt and pepper to taste
•	Olive oil		•	Juice from 2 lemons

Mix the mayonnaise and cheese in a small bowl. Brush a baking sheet lightly with olive oil. Place the fish on the prepared baking sheet. Season the fish with seasoned salt and pepper and drizzle with the lemon juice. Broil for 4 to 5 minutes. Spread 1 to 2 tablespoons of the mayonnaise mixture over each fillet. Broil for 2 minutes or until golden and bubbly.

Baked Maryland Crab Cakes

Serves 4 to 6

4	scallions		1/4	teaspoon paprika
1/2	green bell pepper		1	teaspoon dried parsley
2	teaspoons olive oil		1	pound lump crab meat, shells removed
2	tablespoons drained sliced pimentos		3	to 4 tablespoons mayonnaise
2/3	cup seasoned bread crumbs		•	Soy sauce to taste

Cut the white portion of the scallions into 1/4-inch pieces. Cut the bell pepper into 1/4-inch-wide strips and then cut each strip into small pieces. Heat the olive oil in a skillet over medium heat for 2 minutes. Add the scallions, bell pepper and pimentos and sauté until soft.

Mix the bread crumbs, paprika and parsley in a bowl. Combine the crab meat and scallion mixture in a bowl and mix well. Add 1 tablespoon of the bread crumb mixture, the mayonnaise and soy sauce and mix well. Shape into four to six flat crab cakes. Pour the remaining bread crumb mixture into a shallow pan. Coat the crab cakes with the bread crumb mixture. Place in a 9×9-inch baking pan sprayed with nonstick cooking spray. Bake at 450 degrees for 12 to 15 minutes or until the crab cakes are golden brown.

Note: *Great served with Texas Rémoulade on page 154 or Tarter Sauce on page 153.*

Crawfish Étouffée

Serves 12

1	cup (2 sticks) butter	2	(10-ounce) cans cream of mushroom soup
2	large onions, chopped		
2	green bell peppers, chopped	2	pounds frozen crawfish or shrimp
2	garlic cloves, chopped or minced	1	bunch sliced green onions
2	cups chopped celery	•	Parsley to taste
2	(10-ounce) cans tomatoes with green chiles	•	Hot cooked white rice

Melt the butter in a large stockpot. Add the onions, bell peppers, garlic and celery and sauté until translucent. Add the tomatoes with green chiles and simmer for 1 1/2 hours. Add the soup and cook for 30 minutes or longer. (You may prepare up to 1 day in advance up to this point and reheat before adding the crawfish.) Add the crawfish and cook for 15 minutes. Stir in the green onions and parsley just before serving. Serve over hot cooked white rice.

Note: *You may also serve over grilled fish.*

Crawfish Risotto

Serves 12

3/4	cup (1 1/2 sticks) butter or margarine	3	quarts chicken broth
1	onion, chopped	2	pounds peeled cooked crawfish tails
4	garlic cloves, pressed	8	ounces Pepper Jack cheese, shredded
1	poblano chile, seeded and chopped		
2	pounds uncooked arborio rice	2	tablespoons Creole seasoning

Melt the butter in a Dutch oven over medium heat. Add the onion, garlic and poblano chile and sauté until tender. Add the rice and cook for 5 to 7 minutes, stirring constantly. Add 1 cup of the broth and cook until the liquid is absorbed, stirring constantly. Repeat with the remaining broth, adding 1/2 cup at a time. (The total cooking time is about 1 hour.) Stir in the crawfish and cook for 4 minutes, stirring constantly. Add the cheese and Creole seasoning and cook until the cheese melts, stirring constantly. Garnish with shredded Parmesan cheese and sprigs of fresh Italian parsley.

Note: *You may use 2 pounds of peeled cooked medium shrimp instead of the crawfish.*

Crawfish Fettuccini

Serves 4 to 6

1	cup chopped onion	2	garlic cloves, pressed
1	cup chopped celery	1	tablespoon Creole seasoning
1	large green bell pepper, chopped	1	pound uncooked fettuccini
1/4	cup vegetable oil	2	pounds crawfish tails, peeled and rinsed
8	ounces mushrooms, sliced	1/2	cup (2 ounces) freshly grated Parmesan cheese
2	tablespoons all-purpose flour		
2 1/2	cups evaporated milk	2	tablespoons chopped parsley
8	ounces jalapeño cheese	1	teaspoon paprika

Sauté the onion, celery and bell pepper in the hot oil in a large saucepan until soft. Add the mushrooms and sauté for 2 minutes. Add the flour and cook for 20 minutes, stirring occasionally. Add the evaporated milk, jalapeño cheese, garlic and Creole seasoning. Cook, covered, over low heat until the cheese melts.

Cook the pasta using the package directions; drain. Add to the sauce and stir to coat. Add the crawfish and Parmesan cheese and mix well. Spoon into a baking dish and sprinkle with the parsley and paprika. Bake at 350 degrees for 30 to 40 minutes or until bubbly.

SAUTÉED SHRIMP WITH TOMATOES AND SWISS CHEESE

Sauté 1/2 cup chopped onion and 3 garlic cloves, chopped, in 1/4 cup olive oil in a skillet until the onion is translucent. Add 3/4 cup chopped tomatoes and 1 pound shrimp, peeled and deveined. Sauté until the shrimp turn pink. Add 1/2 cup (2 ounces) shredded Swiss cheese and stir to mix. Season with freshly ground pepper or lemon pepper to taste. Garnish with 2 tablespoons chopped cilantro. Serve over hot cooked rice or alone with a side of vegetables.

Shrimp Creole

Serves 8

1	cup chopped onions	1	tablespoon Worcestershire
1	cup chopped green bell pepper		sauce
1	cup chopped celery	1	tablespoon Tabasco sauce
2	garlic cloves, minced	1 1/2	tablespoons cornstarch
6	tablespoons butter, or 1/2 cup olive oil	1/2	cup water
1	tablespoon paprika	3	pounds shrimp, peeled and halved
1	cup vegetable juice cocktail	•	Hot cooked white rice
2	cups chopped fresh tomatoes, or 1 can crushed tomatoes		

Sauté the onions, bell pepper, celery and garlic in the melted butter in a large saucepan. Add the paprika for color. Stir in the vegetable juice cocktail, tomatoes, Worcestershire sauce and Tabasco sauce. Dissolve the cornstarch in the water and add to the sauce. Add the uncooked shrimp and cook until the shrimp turn pink and are opaque. Serve over fluffy white rice.

Note: *This new, light version of an old favorite does not require a roux. This recipe may be frozen.*

Camarones Ajillo

Serves 10 to 12

4	pounds large shrimp, cleaned	1/4	cup minced onion
2	tablespoons chopped cilantro	1/3	cup olive oil
2	tablespoons chopped parsley	1/2	cup (1 stick) butter, melted
3	to 4 tablespoons minced garlic	•	Salt and pepper to taste

Thread the shrimp onto skewers. Combine the cilantro, parsley, garlic, onion, olive oil, butter, salt and pepper in a shallow dish and mix well. Add the shrimp skewers. Marinate, covered, in the refrigerator for 10 hours or longer. Drain the shrimp, discarding the marinade. Place the shrimp skewers on a grill rack and grill for 15 to 20 minutes or until the shrimp turn pink.

Wooden Skewers

Wooden skewers need to be soaked in water to prevent burning on the grill. Soak your skewers in water in a heavy-duty resealable plastic bag. Seal the bag squeezing out the excess air and then lay flat. No more floating skewers. You can freeze unused skewers. Just thaw before using.

Shrimp de Jonghe

Serves 4

1	pound medium shrimp, peeled and deveined	2	tablespoons chopped parsley
3	tablespoons lemon juice	1/4	cup (1 ounce) grated Parmesan cheese
1/2	cup (1 stick) butter, melted	1/2	teaspoon pepper
1/2	cup seasoned bread crumbs	2	dashes of Tabasco sauce
2	garlic cloves, minced	3	tablespoons sherry (optional)

Place the shrimp in a baking pan and sprinkle with the lemon juice. Combine the butter, bread crumbs, garlic, parsley, cheese, pepper, Tabasco sauce and sherry in a bowl and mix well. Spoon over the shrimp. (You may prepare in advance up to this point and store, covered, in the refrigerator.) Bake, uncovered, at 350 degrees for 15 minutes. Broil for 5 minutes or until the topping is golden brown. Garnish with lemon wedges and parsley.

Shrimp with Sesame Orange Sauce

Serves 4

2	egg whites	1/4	cup (or more) vegetable oil
1/4	cup cornstarch	1	cup fresh orange juice
1/4	cup sesame seeds	2	tablespoons soy sauce
1	teaspoon coarse salt	1	tablespoon sugar
1/2	teaspoon pepper	4	or 5 scallions, trimmed and thinly sliced
1 1/2	pounds medium shrimp, peeled and deveined	•	Hot cooked rice or noodles

Whisk the eggs whites, cornstarch, sesame seeds, 1 teaspoon salt and 1/2 teaspoon pepper in a large bowl until frothy. Add the shrimp and toss to coat. Heat 1/4 cup oil in a large nonstick skillet over medium-high heat. Cook the shrimp in two or three batches for 2 to 3 minutes per side or until crisp and golden, removing the shrimp to paper towels to drain and adding additional oil if needed between batches. Wipe the skillet clean with a paper towel. Combine the orange juice, soy sauce and sugar in the skillet and bring to a boil. Cook for 2 to 3 minutes or until the sauce is syrupy and is reduced to about 1/3 cup. Return the shrimp to the skillet and add the scallions. Cook for 1 minute or until the shrimp are heated through and coated with the sauce. Serve over hot cooked rice or noodles.

Note: *Using egg whites instead of whole eggs or yolks in the batter creates a crispier coating.*

Southwest Agave Lime Shrimp

Serves 4

1	pound fresh shrimp, peeled and deveined	2	tablespoons tequila, 100% agave
1	teaspoon chili powder	•	Juice of 1 lime
4	teaspoons butter	1/2	teaspoon salt
2	garlic cloves, minced	1	jalapeño chile, seeded and chopped
		1	tablespoon chopped cilantro

Mix the shrimp and chili powder in a large bowl. Cook the shrimp with the butter and garlic in a large skillet for 1 minute and turn the shrimp. Stir in the tequila, lime juice, salt, jalapeño chile and cilantro. Cook until the shrimp turn pink. Garnish with additional cilantro.

Shrimp over Wilted Spinach

Serves 2

10	uncooked large shrimp, peeled and deveined	1/2	cup finely chopped shallots (about 2 large)
1/4	cup chopped fresh Italian parsley	2	tablespoons butter
1	tablespoon olive oil	2	tablespoons whipping cream
1	tablespoon fresh lemon juice	1	teaspoon minced peeled fresh ginger
1	teaspoon chopped fresh tarragon	1	tablespoon olive oil
1	teaspoon minced peeled fresh ginger	1	(10-ounce) package baby spinach
•	Salt and pepper to taste	1	tablespoon fresh lemon juice
1	tablespoon olive oil	2	teaspoons chopped fresh tarragon

Combine the shrimp, parsley, 1 tablespoon olive oil, 1 tablespoon lemon juice, 1 teaspoon tarragon and 1 teaspoon ginger in a bowl and toss to mix. Season with salt and pepper. Heat 1 tablespoon olive oil in a large skillet over medium heat. Add the shallots and sauté for 5 minutes. Add the shrimp mixture and sauté for 3 minutes or until the shrimp are almost cooked through. Add the butter and cream and bring just to a simmer. Add 1 teaspoon ginger, salt and pepper. Remove from the heat and set aside.

Heat 1 tablespoon olive oil in a large skillet over high heat. Add the spinach and 1 tablespoon lemon juice. Season with salt and pepper. Cook until the spinach is wilted. Mound equal amounts of the spinach in the center of each serving plate and surround with the shrimp and sauce. Sprinkle the shrimp evenly with 2 teaspoons tarragon.

Shrimp Skillet Supper

Serves 8

5	slices bacon	1	onion, finely chopped
4	eggs	1	(10-ounce) package frozen
1	(7-ounce) package yellow		chopped spinach, thawed
	corn bread mix		and drained
1/2	cup milk	1	pound shrimp, cooked,
1/2	cup (1 stick) butter, melted		peeled and coarsely chopped
	and cooled	2	cups (8 ounces) shredded
•	Hot red pepper sauce to taste		Cheddar cheese

Cook the bacon in a 10-inch cast-iron skillet until crisp. Remove the bacon to paper towels to drain, reserving the drippings in the skillet. Place the reserved drippings in the skillet in a 375-degree oven. Beat the eggs in a mixing bowl until light. Add the corn bread mix, milk, butter, hot sauce, onion, spinach, shrimp and 1 1/2 cups of the cheese and mix well. Pour into the hot bacon drippings. Sprinkle with the remaining 1/2 cup cheese. Bake for 30 minutes. Sprinkle with the crumbled bacon. Garnish with chopped fresh parsley.

Shrimp Bisque in Puff Pastry

Serves 4 to 6

1/4	cup grated onion	3	tablespoons sherry (optional)
2	tablespoons finely chopped	1/2	cup (2 ounces) shredded
	green bell pepper		Cheddar cheese
2	tablespoons butter	2	teaspoons lemon juice
	or margarine	2	cups peeled cooked shrimp
1	(10-ounce) can cream of	•	Salt and pepper to taste
	potato soup	1	(10-ounce) package
3/4	cup cream or half-and-half		puff pastry shells, baked

Sauté the onion and bell pepper in the melted butter in a skillet. Stir in the soup, cream, sherry, cheese, lemon juice, shrimp, salt and pepper. Pour into the baked shells.

Wine Pairing
La Crema Chardonnay

Creamy Shrimp Tortellini

Serves 6 to 8

8	ounces three-cheese tortellini	2	cups whipping cream
1	pound shrimp, peeled	2	tablespoons white wine
6	cups water	1/2	teaspoon pepper
2	garlic cloves, pressed	2	cups (8 ounces) grated
3	tablespoons butter		Parmesan cheese

Cook the pasta and shrimp in boiling water in a large stockpot until the pasta is tender and the shrimp turns pink; drain. Sauté the garlic in the butter in a skillet until light brown. Reduce the heat to low and stir in the cream, wine and pepper. Cook until thickened, stirring constantly. Stir in the cheese gradually. Pour over the pasta and toss to coat.

Shrimp Sauce for Baked Fish

Makes enough sauce for 6 to 8 fish fillets

1	pound frozen peeled tiny shrimp	1	garlic clove, crushed
2	cups water	1/4	cup minced fresh cilantro
1	tablespoon vinegar	1	(10-ounce) can cream of shrimp soup
1	tablespoon shrimp boil		
2	cups sliced fresh mushrooms	1	tablespoon Worcestershire sauce
6	green onions, sliced		
1/4	cup (1/2 stick) butter or olive oil	•	Tabasco sauce to taste
1	or 2 Roma tomatoes, chopped	3	tablespoons sherry or white wine (optional)

Place the shrimp in a large bowl and add the water, vinegar and shrimp boil. Soak for 30 minutes and drain. Sauté the shrimp, mushrooms and green onions in the butter in a skillet until the green onions are tender. Add the tomatoes, garlic and cilantro and stir to mix well. Stir in the soup, Worcestershire sauce and Tabasco sauce. Reduce the heat and simmer for a few minutes. Serve over baked fish or hot cooked rice.

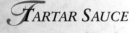

Tartar Sauce

Process 1 cup mayonnaise, 2 tablespoons chopped onion, 2 tablespoons sweet pickle relish, 1 tablespoon horseradish sauce, 1 tablespoon spicy brown mustard, 1 tablespoon capers, chopped (optional), 1 teaspoon dry mustard, juice from 1/2 lime, garlic powder to taste and Tony's Creole Seasoning to taste in a food processor until blended. Spoon into a serving bowl and chill, covered, until ready to serve.

Beurre Blanc Sauce

Beurre Blanc Sauce is made of butter, white wine, and shallots. This is a rendition of a classic sauce used in Italy and France. This is a very versatile sauce and complements any type of baked, poached, sautéed, fried, or grilled meat or vegetables.

As an appetizer, try sliced batter-fried portobello mushrooms over garlic toast drizzled with Beurre Blanc Sauce.

The Italian Café's Beurre Blanc Sauce

CHEF'S RECIPE

Makes 1/2 cup sauce or enough sauce for 4 entrées

2	tablespoons minced shallots	1/4	cup (1/2 stick) unsalted butter, chilled
2	tablespoons white wine vinegar or rice vinegar	•	Salt and white pepper to taste
2	tablespoons dry white wine	1 1/2	tablespoons chopped fresh tarragon
2	tablespoons chicken stock or water		

Simmer the shallots in the vinegar and wine in a saucepan until tender. Remove from the heat and add the stock. Return to very low heat and whisk in the butter 1 tablespoon at a time until the butter melts. (Adjust the heat just enough to melt the butter, but not cook it. This will retain the color and give the sauce a creamy look.) Remove the sauce from the heat and season with salt and white pepper. Stir in the tarragon. Cover to keep warm until ready to serve.

Note: *You may substitute chives, dill, rosemary, or cilantro for the tarragon.*

Texas Rémoulade

Makes 2 cups

1	bunch of cilantro	1/4	cup water
2	tablespoons minced garlic	1/2	teaspoon salt
2	tablespoons minced jalapeño chiles	2	cups mayonnaise
1/4	cup white wine vinegar	•	Dash of Tabasco sauce

Purée the cilantro, garlic, jalapeño chiles, vinegar, water and salt in a food processor. Fold into the mayonnaise in a bowl. Stir in the Tabasco sauce.

Note: *You may also serve this sauce as a salad dressing.*

Main Entrées

LaChance Home in League City

*N*estled in the small town of League City, Texas,
sits this lovely "Gulf Coast Bungalow" constructed of
pine and cypress wood. This turn-of-the-century home,
built in 1909 by the Ferrell Family, is listed in the
League City Historical Registry. The grounds are graced
by one hundred-year-old oak trees planted by the
original owners. This home has had a gazebo added
and has been lovingly refurbished to its original design
by the current owners.

New Year's Eve Dinner for Two

METROPOLITANS, PAGE 45

ONION SOUFFLÉ, PAGE 42

SPINACH SALAD WITH LEMON DRESSING, PAGE 104

CRAPPITO'S CHICKEN IN DIJON CREAM SAUCE, PAGE 183

HORSERADISH ROASTED POTATOES, PAGE 125
MARINATED ASPARAGUS, PAGE 119
GLAZED CARROTS, PAGE 132

FRAISES ROMANOFF, PAGE 218
DARK CHOCOLATE MOUSSE WITH RASPBERRY SAUCE, PAGE 218
COCONUT COOKIES, PAGE 223

WINE PAIRING
GRGICH HILLS CHARDONNAY

Beef Wellington

Serves 6

6	beef tenderloin steaks, 1¹/2 inches thick	8	ounces fresh mushrooms
¹/3	cup soy sauce	¹/4	cup sherry
¹/3	cup red wine	2	(8-count) cans refrigerator crescent rolls
2	garlic cloves, crushed	•	Salt and pepper to taste
1	tablespoon brown sugar	6	tablespoons crumbled blue cheese
1	onion, chopped	1	egg white, lightly beaten
2	tablespoons olive oil		

Place the steaks in a sealable plastic bag. Combine the soy sauce, wine, garlic and brown sugar in a bowl and mix well. Pour over the steaks and seal the bag, turning to coat. Marinate in the refrigerator for 4 to 10 hours. Sauté the onion in the olive oil in a skillet for 4 minutes. Add the mushrooms and sherry and cook for 5 minutes. Unroll the crescent roll dough. Separate into squares, pressing the perforations to seal. Roll out each square on a lightly floured surface with a rolling pin. Drain the steaks, discarding the marinade. Pat the steaks dry with paper towels. Season with salt and pepper. Place each steak on a dough square and top with 1 tablespoon of the onion mixture and 1 tablespoon blue cheese. Fold the dough to enclose the steaks and place on a baking sheet. Brush with the egg white. (You may prepare up to 1 hour in advance up to this point.) Bake at 425 degrees for 20 minutes.

Stuffed Filets Mignons

Serves 4

3	or 4 green onions, chopped	2	tablespoons butter
2	tablespoons butter	2	cups beef stock
8	ounces fresh lump crab meat, shells removed	1	cup madeira
4	(8-ounce) filets mignons, butterflied	2	cups sliced mushrooms, sautéed
		•	Salt and pepper to taste

Sauté the green onions in 2 tablespoons melted butter in a skillet until tender. Stir in the crab meat. Stuff the filling into the filets and close with wooden picks. Carefully sauté the filets in 2 tablespoons melted butter in a skillet until brown on both sides. Place the filets on a rack in a baking pan, reserving the drippings in the skillet. Bake at 450 degrees until the desired degree of doneness. Add the stock, wine and sautéed mushrooms to the reserved drippings in the skillet. Season with salt and pepper. Cook until the stock is reduced by one-half. Serve over the filets.

Wine Pairings
*Becker Chardonnay
Turnbull Cabernet*

Adobo-Marinated Beef Tenderloin with Chimichurri Sauce

Serves 6 to 8

CHIMICHURRI SAUCE

6	garlic cloves
3	bay leaves
1	jalapeño chile, chopped
1	tablespoon salt
1/4	cup white vinegar
1/2	cup minced fresh parsley
1/4	cup minced flat-leaf parsley
1/4	cup finely chopped cilantro
1/4	cup finely chopped oregano
1/3	cup virgin olive oil

BEEF

1 1/2	cups fresh cilantro (leaves and stems)
3	bay leaves
2	teaspoons cumin
2	teaspoons chopped fresh oregano
2	teaspoons chopped fresh thyme
2	teaspoons pepper
1	tablespoon salt
1/2	cup coarsely chopped white onion
1/4	cup coarsely chopped garlic
1	cup white vinegar
1/2	cup vegetable oil
1	(5- to 6-pound) trimmed beef tenderloin

To prepare the sauce, process the garlic, bay leaves, jalapeño chile and salt with 1 teaspoon of the vinegar in a food processor to form a smooth paste. Spoon into a bowl and add the parsley, flat-leaf parsley, cilantro and oregano. Whisk in the remaining vinegar and the olive oil until well mixed.

To prepare the beef, purée the cilantro, bay leaves, cumin, oregano, thyme, pepper, salt, onion, garlic and vinegar at high speed in a blender. Spoon into a bowl and whisk in the oil. Place the tenderloin in a sealable plastic bag and add the marinade. Seal the bag, turning to coat. Marinate in the refrigerator for at least 12 hours, turning the beef occasionally to coat thoroughly. Drain the beef, discarding the marinade. Place the beef on a grill rack. Grill for 8 to 10 minutes or until grill marks form on all sides. Place on a rack in a roasting pan. Bake at 350 degrees until a meat thermometer registers 130 to 135 degrees for medium-rare. Serve with the sauce and Sweet Potato Fries (page 161).

Vodka-Marinated Beef Tenderloin

Serves 8 to 10

1	(4-pound) beef tenderloin, trimmed	1/3	cup vodka (made from grain)
1	tablespoon coarse sea salt	1/4	cup olive oil
2	tablespoons finely crushed black peppercorns	2	tablespoons vegetable oil
3	tablespoons finely chopped fresh parsley	1/2	cup red wine (optional)
		1/4	cup (1/2 stick) unsalted butter, cut into pieces
2	tablespoons finely chopped fresh thyme	1	teaspoon finely chopped fresh thyme
3	garlic cloves, crushed	•	Salt and pepper to taste

Rub the beef with the sea salt and crushed peppercorns. Place in a large sealable plastic bag and add the parsley, 2 tablespoons thyme, the garlic, vodka and olive oil. Seal the bag, pressing out the excess air. Place the bag in a large shallow pan. Marinate in the refrigerator for 2 days, turning the bag twice per day. Remove from the refrigerator and let stand at room temperature for 1 hour. Drain, reserving the marinade. Pat the beef dry with paper towels.

Heat the vegetable oil in a heavy 12-inch skillet over medium-high heat until the oil just begins to smoke. Sear the beef on all sides for 4 minutes or until brown. Place in a large roasting pan. Roast at 425 degrees on the middle oven rack for 25 to 30 minutes or until a meat thermometer inserted diagonally 2 inches into the center registers 130 degrees for medium-rare. Remove to a cutting board and let stand for 20 minutes. Cut into 1/2-inch slices.

Pour the reserved marinade into the drippings in the roasting pan. Bring to a boil, stirring to deglaze the pan by scraping up the brown bits. Stir in the wine if needed for additional sauce. Reduce the heat to low and simmer for 1 minute. Add the butter and heat until melted, stirring constantly. Stir in 1 teaspoon thyme, salt and pepper. Pour the sauce through a sieve into a bowl. Serve the beef drizzled with the sauce.

Sweet Potato Fries

Wrap four large sweet potatoes individually in foil and place on a baking sheet. Bake at 350 degrees for 20 minutes to partially cook through. Remove from the oven to cool. Unwrap the foil and discard. Cut the unpeeled sweet potatoes neatly into thin sticks. Heat 3 cups of canola oil in a deep fryer to 350 degrees. Add the sweet potatoes and deep-fry for 3 to 4 minutes or until golden brown. Remove to paper towels to drain and season with salt to taste.

London Broil

Serves 6

1	(1½- to 2-pound) London broil	¼	cup Worcestershire sauce
¼	cup olive oil	4	dashes of Tabasco sauce
½	cup soy sauce	•	Freshly ground pepper to taste
¼	cup white wine	¼	cup chopped onion
¼	cup lemon juice	1	tablespoon chopped fresh basil
¼	cup prepared mustard	2	garlic cloves, minced

Place the beef in a shallow dish. Combine the olive oil, soy sauce, wine, lemon juice, mustard, Worcestershire sauce, Tabasco sauce, pepper, onion, basil and garlic in a bowl and mix well. Pour over the beef. Cover and marinate in the refrigerator for 24 hours, turning occasionally. Drain the beef, discarding the marinade. Place the beef on a grill rack and grill over medium-high heat to the desired degree on doneness. Do not overcook. Remove to a cutting board and cut diagonally into thin slices.

The King's Prime Rib Roast

Serves 6 to 10

1	(5- to 7-pound) prime rib roast (with ribs)	2	teaspoons salt
		½	teaspoon cayenne pepper
2	tablespoons olive oil	3	or 4 sage leaves, finely chopped
4	or 5 garlic cloves, chopped	1	cup water

Rub the beef with the olive oil and then the garlic, salt, cayenne pepper and sage. Cover and chill in the refrigerator for 8 to 10 hours. Preheat the oven to 325 degrees for 1 hour. Reduce the oven temperature to 300 degrees. Place the beef fat side up on a rack in a roasting pan. Pour the water in the bottom of the pan, making sure the beef is not touching. Insert a meat thermometer into the thickest part of the beef away from fat or bone. Roast until the beef is the desired degree of doneness. (For medium-rare, roast to 130 to 135 degrees on the meat thermometer or check the beef at approximately 18 minutes per pound; for medium, roast to 140 to 150 degrees on a meat thermometer or check the beef at approximately 20 minutes per pound; for medium-well, roast to 155 to 165 degrees or check the beef at approximately 22 minutes per pound.) Turn off the oven and let the beef stand in the closed oven for 1 hour. Remove from the oven. Slice and serve the beef with au jus (pan drippings) on the side.

Beef Roulades

Serves 3 to 4

2	(1¹/₂-pound) round steaks, ¹/₄ inch thick	2	tablespoons all-purpose flour
•	Salt and pepper to taste	¹/₄	cup vegetable oil
1¹/₂	teaspoons brown mustard	¹/₂	cup condensed beef broth
6	tablespoons chopped onion	¹/₂	cup dry red wine
3	slices bacon, chopped	1¹/₂	tablespoons all-purpose flour
2	large dill pickles, cut into 3 strips each	3	tablespoons water

Cut each steak into three equal pieces. Pound with a meat mallet to ¹/₈ inch thick and sprinkle with salt and pepper. Spread about ¹/₄ teaspoon of the brown mustard on each steak piece and sprinkle evenly with the onion and bacon. Place a pickle strip across the narrow end of each steak piece. Roll up beginning at the narrow end and secure with kitchen string. Sprinkle lightly with 2 tablespoons flour. Heat the oil in a heavy skillet or Dutch oven with a tight-fitting lid. Add the roulades to the hot oil and cook for 15 to 20 minutes or until brown on all sides. Add the broth and wine. Bring to a boil and reduce the heat. Simmer, covered, for 1¹/₂ hours or until tender. Remove the roulades to a serving dish. Pour the pan drippings into a 2-cup measure and skim off the fat. Add enough water to measure 1 cup and return to the skillet. Mix 1¹/₂ tablespoons flour with 3 tablespoons water in a bowl to form a smooth paste. Stir into the drippings in the skillet and bring to a boil. Cook until thickened and smooth, stirring constantly. Pour over the roulades and serve with Red Cabbage on page 122, if desired.

MICROWAVE BÉARNAISE SAUCE

Microwave ¹/₂ cup (1 stick) butter in a 5-cup glass measure on High for 1 minute or until melted. Stir in 2 tablespoons lemon juice, 4 egg yolks, ¹/₄ cup half-and-half, 1 teaspoon dry mustard, ¹/₄ teaspoon salt and a dash of Tabasco sauce. Microwave for 1¹/₂ minutes, whisking every 15 seconds.

Simmer ¹/₄ cup tarragon vinegar, 2 tablespoons tarragon, 3 tablespoons chopped onion and 2 tablespoons parsley in a saucepan until no liquid remains. Cool and stir into the sauce.

Rovellini

Serves 4 to 6

MUSHROOM TOMATO SAUCE
1/4 cup dried porcini mushrooms
2 tablespoons olive oil
1 cup finely chopped mushrooms
1 onion, finely chopped
1 or 2 garlic cloves, finely chopped
3/4 cup finely chopped celery
1 (8-ounce) can tomato sauce
1 cup (about) beef broth
1 teaspoon salt
1/2 teaspoon black pepper
1/2 teaspoon red pepper flakes
 (optional)
• Pinch of allspice (optional)
1/2 cup finely chopped parsley
1/4 cup red wine

BEEF
3/4 cup all-purpose flour
1/2 teaspoon salt
1/2 teaspoon black pepper
1/4 teaspoon red pepper
• Vegetable oil
1 or 2 garlic cloves, sliced
1 round steak, tenderized and cut
 into pieces

To *prepare the sauce,* place the porcini mushrooms in boiling water in a bowl and let stand for 30 minutes or until soft and reconstituted; drain and chop. Heat the olive oil in a skillet over medium heat. Add the porcini mushrooms, mushrooms, onion, garlic and celery and sauté until the onion is translucent. Add the tomato sauce and cook for 2 to 3 minutes, stirring constantly to prevent sticking. Stir in the broth and simmer for 30 minutes. Add the salt, black pepper, red pepper flakes, allspice and parsley and mix well. (You may prepare in advance up to this point.) Add the wine to the sauce about 10 minutes before serving. (The sauce will be thick and the consistency of creamed corn. Add additional broth to achieve this consistency if needed.)

To prepare the beef, mix the flour, salt, black pepper and red pepper together in a shallow dish. Pour enough oil into a heavy skillet to cover the bottom and heat over medium-high heat until hot but not smoking. Add the garlic and sauté for 2 to 3 minutes or until the garlic is translucent and begins to brown. Remove the garlic and discard. Dredge the beef in the flour mixture, shaking off the excess. Add to the hot oil and cook for 5 minutes per side, shaking the skillet frequently to prevent sticking and turning once. (The oil has to be hot enough so the flour will not stick and not so hot that it burns.) Serve with the mushroom tomato sauce with mashed potatoes on the side.

Malaysian Beef Satay

Serves 4 to 6

SPICY PEANUT SAUCE

1	tablespoon butter or margarine
1	small onion, finely chopped
1	garlic clove, minced
1/4	cup peanut butter
1/4	cup water
2	drops of Tabasco sauce
2	teaspoons sugar
1/2	teaspoon coriander

BEEF SATAY

1/3	cup soy sauce
1/3	cup peanut oil or vegetable oil
2	onions, finely chopped
2	garlic cloves, crushed
3	tablespoons sesame seeds, toasted
2	pounds sirloin steak, cut into 1-inch cubes
1	teaspoon lemon juice
2	teaspoons cumin
•	Salt and pepper to taste

To *prepare the sauce,* melt the butter in a saucepan and add the onion and garlic. Sauté until light brown. Add the peanut butter, water, Tabasco sauce, sugar and coriander and mix well. Cook until thickened, stirring constantly. (You may prepare in advance up to this point and store, covered, in the refrigerator. Reheat before serving.)

To prepare the satay, combine the soy sauce, peanut oil, onions, garlic and sesame seeds in a large bowl and mix well. Add the beef and toss to coat. Marinate, covered, in the refrigerator for 3 hours. Drain the beef, reserving the marinade. Thread the beef onto skewers and brush with the lemon juice. Sprinkle with the cumin, salt and pepper. Place on a grill rack and grill for 10 minutes, basting with the reserved marinade and turning occasionally. Serve with the spicy peanut sauce for dipping.

Note: *The satay may also be served with hot cooked rice.*

SATAY

Satay is a dish resembling shish kabobs. Satay is found all throughout Southeast Asia with recipes and ingredients varying from country to country, each having traditional favorites. Basically, chunks or slices of meat ranging from chicken, beef or pork, to venison and mutton are skewered on bamboo, and grilled over a wood or charcoal fire. Satay is often served with a spicy peanut sauce, peanut gravy, or slices of vegetables such as onions or cucumbers. A satay sauce for pork incorporates pineapple, and soy-based sauces are found in Indonesia. This hugely popular dish, possibly invented by street vendors, is still sold as "fast food" and is found at many festive celebrations throughout Malaysia.

Reuben Casserole

Serves 6

1	(12-ounce) can corned beef	1/2	cup Thousand Island dressing
4	slices rye bread, toasted and crumbled	2	tablespoons prepared mustard
		1	tomato, sliced
1	(16-ounce) can sauerkraut, drained	1 1/2	to 2 cups (6 to 8 ounces) shredded Swiss cheese

Separate the corned beef with a fork in a bowl. Layer the bread, corned beef, sauerkraut, salad dressing, mustard, tomato and cheese in the order listed in a 1 1/2-quart baking dish. Bake at 350 degrees for 30 minutes or until heated through and bubbly.

Note: *You may microwave on High for 15 minutes instead of baking.*

Tangy Meat Loaf

Serves 8

2	(8-ounce) cans tomato sauce	1	yellow onion, chopped
1/2	cup vinegar	1	egg
1/2	cup packed brown sugar	1/3	cup Italian bread crumbs or crushed club crackers
2 1/2	tablespoons Worcestershire sauce		
2	teaspoons prepared mustard	1	tablespoon minced garlic
2	pounds lean ground round or ground pork	•	Salt, pepper and celery salt to taste

Combine the tomato sauce, vinegar, brown sugar, Worcestershire sauce and mustard in a saucepan and heat until the brown sugar melts. Mix the ground round, onion, egg, bread crumbs, garlic, salt, pepper and celery salt in a large bowl. Add 1/2 to 3/4 cup of the sauce to the ground round mixture and mix well. Shape into a loaf and place in a 5×9-inch loaf pan. Pour the remaining sauce over the loaf. Bake at 350 degrees for 1 hour. Let stand for 10 minutes before slicing. Serve with mashed potatoes and corn.

Note: *You may prepare the meat loaf in advance and bake later. The recipe may also be frozen. You may also pour the entire amount of sauce over the loaf.*

Stuffed Bell Peppers in Tomato Basil Sauce

Serves 8

BELL PEPPERS

8	large green, yellow, red or orange bell peppers, or an assortment of each
1	large yellow onion
2	tablespoons minced garlic
6	tablespoons vegetable oil
2	pounds lean ground round
1	to 1¹/₂ tablespoons Worcestershire sauce
•	Salt and pepper to taste

TOMATO BASIL SAUCE

2	(16-ounce) cans crushed tomatoes
1	large yellow onion, chopped, or 1¹/₂ small onions
2	bay leaves
2	tablespoons oregano
3	tablespoons minced sweet basil, or 6 fresh basil leaves, cut up
1¹/₂	tablespoons minced garlic
•	Salt and pepper to taste
¹/₄	cup olive oil

To prepare the bell peppers, cut the tops from the bell peppers and remove the stems; set aside. Core and seed the bell peppers. Stand the bell peppers in 1 inch of water in a large baking dish. Bake at 450 degrees for 10 to 15 minutes; drain. Process the tops of the bell peppers, onion and garlic in a food processor for 1 minute. Heat the vegetable oil in a large skillet. Add the ground round and processed bell pepper mixture and cook until the ground round is brown, stirring until crumbly. Season with the Worcestershire sauce, salt and pepper; drain. Spoon into the partially cooked bell peppers, spooning any additional ground round mixture around the bell peppers.

To prepare the sauce, simmer the undrained tomatoes, onion, bay leaves, oregano, basil, garlic, salt and pepper in the olive oil in a large skillet for 15 to 20 minutes, stirring frequently. Discard the bay leaves. Pour the sauce around the bell peppers in the baking dish. Bake, covered, at 350 degrees for 25 minutes. Uncover and bake for 15 to 20 minutes longer. Serve with hot cooked white rice and a salad.

Note: You may prepare the bell peppers and sauce a day in advance. The sauce may be frozen.

The Shepherd's Favorite Pie

1 pound lean ground round or ground sirloin
4 or 5 garlic cloves, finely chopped
1 onion, finely chopped
1 bell pepper, finely chopped
4 carrots, peeled and finely chopped
2 cups water
1/4 teaspoon crushed red pepper
1 tablespoon salt
1/4 cup enriched all-purpose flour
1/2 cup water
1 teaspoon Kitchen Bouquet
• Mashed Red Potatoes (below)

Brown the ground round in a skillet, stirring until crumbly. Add the garlic, onion, bell pepper and carrots and sauté for 5 minutes. Add 2 cups water, crushed red pepper and salt. Bring to a boil and reduce the heat to low. Cook for 20 minutes. Dissolve 1 tablespoon of the flour at a time in 1/2 cup water. Stir in the Kitchen Bouquet. Add to the ground round mixture gradually, stirring constantly. Bring to a boil and cook, covered, until thickened, stirring constantly. Adjust the seasonings to taste. Ladle over Mashed Red Potatoes on a serving plate. Serve with small green peas on the side.

Mashed Red Potatoes

• Salt to taste
2 quarts water
5 or 6 large red potatoes, peeled and cubed
3 tablespoons butter
1 cup milk
• Freshly ground pepper to taste

Bring salted water to a boil in a saucepan. Add the potatoes and cook, covered, over low heat for 20 minutes or until tender. Drain the potatoes and remove from the saucepan. Add the butter to the empty saucepan. Return the potatoes to the saucepan and add the milk. Mash with a potato masher, adding additional milk if needed to reach the desired consistency. Season with salt and pepper.

Deep-Dish Pizza

Serves 6 to 8

1	pound ground beef
1/2	cup chopped onion
1	(6-ounce) can tomato paste
1/2	cup chopped mushrooms
1	teaspoon Italian seasoning
1	teaspoon oregano
1/4	teaspoon Tabasco sauce
1	teaspoon salt
•	Pepper to taste
1	(8-count) can refrigerator buttermilk or country-style biscuits
1 1/2	cups (6 ounces) shredded mozzarella cheese or Cheddar cheese

Brown the ground beef and onion in a skillet, stirring until crumbly; drain. Stir in the tomato paste, mushrooms, Italian seasoning, oregano, Tabasco sauce, salt and pepper. Simmer until of the desired consistency. Separate the dough into pieces and press over the bottom and up the side of a 9-inch baking pan. Spoon the ground beef mixture in the prepared pan and sprinkle with the cheese. Bake at 350 degrees for 20 to 25 minutes or until the crust is golden brown.

Exotic Blues Burger

Serves 6

3	pounds ground exotic meat, such as buffalo, ostrich, kangaroo, venison or elk
2	tablespoons House of Blues Seasoning Mix (at right)
6	Kaiser rolls, toasted
6	lettuce leaves
6	slices tomato
6	slices onion
6	slices blue cheese or Pepper Jack cheese

Mix the ground meat and the House of Blues Seasoning Mix in a bowl. Shape into six 8-ounce patties. Place on a grill rack and grill to medium-rare. Place each patty on the bottom of each roll. Top with lettuce, tomato, onion and cheese and replace the roll tops.

Note: *The patties can be prepared ahead of time and frozen until ready to use. Wild game can be purchased at Ditta Meat Food Service.*

House of Blues Seasoning Mix

Mix 1/4 cup kosher salt, 1 tablespoon granulated garlic, 1 tablespoon plus 1 teaspoon granulated onion, 1 tablespoon basil, 1 tablespoon thyme, 1 tablespoon oregano and 1 tablespoon pepper together in a bowl. Store in an airtight container.

Osso Buco

Serves 6

6	(8- to 12-ounce) veal shanks, cut into 2-inch lengths	1	cup dry white wine
•	Salt and pepper to taste	1	(14-ounce) can low-sodium beef broth
1	cup all-purpose flour	1	(28-ounce) can diced tomatoes
1/4	cup (1/2 stick) butter	6	garlic cloves, minced
1/2	cup olive oil	2	carrots, chopped
1	onion, chopped	1/2	teaspoon dried rosemary
3	ribs celery, chopped	1/2	teaspoon Italian seasoning

Trim the excess fat from the veal. Wrap the veal with kitchen string once or twice around and tie. Season with salt and pepper. Dredge in the flour, shaking off the excess. Cook the veal in the butter and olive oil in a large nonreactive Dutch oven or ovenproof sauté pan for 8 to 12 minutes or until brown on all sides. Remove the veal and set aside.

Add the onion and celery to the pan drippings and sauté until soft. Pour off the excess oil. Add the wine and cook for 5 minutes, stirring to deglaze the excess flour from the bottom of the pan. Add the broth, undrained tomatoes, garlic, carrots, rosemary and Italian seasoning. Bring to a boil and reduce to a simmer.

Return the veal to the pan and cover with a tight-fitting lid. (The liquid should come close to the top of the veal shanks.) Bake at 350 degrees for 2 hours. Remove the veal from the pan and discard the kitchen string. Serve the veal with the reduced sauce spooned over the top.

Roasted Leg of Lamb with Apples and Feta Cheese

Serves 6 to 8

1	(2- to 3-pound) leg of lamb, butterflied	1	Granny Smith apple, coarsely chopped
•	Garlic powder, salt and pepper to taste	1	(.6-ounce) package fresh mint, julienned
4	ounces feta cheese, crumbled	•	Pat of butter
4	ounces pine nuts, lightly toasted		

Season the lamb with garlic powder, salt and pepper. Combine the cheese, pine nuts, apple, mint and butter in a bowl and mix well. Place the filling in the center of the butterflied lamb and roll up to enclose the filling; tie with kitchen string. Place on a rack in a roasting pan and insert a meat thermometer in the center. Roast at 375 degrees for 30 minutes per pound or until the meat thermometer registers 120 degrees. Remove from the oven and let stand before carving.

Mint and Brandy Rack of Lamb

Serves 2

1	(8-chop) rack of lamb	1/3	cup honey
1/2	cup mint jelly	1/3	cup brandy
2	teaspoons garlic salt		

Trim the excess fat from the lamb and score the surface. Spread with the mint jelly and sprinkle with the garlic salt. Chill, covered, for 8 to 10 hours. Place the lamb on a rack in a roasting pan. Bake at 375 degrees for 25 to 35 minutes or until of the desired degree of doneness. Remove from the oven and let stand for 5 to 10 minutes before carving.

Drain the lamb, reserving the pan drippings. Combine the pan drippings, honey and brandy in a saucepan and mix well. Cook until the sauce is thickened to a pouring consistency, stirring frequently. Serve over the lamb.

Rosemary Scallion-Crusted Rack of Lamb

Serves 2

1¹/2 tablespoons olive oil
¹/4 teaspoon red pepper flakes
2 teaspoons minced garlic
3 tablespoons thinly sliced scallions (including the green stem)

1 teaspoon crushed dried rosemary
¹/2 cup fresh bread crumbs
• Salt and pepper to taste
1 (1¹/4-pound) rack of lamb, trimmed and frenched

Heat the olive oil in a small skillet until hot, but not smoking. Add the red pepper flakes and sauté for 10 seconds. Add the garlic and sauté for 30 seconds. Add the scallions and rosemary and sauté for 10 seconds. Stir in the bread crumbs, salt and pepper. Remove from the heat.

Heat an ovenproof skillet until hot. Rub the lamb with salt and pepper and place in the hot skillet. Cook until evenly brown on all sides; drain. Place the lamb fat side up in the skillet and pat the crumb mixture evenly over the top. Bake at 475 degrees on the middle oven rack for 15 minutes or until a meat thermometer registers 130 degrees for medium-rare. Remove the lamb to a heated serving platter and let stand, uncovered, for 10 minutes. Garnish with sprigs of fresh watercress and serve.

LAMB

The rack of lamb is like the prime rib of lamb. This is one of the best cuts. Be sure to choose lamb that is more pink than deep red for a fresher cut of meat. Be sure to trim the fat off of the lamb because it is typically very strong.

Braised Lamb Shanks

Serves 4 to 6

4	lamb shanks, trimmed	2	cups full-bodied red wine
•	Salt and pepper to taste	1	cup beef stock
2	tablespoons olive oil	1	tablespoon dried rosemary
2	yellow onions, chopped	3	garlic cloves, crushed
2	ribs celery, chopped	1	bay leaf
2	carrots, chopped		

Season the lamb with salt and pepper. Heat the olive oil in a large ovenproof deep sauté pan over medium-high heat until nearly smoking. Add the lamb and cook for 4 minutes or until brown on all sides. Remove the lamb to a platter, reserving the drippings in the pan. Add the onions, celery and carrots to the reserved drippings and cook for 3 to 5 minutes or until the vegetables are golden and translucent, stirring occasionally. Remove from the heat. Add the wine and return to medium-high heat. Bring to a simmer, stirring to deglaze the brown bits from the bottom of the pan. Add the stock, rosemary, garlic, bay leaf and lamb and bring to a boil. Cover and bake at 350 degrees for 2 hours or until the lamb falls off the bone. Remove the lamb with tongs to a large serving bowl. Remove the bay leaf from the cooking liquid. Purée the liquid with an immersion blender to form a smooth sauce. Season with salt and pepper. Pour some of the sauce over the lamb and serve.

Parmesan-Crusted Baby Lamb Chops

Serves 4

8	single-rib lamb chops, bone ends trimmed of fat and meat	1	cup very fine fresh bread crumbs
3/4	cup freshly grated Parmigiano-Reggiano cheese	•	Olive oil for browning
2	eggs, lightly beaten	•	Fine sea salt and freshly ground pepper to taste

Gently pound the chops to form even but not flat chops. Hold the chops by the bone and turn each in the cheese to coat, shaking off the excess. Dip each chop in the beaten eggs and then coat with the bread crumbs, shaking off the excess after each process. Place on a platter.

Heat olive oil in a large skillet over medium-high heat. Add the chops and cook for 4 minutes or until golden brown. Turn each chop carefully to keep the coating intact and cook for 4 minutes. Season with sea salt and pepper. Garnish with lemon wedges.

Fresh Mint Lamb Chops

Serves 4 to 6

MINT SAUCE
1/3 cup cider vinegar
1/4 cup sugar
1/4 to 1/3 cup chopped mint
• Pinch of baking soda

LAMB CHOPS
1/4 cup white wine
2 tablespoons vegetable oil
1/2 teaspoon salt
1/2 teaspoon pepper
4 to 6 (1-inch) lamb chops

To prepare the mint sauce, bring the vinegar and sugar to a boil in a saucepan. Remove from the heat. Add the mint and mix well. Stir in the baking soda. Cover and chill in the refrigerator.

To prepare the lamb chops, whisk the wine, oil, salt and pepper in a bowl until emulsified. Add the lamb chops. Marinate, covered, in the refrigerator for 45 minutes or longer. Drain the lamb chops, reserving the marinade. Place the lamb chops on a rack in a broiler pan.

Bring the reserved marinade to a boil in a saucepan. Boil for 3 to 4 minutes and remove from the heat. Broil the lamb chops for 6 to 8 minutes on each side or until cooked through, basting with the heated marinade every 2 to 4 minutes. Serve with the mint sauce.

Pork Tenderloin with Honey Bourbon

Serves 8 to 10

3 (12-ounce) pork tenderloins
1/2 cup chopped onion
1/4 cup lemon juice
1/4 to 1/2 cup bourbon
1/4 cup honey

1/4 cup soy sauce
1 tablespoon grated fresh ginger
4 garlic cloves, minced
2 tablespoons olive oil

Place the pork in a large baking dish. Combine the onion, lemon juice, bourbon, honey, soy sauce, ginger, garlic and olive oil in a bowl and mix well. Pour over the pork, turning to coat. Marinate, covered, in the refrigerator for 1 hour or up to 24 hours, turning frequently. Bake the pork with the marinade, covered, at 350 degrees for 1 hour. Uncover and bake for 30 minutes longer or until a meat thermometer inserted into the centers registers 160 degrees.

Note: *You may thicken the marinade with 2 tablespoons all-purpose flour.*

Roasted Pork Tenderloin with Warm Fruit Sauce

Serves 4 to 6

1 (2- to 2¹/2-pound) pork tenderloin
• Salt and pepper to taste
1 (8-ounce) package mixed dried fruit
2 cups orange juice
2 tablespoons orange liqueur (optional)

¹/2 teaspoon ground nutmeg, ground allspice or ground cinnamon
1 tablespoon cornstarch
2 tablespoons water

Season the pork with salt and pepper and place in a shallow baking pan. Bake at 350 degrees for 45 to 60 minutes or until a meat thermometer inserted in the center registers 160 degrees. Remove from the oven and let stand, covered, for 10 minutes.

Cut the fruit into bite-size pieces and place in a saucepan. Add the orange juice, orange liqueur and nutmeg. Bring to a boil and reduce the heat. Simmer, covered, for 5 minutes. Dissolve the cornstarch in the water in a small bowl. Stir into the fruit mixture. Cook until thickened and bubbly, stirring constantly. Cook for 2 minutes longer, stirring constantly. (You may prepare in advance up to this point and reheat before serving.)

Cut the pork into slices and place on individual serving plates. Spoon the sauce over and around the pork. Serve with hot cooked brown and wild rice and fresh asparagus.

Buffet Table

An essential element of your buffet table is creating different focal points to give the presentation of the food added character. Arrange serving dishes in a table setting with various heights and using a variety of bowls and serving pieces. To create height on the table, use books or other sturdy pieces as risers. This allows more serving space and gives depth and visual dimension. Choose a complementary fabric or runner to drape over the risers to add contrast and complete your color theme. Oftentimes, footed cake plates make excellent displays for appetizers or canapés.

When hosting a buffet, the table is the centerpiece and really sets the mood of the party. Sprucing up the table does not require a lot of time or energy, but makes your guests feel that they are worth all the effort.

Marinated Pork Tenderloin

Serves 2 to 3

1	pork tenderloin	2	tablespoons dry mustard
2	garlic cloves, pressed	$2^{1}/_{2}$	teaspoons salt
2	tablespoons parsley	1	tablespoon pepper
$1^{1}/_{2}$	cups vegetable oil	$1/_{2}$	cup wine vinegar
$1/_{4}$	cup Worcestershire sauce	$1/_{3}$	cup lemon juice
$3/_{4}$	cup soy sauce		

Place the pork in a sealable plastic bag. Combine the garlic, parsley, oil, Worcestershire sauce, soy sauce, dry mustard, salt, pepper, vinegar and lemon juice in a bowl and mix well. Pour over the pork and seal the bag. Marinate in the refrigerator for 4 to 5 hours, turning frequently. Drain the pork, discarding the marinade. Grill for 20 minutes or until a meat thermometer inserted in the center registers 160 degrees. Remove from the grill to a cutting board and let stand to cool slightly. Cut into slices to serve.

Pork Medallions in Mustard Sauce

Serves 4

3	tablespoons vegetable oil	$1/_{4}$	cup Chablis or other dry white wine
1	tablespoon whole grain mustard	$1^{3}/_{4}$	cups whipping cream
$1/_{2}$	teaspoon salt	$1/_{4}$	cup whole grain mustard
$1/_{2}$	teaspoon black pepper	$1/_{4}$	teaspoon salt
$2^{3}/_{4}$	pounds pork tenderloins	$1/_{8}$	teaspoon white pepper

Mix the oil, 1 tablespoon mustard, $1/_{2}$ teaspoon salt and the black pepper together and rub over the pork. Place in a large sealable plastic bag and seal the bag. Marinate in the refrigerator for 8 hours, turning occasionally. Drain the pork, discarding the marinade. Place the pork on a lightly greased rack in a shallow roasting pan. Brush with 2 tablespoons of the wine. Insert a meat thermometer into the thickest portion of the pork. Bake at 400 degrees for 25 minutes or until the meat thermometer registers 160 degrees. Brush with the remaining 2 tablespoons wine.

Cook the cream in a saucepan over medium heat for 15 minutes, stirring frequently. Stir in the $1/_{4}$ cup mustard, $1/_{4}$ teaspoon salt and the white pepper. Serve with the pork.

Pork Tenderloin Guiseppina

Serves 6

1 French baguette (very fresh and soft)	• Sliced garlic to taste (optional)
• Olive oil	1 pork tenderloin to fit the length of the bread
• Fresh rosemary leaves to taste	2 to 3 garlic cloves
• Fresh sage leaves to taste	• Salt and pepper to taste
• Fresh thyme leaves to taste	3 (1-inch) pieces of rosemary
• Fresh basil leaves to taste	

Make a slit along the underside of the bread, leaving about 1¹/₂ inches on either end. Scoop out the bread to make a boat, leaving a little around the crust. (Save the scooped out bread to use for another purpose. If you do this step early, you must wrap the bread in plastic wrap to keep it soft and pliable.)

Lay the bread lengthwise on a piece of heavy-duty foil. (The foil should be 3 inches longer than the bread on both ends.) Brush the inside of the bread with enough olive oil to moisten. Lay the fresh herb leaves inside the bread. (You may add additional sliced garlic to the inside of the bread.)

Remove any fat and membrane from the pork. Make a hole about 1 inch deep with a small knife in three equal places down the center of the pork. Stuff a small piece of garlic, salt, pepper and a 1-inch piece of rosemary into each of the holes. Season the entire exterior of the pork with salt and pepper. Stuff the pork into the bread and turn over seam side down. Bring the long sides of the foil together and fold down about 1 inch at the point where the two sides meet. Continue to fold over until the foil is against the pork. Fold the two ends like wrapping a package and fold up to enclose. Place on a baking sheet and bake at 350 degrees for 1 hour. Remove from the oven and let stand for 10 minutes. Unwrap and carve with an electric knife.

Roast Pork with Mushrooms and Shallots

Serves 8

SHALLOTS

Shallots, a relative of the onion, have a less pungent flavor and more tender texture than their more common kin. They are wrapped in a paper-like skin which may range in color from light brown to soft rose. Once this skin is removed, their white flesh may have a pale green or purple color. Each shallot head consists of several cloves. And, like the garlic they resemble, they cook quickly. When selecting shallots, choose a firm, well-shaped head that has no sprouts. Shallots should be stored in a cool, dry place and may keep for up to one month.

They are excellent additions to sauces, soups, stews, salads, and breads.

4	garlic cloves, minced	2	cups whole mushrooms
1	tablespoon olive oil	1/2	cup beef broth
1	tablespoon dried thyme	1	tablespoon cornstarch
3/4	teaspoon salt	2	tablespoons water
1	teaspoon pepper	1	cup beef broth
1/4	teaspoon ground allspice (optional)	1/2	to 1 cup port
1	boneless pork loin	1/2	cup cranberry juice cocktail
1	tablespoon olive oil	1/4	teaspoon salt
2	cups shallots or quartered onion	1/4	teaspoon pepper

Mix the garlic, 1 tablespoon olive oil, the thyme, 3/4 teaspoon salt, 1 teaspoon pepper and the allspice in a bowl. Rub the mixture into the pork. Brown the pork in 1 tablespoon olive oil in a skillet. Place the pork in a roasting pan. Add the shallots and mushrooms to the drippings in the skillet and sauté for 2 to 3 minutes or until soft. Place around the pork, reserving the drippings in the skillet. Add 1/2 cup broth to the roasting pan and cover with foil. Bake at 350 degrees for 45 minutes. Uncover and bake until a meat thermometer inserted into the center registers 155 degrees.

Dissolve the cornstarch in the water in a small bowl. Heat the reserved pan drippings in the skillet and add 1 cup broth, the wine and cranberry juice cocktail. Cook for 3 to 5 minutes. Add the cornstarch mixture and any juices from the roasting pan and cook until thickened, stirring constantly. Season with 1/4 teaspoon salt and 1/4 teaspoon pepper. Serve with the pork.

Cherry Almond-Glazed Pork

Serves 6 to 8

1 (10-ounce) jar black cherry preserves
1 tablespoon light corn syrup
1/4 cup red wine vinegar
1/4 teaspoon salt
1/2 teaspoon ground cinnamon
1/4 teaspoon ground nutmeg
1/4 teaspoon ground cloves
1/2 cup toasted slivered almonds
1 boneless pork loin or pork tenderloins
• Salt and pepper to taste

Combine the preserves, corn syrup, vinegar, 1/4 teaspoon salt, the cinnamon, nutmeg, cloves and almonds in a saucepan and mix well. Bring to a boil, stirring frequently. Reduce the heat and simmer for 3 minutes. Rub the pork with salt and pepper. Place on a rack in a roasting pan. Roast, uncovered, at 325 degrees for 30 minutes per pound, basting periodically with the sauce and basting more frequently toward the end of the roasting time. Bring the remaining sauce to a boil and boil for 2 minutes. Serve with the sliced pork.

Note: *You may freeze any leftovers.*

Tangy Pork Roast

Serves 8 to 10

1 cup apple jelly
1 cup ketchup
2 tablespoons vinegar
2 teaspoons chili powder
1/2 teaspoon salt
1/2 teaspoon garlic salt
1/2 teaspoon chili powder
1 (4-pound) boneless pork roast

Combine the jelly, ketchup, vinegar and 2 teaspoons chili powder in a medium saucepan. Bring to a boil and reduce the heat. Simmer, uncovered, for 2 minutes. Set aside.

Combine the salt, garlic salt and 1/2 teaspoon chili powder in a small bowl. Rub on the pork. Place the pork fat side up on a rack in a shallow roasting pan. Roast at 325 degrees for 2 hours or until a meat thermometer inserted in the center registers 170 degrees, basting with some of the jelly mixture 15 minutes before the pork is done. Remove from the oven and let stand for 10 minutes before carving.

Mix 1/2 cup of the pan drippings with the remaining jelly mixture. Bring to a boil and boil for 2 minutes. Serve with the pork.

Rodeo Ribs

Serves 4

6	pounds pork baby back ribs (3 slabs)	2	tablespoons prepared mustard
1½	cups ketchup	1	teaspoon garlic powder
½	cup honey	½	cup smoky barbecue sauce
		1	to 2 teaspoons Tabasco sauce

Cut the ribs into four-rib serving pieces. Place in a large glass baking dish and do not add any liquid. Cover tightly with foil and bake at 350 degrees for 2 hours. Combine the ketchup, honey, mustard, garlic powder, barbecue sauce and Tabasco sauce in a bowl and mix well. Uncover the ribs and brush the sauce over both sides. Bake, uncovered, with the meaty side up for 30 minutes.

Note: *This recipe may be prepared ahead of time and makes extra sauce.*

Pork Chops with Tomato, Shiitake Mushrooms and Marsala

Serves 4

4	(6-ounce) boneless, center-cut pork loin chops, 1 inch thick	2	tablespoons minced garlic
•	Salt and pepper to taste	8	ounces fresh shiitake mushrooms, sliced
•	All-purpose flour	¾	cup dry marsala
2	eggs, beaten	¾	cup canned low-salt chicken broth
4	cups dry seasoned bread crumbs	1	large tomato, chopped
3	tablespoons olive oil	¼	cup chopped fresh basil
¼	cup (½ stick) margarine		

Pound the pork chops ½ inch thick and sprinkle with salt and pepper. Dip the pork chops into the flour, eggs and then the bread crumbs to coat. Heat the olive oil in a heavy skillet over medium-high heat and sauté for 4 minutes per side or until cooked through. Remove to a platter and keep warm.

Drain the skillet and wipe clean. Heat the margarine in the skillet over medium-high heat. Add the garlic and sauté for 1 minute. Add the mushrooms and sauté for 2 minutes. Add the wine, broth and tomato. Boil for 6 minutes or until thickened, stirring constantly. Stir in the basil and season with salt and pepper. Serve over the pork chops.

Pork Chops Florentine

Serves 6

6	loin pork chops, 3/4 inch thick	•	Dash of ground nutmeg
1 1/2	pounds fresh spinach, chopped and steamed	•	Salt and pepper to taste
1/4	cup minced onion	2	egg yolks, lightly beaten
6	tablespoons butter	1	cup (4 ounces) shredded Swiss cheese
6	tablespoons all-purpose flour	1/4	cup (1 ounce) grated Parmesan cheese
1 1/4	cups chicken stock		
1 3/4	cups milk		

Brown the pork chops in a nonstick skillet and reduce the heat. Cook for 30 minutes or until tender. Remove from the heat and keep warm. Combine the cooked spinach and onion in a bowl and mix well. Melt the butter in a medium saucepan. Stir in the flour and cook over low heat for 3 minutes. Add the stock and milk gradually, stirring constantly. Cook until thickened, stirring constantly. Season with nutmeg, salt and pepper. Pour a small amount of the hot mixture into the beaten egg yolks. Pour the egg yolks into the hot mixture, stirring constantly. Cook until smooth and thickened, stirring constantly. Mix 1 cup of the sauce with the spinach mixture and spread in a greased large shallow baking dish. Arrange the pork chops over the spinach mixture. Stir the Swiss cheese into the remaining sauce and heat until melted. Pour over the pork chops and sprinkle with the Parmesan cheese. Bake at 400 degrees for 20 minutes until light brown.

Bacon Pasta

Serves 4 to 6

12	to 15 slices bacon	1	cup (4 ounces) grated Parmesan cheese
1/2	cup sliced mushrooms	1/2	teaspoon pepper
2	garlic cloves, minced	1/2	cup sliced green onions
1	pound penne, cooked		
2	cups whipping cream		

Cook the bacon in a large skillet over medium heat until crisp. Remove the bacon to paper towels to drain. Reserve 2 tablespoons of the drippings in the skillet. Crumble the bacon when cool. Sauté the mushrooms and garlic in the reserved drippings in the skillet for 3 minutes or until tender. Stir in the cooked pasta, cream, cheese and pepper. Simmer over medium-low heat until thickened, stirring frequently. Fold in the bacon and green onions.

Fusilli with Sausage and Red Bell Peppers

Serves 4

1	tablespoon extra-virgin olive oil	3	tablespoons chopped fresh marjoram
1	pound hot Italian sausage, casings removed	2	(12-ounce) packages cherry tomatoes
2	red bell peppers, chopped (about 2 cups)	•	Salt and pepper to taste
1	large onion, chopped	12	ounces fusilli, cooked
		5	ounces crumbled goat cheese

Heat the olive oil in a large nonstick skillet over medium-high heat. Add the sausage and sauté for 5 minutes or until brown, breaking up with the back of a fork. Drain the sausage, reserving 2 tablespoons of the drippings. Add the bell peppers and onion to the sausage in the reserved drippings and sauté until the bell peppers are soft and the onion is golden brown. Stir in the marjoram and whole tomatoes. Simmer for 8 to 10 minutes or until the tomatoes soften and release their juices, crushing with a fork. Season with salt and pepper. Drain the pasta. Add the sausage mixture and cheese to the pasta and stir to coat. Serve immediately.

Roasted Chicken with Marsala

Serves 6 to 8

1	(4-pound) chicken	•	Seasoned salt and freshly ground pepper to taste
9	fresh sage leaves		
3	sprigs of fresh rosemary	1	cup extra-virgin olive oil
1	teaspoon chopped fresh thyme leaves	1	cup marsala, port or madeira
4	garlic cloves	1	cup Sangiovese or any chianti

Make 1 1/2-inch slits in each side of the chicken breast and on each leg. Stuff each slit with some of the sage, rosemary, thyme, garlic, seasoned salt and pepper. Place the remaining herbs inside the cavity of the chicken. Season the whole chicken with seasoned salt and pepper and place in a baking pan. Infuse with the olive oil. Chill, covered, in the refrigerator for 2 hours. Remove from the refrigerator to the oven and bake at 400 degrees for 30 minutes or until light golden brown. Reduce the oven temperature to 325 degrees. Add the marsala and bake for 30 minutes. Add the Sangiovese. Bake until a meat thermometer inserted into the breast registers 165 degrees. Carve the chicken and arrange in the baking pan. Drizzle with the pan drippings. Bake for 5 minutes, basting with the pan drippings to keep moist.

Champagne Chicken

Serves 4

- 1/4 cup all-purpose flour
- 1 teaspoon salt
- 1/2 teaspoon pepper
- 4 boneless skinless chicken breasts
- 1/2 cup (1 stick) butter
- 3/4 cup sliced mushrooms
- 1 cup cream
- 1/4 cup Champagne
- • Hot cooked rice

Combine the flour, salt and pepper and mix well. Roll the chicken in the flour mixture to coat. Melt the butter in a large skillet and add the chicken. Cook over low heat until light brown. Add the mushrooms and cook for 10 minutes. Add the cream and simmer over low heat for 10 minutes. Add the Champagne and bring to a boil. Serve over hot cooked rice. Garnish with chopped parsley.

Crappito's Chicken in Dijon Cream Sauce

Serves 2

- 1 garlic clove, finely chopped
- 1 tablespoon olive oil
- 1 tablespoon Dijon mustard
- 1 tablespoon finely chopped fresh rosemary
- • Salt and pepper to taste
- 2 (8-ounce) boneless skinless chicken breasts
- 2 tablespoons olive oil
- 1/4 cup dry white wine
- 1/4 cup chicken stock
- 1 tablespoon capers
- 1/4 cup cream
- 1 tablespoon Dijon mustard

Mix the garlic, 1 tablespoon olive oil, 1 tablespoon Dijon mustard, the rosemary, salt and pepper in a sealable plastic bag. Season the chicken with salt and pepper and place in the marinade. Seal the bag and turn to coat. Marinate in the refrigerator for 2 to 10 hours.

Drain the chicken, discarding the marinade. Sauté the chicken in 2 tablespoons olive oil in a skillet until brown on both sides. Remove the chicken to a platter and keep warm, reserving the drippings in the skillet. Add the wine to the pan drippings and cook over medium heat, stirring to deglaze the skillet. Add the stock, capers and cream. Simmer until the sauce is reduced and thickened. Stir in the 1 tablespoon Dijon mustard. Return the chicken to the skillet and cook until heated through. Place the chicken on individual serving plates and spoon the sauce over the top.

Jalapeño Chile Chicken

Serves 6

2   tablespoons minced seeded pickled jalapeño chile

1½ cups (6 ounces) shredded Monterey Jack cheese

½   cup mayonnaise

½   cup sour cream

¼   cup chopped cilantro

1   teaspoon minced garlic

3   whole boneless skinless chicken breasts, cut into halves

•   Seasoned salt to taste

¼   cup mayonnaise

2   corn tortillas

2½ cups corn oil

Combine the jalapeño chile, cheese, ½ cup mayonnaise, the sour cream, cilantro and garlic in a small bowl and mix well. (You may prepare in advance up to this point and chill, covered, in the refrigerator.)

Pound the chicken ½ inch thick between two sheets of waxed paper. Season lightly with seasoned salt. Brush both sides of the chicken with ¼ cup mayonnaise. Cook the chicken in a large skillet over medium-high heat for 4 minutes on both sides or until light brown, turning once. Place on a rack in a broiler pan. Spread equal amounts of the cheese mixture on each chicken breast half. Broil 6 inches from the heat source for 3 to 4 minutes or until the topping begins to brown. Remove from the oven.

Cut the tortillas into strips ¼-inch wide. Heat the corn oil in a heavy saucepan over medium heat to 375 degrees. Add the tortilla strips one-half at a time and cook for 2 minutes or until crisp and light brown, turning once. Drain on paper towels. Serve over the chicken and garnish with additional chopped fresh cilantro. Serve with warm flour tortillas and salsa.

Italian Café Fast Italian Baked Chicken

CHEF'S RECIPE

Serves 6 to 8

1   (16-ounce) bottle Italian
    salad dressing
2   eggs
1/2 teaspoon salt
1   teaspoon freshly
    ground pepper

1   chicken, cut up into pieces
•   Italian-seasoned bread
    crumbs
•   Extra-virgin olive oil

Beat the salad dressing, eggs, salt and pepper in a large glass or stainless steel mixing bowl. Add the chicken, turning to coat. Marinate, covered, in the refrigerator for 30 to 60 minutes. Drain the chicken, discarding the marinade. Coat the chicken with the bread crumbs. Place in a baking pan and drizzle with the olive oil. Cover with foil and bake at 375 degrees for 1 1/2 hours or until the juices run clear. Uncover and continue to bake for 5 to 8 minutes or until the coating becomes golden brown.

Note: *Use a food thermometer to ensure the chicken is cooked to the correct temperature. The internal temperature for chicken pieces with the bone must reach a temperature of 180 degrees. The cooking process will continue after removing the chicken from the oven, so you may want to remove it a little early.*

CHEF FRANK PIAZZA

Frank Piazza, along with his wife Bessilyn, have owned and operated the Italian Café, located in the Clear Lake area, for seventeen years.

Mr. Piazza was a Fine Arts major at the University of Houston, where he developed his creativity as a sculptor, artist, photographer, and now renowned chef. On occasion, he teaches culinary classes as well as conducts tours to Italy with people from all over the United States.

Lake Lure Chicken

Serves 12

12	boneless chicken breasts	1	bottle oil-pack sun-dried tomatoes, or sun-dried tomato spread
1	(16-ounce) bottle Italian salad dressing		
2	packages of goat cheese (not feta cheese)		

Place the chicken in a large sealable plastic bag. Pour the salad dressing over the chicken and seal the bag. Marinate in the refrigerator for 8 to 10 hours. Drain the chicken, discarding the marinade. Place the chicken on a grill rack and grill for 20 minutes or until partially cooked thorough. Place the cheese and sun-dried tomatoes on the chicken and grill until the juices run clear.

Parmesan Chicken with Artichokes

Serves 2 to 3

2	boneless skinless chicken breasts, split into halves	1/2	red bell pepper, cut into 1/4-inch-strips and cut into halves (1/2 cup)
•	Olive oil for brushing	1	(14-ounce) package individually frozen artichokes
•	Salt and pepper to taste		
1	cup (4 ounces) grated Parmesan cheese	•	Juice of 1 lemon
2	tablespoons olive oil	1/2	cup white wine or chicken broth
1	shallot, minced		

Brush each chicken breast half with olive oil and sprinkle with salt and pepper. Dredge in the cheese. Spread 2 tablespoons olive oil in a 9×13-inch baking dish. Place the shallot, bell pepper and frozen artichokes in the prepared dish. Sprinkle with salt and pepper. Drizzle with the lemon juice and add the wine. Place the chicken on top of the vegetables. Cover loosely with foil and bake at 350 degrees for 30 minutes. Uncover and bake for 10 minutes or until the chicken is brown and cooked through.

Lemon Chicken Cutlets

Serves 4 or 5

1/3 cup all-purpose flour
1 tablespoon Cavender's all-purpose Greek seasoning
• Salt and black pepper to taste
• Dash of paprika
4 or 5 boneless chicken breasts
2 tablespoons butter
1 tablespoon vegetable oil
3 tablespoons butter

1 tablespoon Tony Chachere's instant brown gravy mix
1 bunch green onions, chopped
2 tablespoons fresh lemon juice
1 (10-ounce) can chicken broth
1 tablespoon capers
1 tablespoon chopped parsley
• Slivered almonds
2 tablespoons butter

Mix the flour, Greek seasoning, salt, black pepper and paprika together. Pound the chicken with a meat mallet until thin. Coat the chicken in the flour mixture, shaking off the excess and reserving the remaining flour mixture. Melt 2 tablespoons butter in the oil in a large skillet. Add the chicken and sauté over medium-high heat until brown and cooked through, turning once. Place the chicken in a baking dish sprayed with nonstick cooking spray, reserving the drippings in the skillet.

Melt 3 tablespoons butter in the reserved drippings. Add a mixture of the gravy mix and reserved flour mixture and cook to form a roux, stirring constantly. Add the green onions, lemon juice and broth. Cook for 1 minute or until thickened, stirring constantly. Add the capers and chopped parsley and stir to mix well. Pour over the chicken and bake at 350 degrees for 1 hour.

Sauté the almonds in 2 tablespoons butter in a skillet until brown and toasted. Sprinkle over the top of the chicken mixture when ready to serve.

Chicken Marsala

Serves 6 to 8

6	whole chicken breasts, boned, skinned and quartered
1/2	cup all-purpose flour
1	cup (2 sticks) butter or margarine
•	Salt and pepper to taste
1 1/2	cups sliced mushrooms
3/4	cup marsala
1/2	cup chicken stock
1/2	teaspoon salt
1/8	teaspoon pepper
1/2	cup (2 ounces) shredded fontina cheese or mozzarella cheese
1/2	cup (2 ounces) grated Parmesan cheese

Dredge the chicken lightly in the flour. Cook four pieces of chicken at a time in 2 tablespoons of the butter in a large skillet over low heat for 3 to 4 minutes on each side or until golden brown, adding more of the remaining butter as needed. Place the chicken in a greased 9×13-inch baking dish, overlapping the edges and reserving the drippings in the skillet. Season the chicken with salt and pepper to taste.

Melt the remaining 1/4 cup butter in the reserved drippings in the skillet. Add the mushrooms and sauté until tender. Drain, reserving the drippings in the skillet. Sprinkle the mushrooms over the chicken. Add the wine and stock to the reserved drippings. Simmer for 10 minutes, stirring occasionally. Stir in 1/2 teaspoon salt and 1/8 teaspoon pepper. Spoon one-third of the sauce over the chicken, reserving the remaining sauce. Mix the fontina cheese and Parmesan cheese together and sprinkle over the chicken. Bake at 450 degrees for 10 to 12 minutes. Broil for 1 to 2 minutes or until light brown. Serve with the reserved sauce.

Chicken Supreme

Serves 4 to 6

1	cup sour cream
2	tablespoons lemon juice
2	teaspoons celery salt
1	teaspoon paprika
1	garlic clove, crushed
1	teaspoon salt
1/4	teaspoon pepper
6	chicken breasts
1	cup (or more) soft bread crumbs
1/2	cup (1 stick) butter, melted

Mix the sour cream, lemon juice, celery salt, paprika, garlic, salt and pepper in a bowl. Coat the chicken with the mixture and place on a platter. Chill, uncovered, in the refrigerator for 8 to 10 hours. Roll the chicken in the bread crumbs. Arrange in a shallow baking pan. Pour half the butter over the chicken. Bake at 350 degrees for 40 minutes. Top with the remaining butter and bake for 15 minutes longer. You may add grated Parmesan cheese to the bread crumbs.

Stuffed Pistolettes

Serves 6 to 8

PISTOLETTES

8	Pistolette buns
1	egg
3	tablespoons water
4	garlic cloves, pressed
6	tablespoons butter
•	Grated Parmesan cheese

FILLING

3	chicken breasts, cut into bite-size pieces
1	pound shrimp, peeled, deveined and chopped
1/3	cup butter
1/2	cup chopped green onions
1/2	cup chopped celery
3	garlic cloves
1/3	cup fresh parsley, finely chopped
•	Salt and pepper to taste
1/3	cup butter
1	(4-ounce) can mushrooms, drained
1/3	cup cooking sherry
3	tablespoons butter
3	tablespoons all-purpose flour
2	cups milk
1	cup (4 ounces) shredded Swiss cheese
1/4	cup (1 ounce) grated Parmesan cheese
1 1/2	teaspoons Worcestershire sauce

To *prepare the pistolettes,* hollow out the buns from the bottom. Beat the egg and water in a bowl. Brush the buns inside and out with the egg mixture and place on a baking sheet. Bake at 350 degrees until brown and crisp. Remove from the oven to cool. Sauté the garlic in the butter in a small skillet over low heat for 5 minutes. Brush over the buns and sprinkle with the cheese.

To prepare the filling, sauté the chicken and shrimp in 1/3 cup butter until the chicken juices run clear and the shrimp turns pink. Remove from the skillet to drain. Sauté the onions, celery, garlic, parsley, salt and pepper in 1/3 cup butter in the skillet until tender. Remove from the heat and drain well. Return the chicken and shrimp mixture and drained vegetables to the skillet. Add the mushrooms and sherry and stir to mix well. Melt 3 tablespoons butter in a saucepan over low heat. Add the flour, salt and pepper gradually, stirring until smooth. Add the milk gradually, stirring constantly. Cook until thick and creamy, stirring constantly. Remove from the heat. Add the Swiss cheese, Parmesan cheese and Worcestershire sauce and stir until melted and smooth. Add to the chicken and shrimp mixture in the skillet and stir until well mixed.

To assemble, spoon the hot filling into the pistolettes on a baking sheet. Broil for 5 minutes or until heated through. Garnish with additional chopped fresh parsley and serve warm.

Note: *You may use fresh mushrooms instead of canned and sauté with the chicken and shrimp. Puff pastry shells may be used instead of the pistolettes.*

Chicken Enchiladas

Serves 6 to 8

1	cup chopped onion	4	chicken breasts, cooked and chopped
1/2	cup (1 stick) butter	6	to 8 flour tortillas
1	cup chopped green chiles	2 1/2	pints whipping cream
1/2	cup chicken broth	1 1/2	cups (6 ounces) shredded jalapeño Jack cheese
8	ounces cream cheese, softened		

Sauté the onion in the butter in a skillet until translucent. Add the green chiles and broth. Add the cream cheese and cook until melted, stirring constantly. Stir in the chicken. Spoon into the tortillas and roll up. Place in a single layer in a greased baking dish. Pour the cream over the top and sprinkle with the jalapeño Jack cheese. Bake, covered, at 350 degrees for 45 minutes. Serve with hot cooked rice and Charro Beans, page 119.

Spinach Enchiladas

Serves 6

1/2	cup finely chopped onion	1/2	cup Alfredo sauce
1/2	cup finely chopped celery	1	pound Velveeta cheese, cut into cubes
1/2	cup finely chopped mushrooms	1	(4-ounce) can chopped green chiles
1	tablespoon olive oil	1/2	cup water
1	tablespoon butter	6	flour tortillas
2	(10-ounce) packages frozen chopped spinach, thawed and drained	1	cup (4 ounces) shredded Monterey Jack cheese

Sauté the onion, celery and mushrooms in the olive oil and butter in a skillet until soft. Squeeze all of the liquid from the spinach. Add the spinach and Alfredo sauce to the sautéed vegetables and stir to mix well. Melt the Velveeta cheese in a nonstick saucepan. Stir in the green chiles and water. (You may add additional water for a thinner sauce, if desired.) Spoon about a 1-inch round of spinach mixture onto each of the tortillas and roll up. Place in an 8×11-inch glass baking dish. Pour the cheese sauce over the top and sprinkle with the Monterey Jack cheese. Bake at 350 degrees for 30 minutes.

Note: *Instead of using purchased Alfredo sauce in this recipe, make your own using the recipe on page 191.*

Spicy Mexican Chicken

Serves 6

4	whole chicken breasts, cut into halves, skinned and boned	1	tablespoon chili powder
1	(7-ounce) can chopped green chiles	1/2	teaspoon salt
4	ounces Monterey Jack cheese, cut into 8 strips	1/4	teaspoon cumin
1/2	cup bread crumbs	1/4	teaspoon pepper
1/4	cup (1 ounce) freshly grated Parmesan cheese	1/4	cup (1/2 stick) plus 2 teaspoons butter, melted
		1	(16-ounce) can tomato sauce
		1/3	cup sliced green onions
		1/2	teaspoon cumin
		•	Salt and pepper to taste

Place the chicken between two sheets of waxed paper. Pound with a meat mallet until the chicken is 1/4 inch thick. Place 2 tablespoons of the green chiles and one strip of Monterey Jack cheese in the center of each chicken piece and roll up, tucking the ends under and securing with wooden picks. Mix the bread crumbs, Parmesan cheese, chili powder, 1/2 teaspoon salt, 1/4 teaspoon cumin and 1/4 teaspoon pepper in a small bowl. Place 1/4 cup of the melted butter in a shallow bowl. Dip each chicken roll in the butter and then in the bread crumb mixture to coat. Place seam side down in an oblong baking dish and drizzle with the remaining 2 teaspoons butter. Chill, covered, for 4 hours. Uncover and bake at 400 degrees for 35 minutes or until the juices run clear.

Combine the tomato sauce, green onions, 1/2 teaspoon cumin, salt and pepper in a small saucepan and mix well. Cook until heated through. Place a small amount of the sauce on each serving plate and top with a chicken roll. Serve with the remaining sauce.

Alfredo Sauce

Sauté 1 pound sliced fresh mushrooms and 4 crushed garlic cloves in 1/2 cup (1 stick) butter in a saucepan for 5 minutes or until tender. Add 2 quarts half-and-half, 2 cups (8 ounces) grated Parmesan cheese, 1 teaspoon seasoned salt and 4 to 6 tablespoons chopped fresh parsley. Cook until heated through. Do not boil.

Lasagna Florentine

Serves 8

VELOUTÉ SAUCE

1/2 cup (1 stick) unsalted butter
1/2 cup all-purpose flour
3 cups chicken broth or
   turkey broth
1 cup heavy cream
2 teaspoons salt
1 teaspoon ground nutmeg
• Pepper to taste

LASAGNA

8 ounces lasagna noodles
1 tablespoon vegetable oil
2 (10-ounce) packages frozen
   chopped spinach
2 to 3 cups chopped cooked chicken
   or turkey
1 cup (4 ounces) grated Munster
   cheese or Baby Swiss cheese
3/4 cup (3 ounces) freshly grated
   Parmesan cheese

To *prepare the sauce,* melt the butter in a saucepan. Stir in the flour gradually. Add the broth gradually, stirring constantly. Cook over medium heat until the mixture comes to a boil, stirring constantly. Remove from the heat. Stir in the cream, salt, nutmeg and pepper.

To prepare the lasagna, cook the noodles with the oil using the package directions. Drain and immediately place in cold water to cool; drain well. Microwave the spinach using the package directions; drain and squeeze dry. Combine the spinach and one-half of the velouté sauce in a bowl and mix well. Reserve some of the velouté sauce for the top layer. Spread a thin layer of the spinach mixture in a baking dish. Layer the noodles, remaining spinach mixture, chicken, remaining velouté sauce, Munster cheese and Parmesan cheese one-half at a time in the prepared dish. Spread the reserved velouté sauce over the top. Bake at 350 degrees for 30 minutes. Let stand for 15 minutes before serving.

Note: *This recipe may be prepared in advance and frozen before baking. Thaw completely before baking.*

Spicy Chicken Spinach Casserole

Serves 10 to 15

2 large chickens
• Salt and black pepper to taste
1/4 cup (1/2 stick) butter
1/4 cup all-purpose flour
1 cup milk
2 cups sour cream
1/3 cup lemon juice
1 teaspoon salt
1 teaspoon MSG
2 teaspoons seasoned salt
1/2 teaspoon cayenne pepper
2 teaspoons black pepper
1 teaspoon paprika
10 ounces small flat egg noodles, cooked and drained
1 (10-ounce) package frozen chopped spinach, cooked and drained
1 (6-ounce) can mushroom pieces, drained
1 (8-ounce) can water chestnuts, drained and chopped
1 small jar chopped pimentos, drained
1/2 cup chopped onion
1/2 cup chopped celery
1 1/2 cups (6 ounces) Monterey Jack cheese

Place the chicken in a large stockpot. Add enough water to cover and season with salt and black pepper. Bring to a boil and reduce the heat. Simmer until the chicken is cooked through and tender. Drain, reserving 1 cup of the stock. Cut the chicken into bite-size pieces, discarding the skin and bones. (You should have at least 4 cups of chicken.)

Melt the butter in a large saucepan and stir in the flour. Add the milk and the reserved stock. Cook over low heat until thickened, stirring constantly. Add the sour cream, lemon juice, 1 teaspoon salt, the MSG, seasoned salt, cayenne pepper, 2 teaspoons black pepper and the paprika and mix well. Stir in the egg noodles, spinach, mushrooms, water chestnuts, pimentos, onion and celery. Layer the noodle mixture and chicken one-half at a time in a buttered 3-quart baking dish. Sprinkle with the Monterey Jack cheese. Bake at 350 degrees for 25 minutes or until bubbly.

Chicken Puffs

Serves 4 to 6

4	chicken breasts	2	sprigs of thyme
6	cups water	1	teaspoon whole black peppercorns
1	rib celery, finely chopped	3	to 4 tablespoons cornstarch
1	carrot, finely chopped	6	to 8 tablespoons wine
1	tablespoon butter	•	Salt and pepper to taste
4	shallots, finely chopped	1	package long grain and wild rice, cooked
1	rib celery, finely chopped		
1	carrot, finely chopped	1	package frozen puff pastry
1	(750-mililiter) bottle dry white wine	1	egg white, beaten

Place the chicken, water, 1 rib celery and 1 carrot in a large saucepan. Boil for 30 minutes or until tender. Drain the chicken, reserving 1 quart of the broth. Strain the broth, discarding the solids. Cut the chicken into bite-size pieces, discarding the skin and bones.

Heat the butter in a sauté pan. Add the shallots, 1 rib celery and 1 carrot and sauté briefly. Add the bottle of wine, thyme and peppercorns. Cook over medium heat for 45 minutes or until reduced to 1 1/2 cups. Add the reserved broth and bring to a boil. Reduce the heat and simmer for 15 minutes. Strain the mixture, discarding the solids. Return the liquid to the pan. (You may prepare up to 24 hours in advance at this point and store in the refrigerator.) Reheat the liquid slightly. Stir in a mixture of the cornstarch and 6 to 8 tablespoons wine. Cook until thickened, stirring constantly. Season with salt and pepper.

Combine the chicken and rice in a bowl and mix well. Let stand until cool. Stir in 1/2 cup of the sauce or enough to hold the mixture together. Thaw the pastry using the package directions. Unfold the pastry and place on a pastry sheet lightly dusted with flour. Roll out the pastry, but not too thin to handle. Cut into 8-to 10-inch squares. Place 1 cup of the chicken mixture onto each square and fold the pastry over the filling to form a bundle, enclosing all openings. Place the bundles on a baking sheet with the smooth side facing up. Cut leaves for decoration out of the remaining pastry and place on top of each puff. Brush with the egg white. Bake at 350 degrees for 30 minutes or until light brown.

Serve with the remaining sauce drizzled over the top with steamed broccoli or asparagus.

Note: *This is an excellent recipe to prepare for a dinner party since minimum preparation is required prior to serving..*

Frenchie's Quail in Red Wine Sauce

CHEF'S RECIPE

Serves 6

12	quail, washed	2	cups chicken broth
•	Brandy	1	cup dry red wine
•	All-purpose flour	1	rib celery, cut into quarters
5	tablespoons butter	•	Salt and pepper to taste
2	cups sliced mushrooms	•	Strained juice of 2 oranges
1/4	cup (1/2 stick) butter	•	Hot cooked angel hair pasta

Brush the quail with brandy and lightly sprinkle with flour. Melt 5 tablespoons butter in a heavy skillet. Add the quail and sauté for 10 minutes.

Sauté the mushrooms in 1/4 cup butter in a skillet until tender. Pour over the quail. Add the broth, wine, celery, salt and pepper. Cover and simmer for 30 minutes or until tender. Remove the celery. Stir in the orange juice. Cook until heated through. Spoon over the pasta.

ORIENTAL CHICKEN

Place one hen, or six chicken breasts and six chicken thighs in a large saucepan. Cover with water and season with salt and pepper to taste. Bring to a boil and cook until the chicken tests done. Drain and chop the chicken, discarding the skin and bones.

Combine the chicken, three (10-ounce) packages frozen chopped broccoli, 4 ounces sliced mushrooms, one (8-ounce) can sliced water chestnuts, 1/2 teaspoon white pepper, 1/4 teaspoon cayenne pepper, two (10-ounce) cans cream of chicken soup, one-half soup can water, 1 1/2 cups Hellman's mayonnaise, 2 tablespoons lemon juice and 1/3 cup white wine in a large bowl and mix well. Spoon into a large baking dish. Sprinkle with herb-seasoned bread crumbs. Bake at 350 degrees until hot and bubbly.

Penne with Tomatoes and Cheese

Serves 6 to 8

2	cups chopped onions		2	cups chicken broth
2	teaspoons minced garlic		•	Salt and black pepper to taste
3	tablespoons olive oil		1	pound penne or rigatoni
3	(28-ounce) cans Italian plum tomatoes, drained		3	tablespoons olive oil
1/2	cup white wine		2	to 3 cups (8 to 12 ounces) shredded Havarti cheese
2	teaspoons dried basil		1/2	cup (2 ounces) grated Parmesan cheese
1	teaspoon Italian seasoning		1/4	cup finely chopped fresh basil
1	to 1 1/2 teaspoons dried crushed red pepper			

Sauté the onions and garlic in 3 tablespoons olive oil in a large heavy saucepan over medium heat until the onions are translucent but not brown. Stir in the tomatoes, wine, dried basil, Italian seasoning and crushed red pepper. Bring to a boil, breaking up the tomatoes with the back of the spoon. Add the broth and return to a boil. Reduce the heat to medium. Simmer for 70 minutes or until the mixture thickens slightly and is reduced to about 6 cups, stirring occasionally. Season with salt and black pepper.

Cook the pasta in a large stockpot using the package directions; drain. Return the pasta to the stockpot and toss with 3 tablespoons olive oil to coat. Add the sauce and toss well. Stir in the Havarti cheese. Spoon into a 9×13-inch glass baking dish. Sprinkle with the Parmesan cheese. Bake at 375 degrees for 30 minutes or until the pasta is heated through. Sprinkle with the fresh basil just before serving.

Note: *You may break up the tomatoes before adding to the saucepan. You may make the sauce two days in advance and store in the refrigerator. Warm the sauce before preparing the dish.*

Desserts

Helen's Garden

Located among majestic oaks in the heart of the historic district in League City is Helen's Garden. This delightful, flower-filled park was dedicated on April 8, 1999, to Helen Lewis Hall and given to the community by her husband Walter Hall. On a plaque in the park the inscription reads, Helen's Garden is "to honor the memory of one who gave selflessly for the betterment of her family and the folks of League City." The park is filled with benches and birdhouses given by families and dedicated to their loved ones. This special gift is a place to be with family and enjoy the outdoors.

Tea with the Easter Bunny

Helen's Garden

PINEAPPLE MINT TEA, PAGE 66
PINEAPPLE PUNCH, PAGE 46
STRAWBERRY SLUSH, PAGE 47

HEART-SHAPED PEANUT BUTTER AND JELLY SANDWICHES

CHOCOLATE CHIP CHEESE BALL WITH GRAHAM CRACKERS, PAGE 220
FRUIT KABOBS WITH PIÑA COLADA DIP, PAGE 220

CARAMEL CORN, PAGE 221
PEPPERMINT SWIRL BARK, PAGE 227
ICE CREAM CAKE, PAGE 214
APRICOT LEMON CAKE, PAGE 208

Apple Cake with Caramel Sauce and Bourbon Whipped Cream

Serves 16

CAKE
1/2 cup granulated sugar
1 tablespoon ground cinnamon
3 cups all-purpose flour
1 tablespoon baking powder
1/2 teaspoon salt
2 cups granulated sugar
1 cup vegetable oil
3/4 cup sour cream
4 eggs
1/2 cup orange juice
2 teaspoons vanilla extract
4 cups chopped peeled Granny Smith apples (about 3 large)
1 cup chopped walnuts
• Confectioners' sugar

CARAMEL SAUCE
1 1/2 cups whipping cream
1 cup packed dark brown sugar
1/2 cup dark corn syrup
1/4 cup (1/2 stick) unsalted butter
1 teaspoon vanilla extract

BOURBON WHIPPED CREAM
3 cups chilled heavy whipping cream
1/2 cup packed light brown sugar
1/3 cup bourbon

To *prepare the cake,* mix 1/2 cup granulated sugar and the cinnamon in a small bowl. Mix the flour, baking powder and salt in a medium bowl. Whisk 2 cups granulated sugar, the oil, sour cream, eggs, orange juice and vanilla in a large bowl until blended. Stir in the flour mixture. Pour half the batter into a greased and floured 12-cup nonstick bundt pan. Sprinkle half the apples over the batter. Sprinkle with half the walnuts and half the cinnamon-sugar. Spoon the remaining batter over the layers. Sprinkle with the remaining apples, walnuts and cinnamon-sugar. Bake at 350 degrees for 55 minutes. Cover the pan loosely with foil and bake for 30 minutes longer or until a cake tester inserted near the center comes out clean. Cool in the pan on a wire rack for 10 minutes. Loosen the edge from the side of the pan and invert onto a wire rack to cool completely. Remove to a cake plate and sprinkle with confectioners' sugar.

To prepare the sauce, bring the cream, brown sugar, corn syrup and butter to a boil in a heavy saucepan, stirring occasionally. Reduce the heat to medium-high. Boil for 8 minutes or until reduced to 2 cups, stirring occasionally. Whisk in the vanilla and cool.

To prepare the whipped cream, beat the whipping cream and brown sugar in a large mixing bowl until soft peaks form. Add the bourbon and beat until stiff peaks form.

To serve, cut the cake into slices and serve with the warm sauce and whipped cream.

Absolutely Divine Carrot Cake

Serves 12

CAKE

1 1/2 cups whole wheat flour
2/3 cup all-purpose flour
2 teaspoons baking soda
2 teaspoons ground cinnamon
1/2 teaspoon salt
1/2 teaspoon ground nutmeg
1/4 teaspoon ground ginger
1 cup granulated sugar
1 cup packed brown sugar
1 cup buttermilk
3/4 cup vegetable oil
4 eggs
1 1/2 teaspoons vanilla extract
1 pound baby carrots, peeled and grated
1 (15-ounce) can crushed pineapple, drained thoroughly
1 cup chopped pecans
1 cup flaked coconut
1/2 cup dark raisins

CREAM CHEESE FROSTING

1/2 cup (1 stick) butter or margarine, softened
8 ounces cream cheese, softened
1 (1-pound) package confectioners' sugar
2 teaspoons grated orange zest (grated zest of 2 oranges)
1 teaspoon vanilla extract

To *prepare the cake,* grease three 8-inch cake pans and line the bottoms with waxed paper. Grease and flour the waxed paper. Mix the whole wheat flour, all-purpose flour, baking soda, cinnamon, salt, nutmeg and ginger in a medium bowl. Combine the granulated sugar, brown sugar, buttermilk, oil, eggs and vanilla in a large bowl and stir until blended. Add the flour mixture, carrots, pineapple, pecans, coconut and raisins and stir until well blended. Pour into the prepared cake pans. Bake at 350 degrees for 30 minutes or until a wooden pick inserted in the centers comes out clean. Cool in the pans for 20 minutes. Loosen the layers from the side of the pans with a sharp knife. Invert onto wire racks and remove the waxed paper. Cool completely.

To prepare the frosting, beat the butter and cream cheese in a large mixing bowl until light and fluffy. Add the confectioners' sugar, orange zest and vanilla and mix well. Spread the frosting between the layers and over the top and side of the cake. Garnish with marzipan carrots. Cover and chill for 8 to 10 hours before cutting.

Note: *Do not substitute all-purpose flour for the whole wheat flour. Use only freshly grated orange zest for the best flavor. Do not substitute golden raisins for the dark raisins.*

Texas Chocolate Cake

Serves 16

2 cups all-purpose flour	1 cup (2 sticks) butter or margarine
2 cups granulated sugar	1 (1-pound) package
1 teaspoon baking soda	confectioners' sugar
1/2 teaspoon salt	1 teaspoon vanilla extract
1/2 cup sour cream	1 cup chopped walnuts
2 eggs	1/2 cup (1 stick) butter or margarine
6 tablespoons baking cocoa	6 tablespoons milk
1 cup water	1/4 cup baking cocoa

Combine the flour, granulated sugar, baking soda, salt, sour cream and eggs in a large bowl and mix well. Melt 6 tablespoons baking cocoa, the water and butter in a 1-quart saucepan. Bring to a boil, stirring constantly. Pour immediately into the flour mixture and mix until smooth. Pour into a greased 9×13-inch cake pan. Bake at 350 degrees for 30 minutes or until the cake tests done. Mix the confectioners' sugar, vanilla and walnuts in a bowl. Bring the butter, milk and 1/4 cup baking cocoa to a boil in a saucepan. Add immediately to the confectioners' sugar mixture and mix well. Spread immediately over the warm cake.

Chocolate Torte with Coffee Cream Filling
Serves 12

11/4 cups sifted confectioners' sugar	• Dash of salt
1/2 cup baking cocoa	2 cups heavy whipping cream
8 egg yolks	3 tablespoons granulated sugar
1 teaspoon vanilla extract	1 tablespoon instant coffee powder
8 egg whites	

Sift the confectioners' sugar and baking cocoa together. Beat the egg yolks and vanilla in a small mixing bowl for 5 minutes or until thick and pale yellow. Add the confectioners' sugar mixture and beat until blended. Beat for 1 minute longer. Beat the egg whites with the salt in a large mixing bowl until stiff peaks form. Fold into the batter gently. Pour into an ungreased 9-inch springform pan. Bake at 325 degrees for 45 to 50 minutes or until the torte tests done. Remove from the oven and cool in the pan on a wire rack. (The center of the torte will fall while cooling.) Gently loosen the torte from the side of the pan and remove the side. Place on a serving plate. Whip the whipping cream, granulated sugar and coffee powder in a mixing bowl until stiff peaks form. Spoon into the center of the torte. Garnish with semisweet chocolate curls.

Flourless Fudge Cake

Serves 8

1/3 cup water
1/2 cup sugar
1/2 cup (1 stick) butter
12 ounces semisweet chocolate, chopped into small pieces

1/3 cup orange liqueur (Cointreau or Grand Marnier) or raspberry liqueur (Chambord)
6 eggs

Butter the bottom and side of an 8-inch cake pan. Line the bottom of the pan with baking parchment. Bring the water and sugar to a boil in a saucepan. Cook until the sugar dissolves, stirring constantly. Remove from the heat. Add the butter and chocolate. Let stand for 2 minutes to melt and stir until smooth. Whisk in the liqueur. Whisk in the eggs one at a time. Pour into the prepared cake pan. Place the cake pan in a larger pan. Add warm water to the larger pan. Bake at 325 degrees for 40 to 45 minutes or until the center is slightly puffed and soft when pressed in the center. Remove from the oven and cool in the pan. Invert onto a wire rack and smooth the side with a spatula. Let stand for 30 minutes. Serve with whipped cream and oranges or raspberries.

Note: *The water bath helps the delicate cake set to a smooth consistency. Do not chill the cake if serving the same day. The flavor is better at room temperature. You may wrap the cake in plastic wrap and store in the freezer. Defrost and serve at room temperature.*

Frozen Kahlúa Cake

Serves 12

1 teaspoon baking soda	4 egg yolks
2 tablespoons cold water	1 1/3 cups all-purpose flour
1/2 cup cold coffee	2 tablespoons vanilla extract
1/2 cup Kahlúa	4 egg whites, stiffly beaten
3/4 cup (1 1/2 sticks) butter, softened	1 cup confectioners' sugar
2 cups granulated sugar	1/2 cup Kahlúa
3/4 cup baking cocoa	

Dissolve the baking soda in the cold water in a bowl. Add the cold coffee and 1/2 cup Kahlúa and mix well. Cream the butter and granulated sugar in a mixing bowl until light and fluffy. Add the baking cocoa and egg yolks and mix well. Add the coffee mixture alternately with the flour, beating constantly. Beat in the vanilla. Fold in the stiffly beaten egg whites. Pour into a greased and floured bundt pan. Bake at 325 degrees for 1 hour.

Combine the confectioners' sugar and Kahlúa in a bowl and mix well. Invert the warm cake onto a cake plate. Pour the Kahlúa mixture over the warm cake. Cover the cake with foil and freeze. Remove the cake from the freezer 1 hour before serving. Cut into slices and serve with dollops of whipped cream.

Note: *This cake was voted one of the best cakes in Texas in 1985 and it is still tops. It is so convenient to have a frozen cake for company.*

Classic Milky Way Cake
Serves 12 to 14

Many of you have had the Milky Way Cake recipe in your collection for a very long time. In testing this recipe, many of the younger members of our organization had never tasted it before. They loved it! One lady in our group has made this cake every year for her son's birthday and he is now twenty-two. This recipe is for everyone, young and old alike.

CAKE
8   (13/4-ounce) Milky Way candy bars
11/2 cups (3 sticks) butter
1/4   teaspoon baking soda
11/4 cups buttermilk
2   cups sugar
4   eggs
21/2 cups all-purpose flour

FUDGE ICING
21/2 cups sugar
1   cup evaporated milk
1   cup (6 ounces) semisweet chocolate chips
1   cup marshmallow creme
1/2   cup (1 stick) butter

To *prepare the cake*, melt the candy bars with 1/2 cup of the butter in a saucepan, stirring constantly. Remove from the heat and let stand until cool. Dissolve the baking soda in the buttermilk. Cream the remaining butter and sugar in mixing bowl until light and fluffy. Add the eggs one at a time, beating well after each addition. Add the flour alternately with the buttermilk mixture, beating constantly. Add the melted candy bar mixture and mix well. Spoon into three greased and floured 9-inch cake pans. Bake at 325 degrees for 30 to 40 minutes or until the layers test done. Cool in the pans for 10 minutes. Invert onto wire racks to cool completely.

To prepare the icing, combine the sugar and evaporated milk in a saucepan and mix well. Cook over medium heat to 234 to 240 degrees on a candy thermometer, soft-ball stage. Remove from the heat. Add the chocolate chips, marshmallow creme and butter and stir until smooth. Spread between the layers and over the top and side of the cake. Let stand until cool before serving.

Note: *The cake is also delicious served without the icing.*

Laura's Tea Room Deep-Dish Coconut Cake

CHEF'S RECIPE

Serves 12

1	(2-layer) package white cake mix	1	(8-ounce) can cream of coconut
3	eggs	1	(14-ounce) can sweetened
1/4	cup granulated sugar		condensed milk
1/4	cup vegetable oil	2	cups heavy whipping cream
1 1/4	cups half-and-half	1/4	cup confectioners' sugar
2 1/2	cups shredded coconut	2	teaspoons vanilla extract
1	cup pecans, chopped		

Combine the cake mix, eggs, granulated sugar, oil and half-and-half in a mixing bowl and beat until blended. Stir in 2 cups of the shredded coconut and 3/4 cup of the pecans. Spoon into a greased 9×13-inch cake pan. Bake at 350 degrees for 45 minutes. (Do not use a convection oven.) Punch holes in the hot cake with a wooden spoon handle. Pour a mixture of the cream of coconut and condensed milk into the holes. Chill completely in the refrigerator. (You may also freeze at this point.) Beat the whipping cream, confectioners' sugar and vanilla in a mixing bowl until stiff peaks form. Spread over the top of the chilled cake. Sprinkle with the remaining 1/2 cup shredded coconut and remaining 1/4 cup pecans.

Cranberry Cake

Serves 8 to 10

2 1/4	cups unbleached flour	2	eggs
1	teaspoon baking powder	1	cup buttermilk
1	teaspoon baking soda	•	Grated zest of 2 oranges
1/4	teaspoon salt	1	cup fresh cranberries, chopped
3/4	cup (1 1/2 sticks) butter, softened	1	cup chopped dates
1	cup sugar	1	cup walnuts, finely chopped

Sift the flour, baking powder, baking soda and salt together. Cream the butter and sugar in a mixing bowl until light and fluffy. Beat in the eggs one at a time. Add the flour mixture and buttermilk alternately, beating at low speed for 2 minutes. Beat in the orange zest. Stir in the cranberries, dates and walnuts. Pour into a greased bundt or tube pan. Bake at 350 degrees for 1 hour or until a wooden pick inserted near the center comes out clean. Cool in the pan for 10 minutes. Invert onto a wire rack to cool completely. Store in an airtight container for 24 hours to enhance the flavor. Serve with whipped cream, if desired.

French Holiday Cake

Serves 12

1	(12-ounce) package vanilla wafers	1/2	cup milk
1	cup (2 sticks) butter, softened	1 1/2	cups broken pecans
2	cups sugar	1	(7-ounce) can flaked coconut
6	eggs		

Process the vanilla wafers in a blender until finely crushed or place in a sealable plastic bag and finely crush with a rolling pin. Cream the butter and sugar in a mixing bowl until light and fluffy. Add the eggs one at a time, beating well after each addition. Add the vanilla wafer crumbs and milk alternately, beating well after each addition. Stir in the pecans and flaked coconut. Pour into a greased and floured bundt pan. Bake at 350 degrees for 1 1/2 hours. Cool completely in the pan on a wire rack. Invert onto a cake plate to serve.

Note: *Test the cake for doneness after 1 hour if you are using a dark, Teflon-lined bundt pan.*

Apricot Lemon Cake

Serves 12

1	(2-layer) package yellow cake mix	3/4	cup vegetable oil
1	(3-ounce) package lemon gelatin	1	(1 1/2-ounce) bottle lemon extract
4	eggs	1	cup confectioners' sugar
3/4	cup apricot nectar	3	tablespoons lemon juice

Combine the cake mix, gelatin, eggs, apricot nectar, oil and lemon extract in a mixing bowl and beat until smooth. Pour into a greased and floured tube pan or bundt pan. Bake at 350 degrees for 45 minutes. Cool slightly and invert onto a cake plate.

Combine the confectioners' sugar and lemon juice in a bowl and mix until smooth. Drizzle over the warm cake.

Note: *This cake may be frozen.*

Lemon Angel Cake

Serves 12

1	angel food cake	1/2	teaspoon vanilla extract
1/3	cup lemon juice	1/2	teaspoon almond extract
1	(14-ounce) can sweetened	12	ounces whipped topping
	condensed milk	•	Sliced almonds

Cut the cake into three layers with a serrated knife. Whip the lemon juice, condensed milk, vanilla and almond extract in a bowl until the consistency of thick icing. Spread between the layers and on top of the cake. Frost with the whipped topping and sprinkle with almonds. Store in the refrigerator.

Note: *You may use a purchased angel food cake or an angel food cake made from a mix. The latter makes a prettier and more delicious cake.*

Molasses Cake

Serves 15

2	cups all-purpose flour	1	cup molasses
1	teaspoon salt	1	teaspoon ground cloves
1	teaspoon baking soda	1	teaspoon ground ginger
1/2	cup sugar	1	teaspoon ground cinnamon
1/2	cup shortening, melted	1	cup boiling water
2	eggs		

Mix the flour, salt and baking soda together in a mixing bowl. Add the sugar, shortening, eggs, molasses, cloves, ginger and cinnamon and beat until smooth. Add the boiling water and mix thoroughly. Pour into a 9×13-inch greased and floured cake pan. Bake at 350 degrees for 30 to 35 minutes or until a wooden pick inserted in the center comes out clean. Cut into squares. Serve with whipped cream and garnish with lemon zest.

Note: *You may use melted butter or vegetable oil instead of the shortening.*

Pecan Cake Squares

Makes about 28 squares

1	cup (2 sticks) butter, softened	3/4	teaspoon baking powder
1/2	cup confectioners' sugar	1	teaspoon vanilla extract
2	cups all-purpose flour	1 1/2	cups pecans
3	eggs	1 1/2	cups shredded coconut
1 1/2	cups packed brown sugar		

Cream the butter and confectioners' sugar in a mixing bowl until light and fluffy. Add the flour and mix well. Spread into a thin layer in a 9×13-inch cake pan. Bake at 350 degrees for 25 to 30 minutes or until golden brown. Maintain the oven temperature. Beat the eggs and brown sugar in a mixing bowl. Add the baking powder and vanilla and mix well. Stir in the pecans and shredded coconut. Spread over the baked layer. Bake for 20 to 25 minutes or until golden brown. Cool and cut into 2-inch squares.

Pumpkin Spice Cake

Serves 12

2	cups unbleached flour	1	(16-ounce) can pumpkin purée
2	teaspoons baking powder	3/4	cup raisins
1	teaspoon baking soda	3	ounces cream cheese, softened
3/4	teaspoon salt	1/4	cup (1/2 stick) unsalted
2	teaspoons ground cinnamon		butter, softened
1/4	teaspoon ground ginger	1/8	teaspoon ground ginger
1/4	teaspoon ground cloves	2 1/2	cups confectioners' sugar
4	eggs	2	tablespoons fresh lemon juice
2	cups granulated sugar	3/4	cup walnuts, finely chopped
1	cup vegetable oil		

Sift the flour, baking powder, baking soda, salt, cinnamon, 1/4 teaspoon ginger and the cloves together. Beat the eggs in a large mixing bowl until pale yellow. Beat in the granulated sugar gradually. Add the oil in a thin stream, beating constantly. Blend in the pumpkin purée. Add the flour mixture 1/2 cup at a time, beating well after each addition. Stir in the raisins. Pour into a greased 9×13-inch cake pan. Bake at 350 degrees for 45 to 50 minutes. Cool in the pan. Beat the cream cheese, butter and 1/2 teaspoon ginger in a mixing bowl until light and fluffy. Add the confectioners' sugar and lemon juice alternately, beating constantly. Spread over the cooled cake. Sprinkle with the walnuts.

Rum Cake

Serves 12

CAKE
1   (2-layer) package yellow cake mix
1   (4-ounce) package vanilla instant
    pudding mix
1/2 cup vegetable oil
1/4 cup water
1/4 cup brandy
1/4 cup rum

4   eggs
1/2 to 1 cup chopped pecans

RUM GLAZE
1/2 cup (1 stick) butter
1   cup sugar
1/4 cup rum
1/4 cup water

To *prepare the cake,* combine the cake mix, pudding mix, oil, water, brandy, rum and eggs in a mixing bowl and beat well. Layer the pecans in the bottom of a greased and floured bundt pan. Pour the batter into the prepared pan. Bake at 350 degrees for 25 to 30 minutes or until a knife inserted near the center comes out clean.

To prepare the glaze, melt the butter in a saucepan. Add the sugar, rum and water and mix well. Bring to a boil, stirring frequently. Make small cuts with a sharp knife in the warm cake. Pour the glaze over the warm cake. Let stand until cool before removing the cake from the pan.

Tres Leches Cake

Serves 12

1   (2-layer) package white cake mix
•   Butter
2   (14-ounce) cans coconut milk
1   teaspoon rum extract
1   teaspoon vanilla extract
1/2 cup coconut rum

1   (14-ounce) can sweetened
    condensed milk
16 ounces whipped topping
1   (4-ounce) package cheesecake
    instant pudding mix
1/4 cup coconut rum

Prepare the cake mix using the package directions, substituting butter for the oil and coconut milk for the water, and adding the rum extract and vanilla. Pour into a greased 9×13-inch cake pan and bake using the package directions. Cool in the pan for 15 minutes. Punch holes with the handle of a wooden spoon in the warm cake. Pour the remaining 1 can of coconut milk over the cake. Let soak for 15 minutes. Pour 1/2 cup coconut rum evenly over the cake. Top with the condensed milk. Let soak for 15 minutes. Cover with plastic wrap and chill for 12 to 24 hours. Mix the whipped topping and pudding mix in a bowl. Stir in 1/4 cup coconut rum. Spread evenly over the top of the cake. Chill in the refrigerator until ready to serve.

Tommy's Seafood Steakhouse Black and White Bread Pudding

CHEF'S RECIPE

Serves 12

1	loaf French bread, crusts trimmed	4	egg yolks
3/4	cup white chocolate chunks	1 1/2	cups sugar
3/4	cup dark chocolate chunks	1	tablespoon vanilla extract
1/2	cup pecan pieces	2 1/2	cups milk
8	eggs	2 1/2	cups heavy cream

Cut the bread into 1 1/2-inch pieces. Layer the bread, white chocolate, dark chocolate and pecan pieces evenly in a 10×15-inch buttered baking pan. Whisk the eggs and sugar in a bowl until a ribbon forms. Add the vanilla. Stir in the milk and cream. Pour the mixture through a fine sieve into a bowl. Pour over the layers in the prepared pan and press the bread down to submerge. Place the pan in a larger pan and add enough water to come halfway up the sides of the larger pan. Bake at 350 degrees until brown.

Frozen Mocha Cheesecake

Serves 15 to 16

1 1/4	cups chocolate wafer crumbs (about 24 cookies)	1	(14-ounce) can sweetened condensed milk
1/4	cup sugar	2	tablespoons instant coffee
1/4	cup (1/2 stick) margarine, melted	1	teaspoon hot water
8	ounces cream cheese, softened	2	cups heavy whipping cream, whipped
2/3	cup chocolate syrup		

Mix the wafer crumbs, sugar and margarine in a bowl. Press over the bottom of a greased 10-inch springform pan. Chill in the refrigerator. Beat the cream cheese in a mixing bowl until fluffy. Add the chocolate syrup and condensed milk. Dissolve the instant coffee in the hot water in a cup. Add to the cream cheese mixture and mix well. Fold in the whipped cream. Pour into the prepared pan. Cover with plastic wrap and freeze for 6 hours or until firm. Serve with additional whipped cream and garnish with chocolate curls.

Luscious Lemon Cheesecake

Serves 12

CHEESECAKE
1   cup graham cracker crumbs
3   tablespoons sugar
3   tablespoons butter, melted
24   ounces cream cheese, softened
3/4   cup sugar
3   eggs
1/4   cup fresh lemon juice
1   tablespoon grated lemon zest
1   cup sour cream
2   tablespoons sugar
1   teaspoon vanilla extract

LEMON GLAZE
1/2   cup sugar
2   tablespoons cornstarch
1/3   cup lemon juice
3/4   cup water
1   tablespoon grated lemon zest

To prepare the cheesecake, mix the graham cracker crumbs, 3 tablespoons sugar and the butter in a bowl. Press over the bottom of a 9-inch springform pan. Bake at 325 degrees for 10 minutes. Remove from the oven and increase the oven temperature to 350 degrees. Beat the cream cheese, 3/4 cup sugar, the eggs, lemon juice and lemon zest in a mixing bowl until smooth. Pour into the prepared crust. Bake for 35 minutes. Remove from the oven. Mix the sour cream, 2 tablespoons sugar and the vanilla in a bowl. Spread over the cheesecake. Bake for 10 minutes. Remove from the oven to cool.

To prepare the glaze, combine the sugar, cornstarch, lemon juice, water and lemon zest in a saucepan and mix well. Cook over low heat until thickened and clear, stirring constantly. Remove from the heat to cool slightly. Spread over the top of the cheesecake. Chill, covered, in the refrigerator for 8 to 10 hours before serving.

Miniature Cheesecakes

Makes 3 dozen

- Graham cracker crumbs
- 24 ounces cream cheese, softened
- 3/4 cup sugar
- 3 egg yolks
- 3 egg whites, stiffly beaten
- 3/4 cup sour cream
- 2 tablespoons sugar
- 1 teaspoon vanilla extract
- 18 maraschino cherries, cut into halves

Line thirty-six miniature muffin cups with miniature baking cups and spray lightly with nonstick cooking spray. Dust with graham cracker crumbs. Beat the cream cheese, 3/4 cup sugar and the egg yolks in a mixing bowl until smooth. Fold in the stiffly beaten egg whites. Spoon into the prepared cups. Bake at 350 degrees for 15 minutes. (The centers will fall.)

Combine the sour cream, 2 tablespoons sugar and the vanilla in a bowl and mix well. Spoon 1 teaspoonful of the mixture on top of each cheesecake. Bake for 5 minutes. Cool completely before removing from the muffin cups. Place a maraschino cherry half on top of each. Chill in the refrigerator or freeze until ready to serve.

Ice Cream Cake

Serves 12

- 1 regular-size frozen pound cake
- 1 quart coffee ice cream, softened enough to spread
- 1 bottle chocolate fudge sauce
- 4 Heath candy bars, chopped

Cut the cake into 1/4-inch slices. Line a 9-inch springform pan with a layer of the cake slices, cutting some of the cake slices into pieces to fit into the openings. Spread half the ice cream over the cake. Freeze for at least 2 to 10 hours. Spread half the fudge sauce and half the candy over the ice cream layer. Repeat the layers using the remaining ingredients. Freeze until firm.

To serve, loosen the cake from the side of the pan and release the side. Cut into slices. Store in the freezer.

Pecan Cream Cake

Serves 12

CAKE

3/4 cup graham cracker crumbs
3/4 cup pecans
3 tablespoons granulated sugar
1/3 cup butter, melted
3 eggs
1/2 cup heavy cream
1/2 cup dark corn syrup
1/4 teaspoon salt
1/4 teaspoon ground cinnamon

1 cup granulated sugar
1/2 teaspoon vanilla extract
2 tablespoons butter, softened
1 1/2 cups pecans

RUM WHIPPED CREAM

2 cups heavy whipping cream
1/4 cup confectioners' sugar
3 tablespoons rum, or to taste

To *prepare the cake,* combine the graham cracker crumbs, 3/4 cup pecans, 3 tablespoons granulated sugar and 1/3 cup butter in a food processor or blender and process until finely ground. Press over the bottom and 1/2- to 1-inch up the side of a 9- or 10-inch springform pan. Process the eggs, 1/2 cup cream, the corn syrup, salt, cinnamon, 1 cup granulated sugar, the vanilla, 2 tablespoons butter and 1 1/2 cups pecans in a food processor or blender until the pecans are coarsely chopped. Pour into the prepared pan. Bake at 400 degrees for 35 to 40 minutes or until the side appears brown and the filling is puffed. Remove from the oven to cool. Chill in the refrigerator until ready to serve.

To prepare the topping, combine the whipping cream, confectioners' sugar and rum in a mixing bowl. Whip at high speed until stiff peaks form.

To serve, loosen the cake from the side of the pan and release the side. Cut the cake into slices and spoon the topping over each slice.

Note: *Do not grease the springform pan. If you use a dark or coated springform pan, reduce the baking temperature to 375 degrees. You may substitute Kahlúa or amaretto for the rum.*

WHIPPED CREAM

Heavy whipping cream may be whipped with an electric mixer or rotary beater. To get the best results, start with a chilled bowl and beaters. Do not whip the cream too far ahead of time. If it begins to separate, it can be easily reincorporated by mixing it briefly with a wire whisk.

Pear Galette

Serves 10

5 cups (1/4-inch-lengthwise-slices) peeled Bartlett pears

3/4 to 1 cup brandy

6 tablespoons golden raisins

6 tablespoons dried cranberries

1 1/2 cups all-purpose flour

6 tablespoons granulated sugar

1/8 teaspoon salt

1/3 cup chilled butter, chopped

5 to 6 tablespoons ice water

3 tablespoons brown sugar

2 1/2 tablespoons cornstarch

2 teaspoons confectioners' sugar

1 cup heavy whipping cream, whipped

Mix the pears, brandy, raisins and cranberries in a bowl. Cover and let stand for 1 hour; drain. Pulse the flour, 1 tablespoon of the granulated sugar and salt in a food processor two times. Add the butter and pulse four times or until the mixture resembles coarse cornmeal. Add the ice water through the food chute, processing constantly until combined. Gently press the dough into a 4-inch circle on plastic wrap. Cover and chill for 15 minutes.

Slightly overlap two pieces of plastic wrap on a slightly damp surface. Unwrap the chilled dough and place on the plastic wrap. Cover with two additional pieces of plastic wrap. Roll the dough while still covered into a 14-inch circle. Freeze until the plastic wrap can be easily removed. Remove only the top sheets of the plastic wrap. Fit the dough, plastic wrap side up, into a 10-inch tart pan with a removable bottom coated with nonstick cooking spray. Press the dough over the bottom and up the side of the pan, allowing the dough to extend over the edge of the pan. Remove the plastic wrap.

Whisk 3 tablespoons of the granulated sugar, the brown sugar and cornstarch together in a bowl. Sprinkle 1/2 cup of the sugar mixture into the prepared pan. Cover with half the fruit mixture. Repeat the layers with the remaining sugar mixture and fruit. Fold the edge of the dough over the fruit. (The dough will only partially cover the fruit.) Sprinkle the remaining 2 tablespoons granulated sugar over the fruit. Bake at 425 degrees for 20 minutes. Reduce the oven temperature to 350 degrees and bake for 45 minutes or until the pastry is golden brown. Cool on a wire rack for 10 minutes. Sift the confectioners' sugar over the top. Serve warm or at room temperature with a dollop of the whipped cream on each piece.

Galette

A galette is a tart that is French in origin. This tart is traditionally baked in a plate, pan, or mold, or can be baked free form, like a pizza. In America, we often make them in a tart pan but still might call them a galette. Of all the tart variations, galettes are by far the easiest to make. These no fuss, individual-size desserts are prepared with store-bought puff pastry and are ready to eat in about an hour. Frozen puff pastry thaws in about 8 hours in the refrigerator. It is important to keep it chilled while thawing to ensure that it will puff up nicely and have a crisp texture.

Poached Pears with Caramel Sauce

Serves 4

1	vanilla bean
1	cup white wine
4	Bosc pears with stems intact (not quite ripe)

2/3	cup sugar
1/4	cup water
1/2	cup (35%) whipping cream

Split the vanilla bean in half lengthwise and scoop out the center into a saucepan. Add the wine. Peal the pears with a paring knife, keeping their shape. Scoop out the cores from the bottom using a parisienne knife or melon baller. Place the pears stems up in the wine. Cover and poach gently for 20 minutes or until soft. (The degree of ripeness will determine the cooking time.) Remove the pears, reserving one-half of the poaching liquid for the sauce.

Bring the sugar and water to a boil in a saucepan. Boil vigorously without stirring until the sugar begins to change color, watching carefully to prevent burning. Remove the pan from the heat when the sugar is light amber in color. Add the poaching liquid all at once. (It will hiss and spatter.) Return to the heat and add the cream. Simmer the sauce until all of the lumps disappear.

To serve, pour the warm sauce onto dessert plates and stand the pears up in the center.

Note: *You can also serve with vanilla ice cream.*

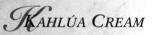

Kahlúa Cream

Whip 1 quart heavy whipping cream in a mixing bowl until stiff peaks form. Fold in 1/2 cup chocolate syrup and 1/2 cup Kahlúa. Pour into two 9-inch foil pans and sprinkle with 1/2 cup chopped pecans. Freeze until firm. Cut into slices to serve. Store in the freezer. This recipe may be made one day in advance.

Dark Chocolate Mousse with Raspberry Sauce

Serves 6

FRAISES ROMANOFF

Rinse 1 quart of fresh strawberries and remove the caps. Place in a container and add 1/2 cup Grand Marnier and 1/2 cup orange juice. Cover and chill for several hours, turning occasionally. Whip 1 cup heavy whipping cream in a mixing bowl until soft peaks form. Add 1/4 cup confectioners' sugar and 1/2 teaspoon vanilla extract and whip until stiff peaks form. Place the strawberries and some of the juice in individual glass dishes and dollop with the whipped cream.

MOUSSE

2   (3- to 5-ounce) bars dark Swiss chocolate, coarsely chopped
1/4   cup sugar
2   tablespoons butter
2   eggs
3/4   cup milk

RASPBERRY SAUCE

1   (10-ounce) package frozen raspberries in syrup, thawed
1   teaspoon cornstarch
2   tablespoons sugar

To *prepare the mousse*, cook the chocolate, sugar and butter in a heavy saucepan over low heat until the chocolate melts, stirring constantly. Whisk the eggs in a mixing bowl. Add the milk and blend well. Whisk about 1/2 cup of the hot chocolate mixture gradually into the egg mixture. Add to the remaining chocolate mixture, stirring constantly. Cook over low heat for 5 to 8 minutes or until thickened, stirring constantly. Remove from the heat to a glass bowl and let stand for 45 minutes. Spoon into six stemmed glasses and chill for 2 hours.

To prepare the sauce, purée the raspberries in a blender. Press the mixture through a wire-mesh strainer into a small saucepan, using the back of a spoon to squeeze out the juice. Discard the pulp and seeds. Whisk the cornstarch into the raspberry liquid until smooth. Whisk in the sugar. Bring to a boil over medium heat, stirring constantly. Boil for 1 minute, stirring constantly. Remove from the heat to cool.

To serve, spoon 2 tablespoons of the raspberry sauce over each serving of mousse. Garnish with fresh raspberries.

Note: *This mousse is not very sweet. If a sweeter mousse is desired, use semisweet chocolate and increase the sugar to 1/2 to 1 cup.*

Grasshopper Mousse

Serves 12

2²/₃ cups cold milk	1 (6-ounce) package vanilla instant pudding mix
1/3 cup crème de menthe	
2 tablespoons crème de cacao	8 ounces frozen whipped topping, thawed

Blend the milk, crème de menthe and crème de cacao in a mixing bowl. Add the pudding mix and stir until completely dissolved. Stir in the whipped topping. Chill for 8 to 10 hours. Serve in small chocolate shells or baked pastry shells. Garnish with shaved semisweet chocolate.

Note: *You may spoon the mousse into martini glasses and garnish with chocolate shavings and a chocolate stick.*

Tiramisu

Serves 10 to 12

40 ladyfingers (about)	2 cups heavy whipping cream
2 cups brewed espresso or very strong coffee	1/4 cup amaretto
	1/4 cup rum
1/4 cup amaretto	1 teaspoon vanilla extract
1/4 cup Kahlúa	2 or 3 egg whites
3 pounds mascarpone cheese	4 ounces chocolate or chocolate mint, shaved
1¹/₂ cups sugar	

Place the ladyfingers on a baking sheet. Bake at 350 degrees until light brown. Remove to a wire rack to cool. Combine the espresso, 1/4 cup amaretto and the Kahlúa in a bowl and blend well. Let stand until cool. Dip the cooled ladyfingers into the espresso mixture. Line a 10×15-inch pan or trifle bowl with about twenty of the ladyfingers. Combine the mascarpone cheese, sugar, whipping cream, amaretto, rum, vanilla and egg whites in a 12-quart bowl of an electric mixer fitted with a wire whip. Beat at high speed until fluffy and creamy, scraping the side of the bowl with a rubber spatula. Do not overbeat. Spread one-half of the mascarpone mixture over the ladyfingers. Sprinkle one-half of the shaved chocolate evenly over the mascarpone layer. Repeat the layers with the remaining ladyfingers, mascarpone mixture and shaved chocolate until all of the ingredients are used. Cover with a domed lid and chill for at least 2 hours.

Note: *Mascarpone cheese may be found in the deli section of your favorite grocery.*

Gaido's Wooden Shoe

CHEF'S RECIPE

Serves 1

1	ounce dark crème de cacao	1.5	ounces Coco Lopez
1	tablespoon piña colada mix		cream of coconut
		3	scoops vanilla ice cream

Blend the crème de cacao, piña colada mix, cream of coconut and ice cream in a blender until smooth. Pour into a tall glass and garnish with whipped cream and chocolate sprinkles.

Chocolate Chip Cheese Ball

Serves 8

8	ounces cream cheese, softened	2	tablespoons brown sugar
1/2	cup (1 stick) butter, softened	3/4	cup miniature semisweet
1/4	teaspoon vanilla extract		chocolate chips
3/4	cup confectioners' sugar	3/4	cup finely chopped pecans

Beat the cream cheese, butter and vanilla in a mixing bowl until fluffy. Add the confectioners' sugar and brown sugar gradually, beating constantly. Stir in the chocolate chips and 1/2 cup of the pecans. Shape into a ball. Cover and chill for one hour. Roll in the remaining pecans. Serve with graham crackers or apple slices.

Piña Colada Dip

Serves 8

8	ounces cream cheese, softened	1/4	cup pineapple juice
1 1/2	cups confectioners' sugar	1	envelope dry piña colada mix

Beat the cream cheese in a mixing bowl until fluffy. Add the confectioners' sugar and pineapple juice alternately, beating constantly. Add the piña colada mix and mix well. Spoon into a serving bowl. Chill, covered, in the refrigerator. Serve with fresh fruit.

Gaido's Seafood Restaurant in Galveston, Texas, was founded in 1911 by S. J. Gaido. He believed in the concept of using only the freshest ingredients. Today that concept still exists with the fourth generation of Gaidos who are now running the restaurant. Originally in the Murdoch's Bath House on Seawall Boulevard, it was relocated in 1947 to its current location at 39th and Seawall Boulevard. The restaurant now seats up to 1,000 people.

Caramel Corn

Makes 8 quarts

8	quarts popped popcorn	1	teaspoon salt
2	cups packed brown sugar	1/2	teaspoon baking soda
1	cup (2 sticks) butter	•	Salted peanuts (optional)
1/2	cup white corn syrup		

Divide the popcorn into two large baking pans. Mix the brown sugar, butter, corn syrup and salt in a large saucepan and bring to a boil. Boil for 5 minutes, stirring constantly. Remove from the heat and stir in the baking soda. Pour one-half of the mixture over each pan of popcorn and mix well with a rubber spatula. Bake at 250 degrees for 1 hour, stirring well from the bottom every 20 minutes to evenly coat all pieces and adding the peanuts during the last 20 minutes. Remove from the oven to cool. Store in an airtight container or sealable plastic bags.

Iced Brownies

Makes 4 dozen

BROWNIES		FUDGE ICING	
1	cup (2 sticks) butter	1	ounce semisweet chocolate
4	ounces semisweet chocolate	1/4	cup (1/2 stick) butter
1	cup all-purpose flour	1	cup sugar
1 1/2	teaspoons baking powder	1/4	cup milk
2	cups sugar	•	Pinch of salt
4	eggs, beaten	1/2	teaspoon vanilla extract
1	teaspoon vanilla extract	1	teaspoon milk (optional)

To *prepare the brownies,* melt the butter and chocolate in a heavy saucepan. Sift the flour and baking powder into the chocolate mixture. Stir in the sugar, eggs and vanilla. Pour into an oiled 9×13-inch baking pan. Bake at 350 degrees for 30 minutes. Remove from the oven to cool.

To prepare the icing, combine the chocolate, butter, sugar, 1/4 cup milk, salt and vanilla in a saucepan and slowly bring to a boil. Boil for 1 minute, stirring constantly. Remove from the heat to cool. Add the vanilla and beat with a spoon until the mixture thickens and loses its gloss, adding 1 teaspoon milk if the mixture becomes too thick. Spread over the brownies and cut into squares.

Caramel Layer Chocolate Squares

Makes 3 dozen

1 (14-ounce) package caramels (about 50 pieces)	3/4 cup (1 1/2 sticks) margarine, melted
1/3 cup evaporated milk	1/3 cup evaporated milk
1 (2-layer) package German chocolate cake mix	1 cup pecans, chopped
	1 cup (6 ounces) semisweet chocolate chips

Unwrap the caramels. Cook the caramels and 1/3 cup evaporated milk in a saucepan over low heat until the caramels melt, stirring constantly. Combine the cake mix, margarine, 1/3 cup evaporated milk and the pecans in a bowl and stir by hand until the dough holds together. Press half the dough into a greased and floured 9×13-inch baking pan. Bake at 350 degrees for 8 minutes. Sprinkle the chocolate chips over the baked layer. Spread the caramel mixture over the chocolate chips to within 1/2 inch of the edge. Drop and pat the remaining dough over the caramel mixture. Bake for 20 to 25 minutes or until the mixture pulls away from the sides of the pan. Remove from the oven and cool slightly. Chill in the refrigerator for 20 minutes or until the caramel layer sets. Cut into bars.

Fudgy Chocolate Cookies

Makes 5 dozen

1 3/4 cups all-purpose flour	2 eggs, at room temperature
1/3 cup baking cocoa	1 teaspoon vanilla extract
1/2 teaspoon baking soda	1 1/2 cups semisweet chocolate chunks
3/4 cup (1 1/2 sticks) butter, softened	3/4 cup coarsely chopped walnuts or pecans
1 cup packed dark brown sugar	• Confectioners' sugar
1/2 cup granulated sugar	

Cover cookie sheets with baking parchment or lightly grease. Mix the flour, baking cocoa and baking soda together. Cream the butter, brown sugar and granulated sugar in a mixing bowl. Add the eggs and vanilla and beat until fluffy. Add the flour mixture and beat at low speed until combined. Stir in the chocolate chunks and walnuts. Drop the dough by scant tablespoonfuls 2 inches apart onto the prepared cookie sheets. Bake at 350 degrees for 8 minutes or until the centers are no longer wet. Cool on the cookie sheets for 5 minutes. Sprinkle with confectioners' sugar.

Note: *Do not substitute the butter and have all ingredients at room temperature before beginning the recipe. This recipe may be frozen.*

Coconut Cookies

Makes 3 dozen

1 cup (2 sticks) butter, softened	3 ounces shredded coconut
1/2 cup granulated sugar	1 teaspoon vanilla extract
2 cups all-purpose flour	• Confectioners' sugar

Cream the butter and granulated sugar in a mixing bowl. Add the flour, coconut and vanilla and mix well. (You may prepare in advance up to this point and refrigerate.) Roll into small balls and place 1 inch apart on cookie sheets. Flatten the balls with a fork which has been dipped in cold water. Bake at 350 degrees for 20 minutes or until golden brown. Remove from the oven and sprinkle with confectioners' sugar. Cool on wire racks.

Note: *This recipe may be frozen.*

Crunchy Cookies

Makes 3 1/2 dozen

1 cup (2 sticks) butter, softened	1 cup crushed potato chips
3/4 cup granulated sugar	1 cup chopped pecans
1 1/2 cups all-purpose flour	• Confectioners' sugar
1 teaspoon vanilla extract	

Cream the butter and granulated sugar in a mixing bowl until light and fluffy. Add the flour gradually, beating constantly. Stir in the vanilla, potato chips and pecans. Chill the dough for 15 minutes. Drop the dough by teaspoonfuls onto ungreased cookie sheets. Bake at 325 degrees for 15 to 20 minutes or until light brown on the bottom. Remove from the oven and sprinkle with confectioners' sugar. Cool on wire racks.

Note: *This recipe may be frozen.*

Gingersnaps

Makes 3 to 4 dozen

1/4	cup molasses	1	teaspoon ground ginger
3/4	cup shortening	1	teaspoon ground cinnamon
1	cup sugar	1/2	teaspoon ground cloves
1	egg	1/4	teaspoon salt
2	cups all-purpose flour	•	Sugar for rolling
2	teaspoons baking soda		

Combine the molasses, shortening, 1 cup sugar and egg in a mixing bowl and mix well. Add the flour, baking soda, ginger, cinnamon, cloves and salt and mix well. Chill the dough for 1 hour. Shape the dough into walnut-size balls. Roll in additional sugar and place on foil-lined cookie sheets. Do not press down. Bake at 350 degrees for 10 minutes or until the cookies crack and flatten. Remove to wire racks to cool.

Note: *If you prefer a chewy cookie, reduce the baking time.*

Old-Fashioned Oatmeal Cookies

Makes 4 dozen

1 1/4	cups sifted all-purpose flour	1	cup granulated sugar
1	teaspoon baking soda	1	teaspoon vanilla extract
1/2	teaspoon salt	2	eggs
1	teaspoon ground cinnamon	3	cups rolled oats
1/2	teaspoon ground nutmeg	2/3	cup chopped nuts
1/2	teaspoon ground cloves	1/2	cup raisins
1	cup shortening	1/2	cup shredded coconut (optional)
1	cup packed brown sugar		

Sift the flour, baking soda, salt, cinnamon, nutmeg and cloves together. Mix the shortening, brown sugar, granulated sugar, vanilla and eggs in a mixing bowl and mix well. Add the flour mixture and stir to mix well. Stir in the oats, nuts, raisins and shredded coconut. Drop by rounded teaspoonfuls 2 inches apart onto ungreased cookie sheets. Bake at 350 degrees for 12 to 15 minutes or until golden brown. Cool on wire racks.

Note: *This recipe may be frozen.*

Lemon Melting Moments

Makes 4 dozen

COOKIES
2/3 cup cornstarch
1 cup all-purpose flour
1 cup (2 sticks) butter, softened
1/3 cup confectioners' sugar
1 teaspoon lemon extract

LEMON FROSTING
1/3 cup butter, softened
1 1/2 cups (or more) confectioners' sugar
3 tablespoons lemon juice
1 teaspoon lemon zest

To prepare the cookies, sift the cornstarch and flour together. Cream the butter, confectioners' sugar and lemon extract in a mixing bowl until light and fluffy. Add the flour mixture and mix well. Drop by small teaspoonfuls onto ungreased cookie sheets. Bake at 325 degrees for 15 minutes. Do not brown. Cool on wire racks.

To prepare the frosting, combine the butter, confectioners' sugar, lemon juice and lemon zest in a mixing bowl and mix well, adding additional confectioners' sugar to reach the desired spreading consistency. (This makes two batches of frosting.) Drizzle the frosting over the cool cookies.

Note: These cookies are very delicate, so handle gently.

Caramel Pecan Delights

Makes about 4 dozen

2 1/4 cups packed brown sugar
1 cup (2 sticks) butter
1 cup light corn syrup
1/8 teaspoon salt
1 (14-ounce) can sweetened condensed milk
1 teaspoon vanilla extract
1 1/2 pounds pecan halves
1 cup (6 ounces) semisweet chocolate chips
1 cup (6 ounces) milk chocolate chips
2 tablespoons shortening

Combine the brown sugar, butter, corn syrup and salt in a large saucepan. Cook over medium heat until the brown sugar dissolves. Add the condensed milk gradually, stirring constantly to mix well. Cook to 248 degrees on a candy thermometer, firm-ball stage. Remove from the heat and stir in the vanilla. Fold in the pecans. Drop by spoonfuls onto baking sheets lined with waxed paper. Chill until firm. Melt the semisweet chocolate chips, milk chocolate chips and shortening in the microwave or over a double boiler. Drizzle the melted chocolate over each cluster.

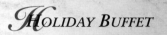

Swedish Cocoa Balls

Makes 2 dozen

1/2	cup (1 stick) butter, softened	1/2	teaspoon rum flavoring or vanilla extract
2/3	cup sugar	13/4	cups quick-cooking oats
3	tablespoons baking cocoa		
1	tablespoon strong coffee		

Cream the butter and sugar in a mixing bowl until light and fluffy. Add the baking cocoa, coffee, rum flavoring and oats and mix well. Chill, covered, in the refrigerator. Roll into small balls, pressing firmly.

Note: *This recipe may be frozen.*

Pralines à la Microwave

Makes 2 dozen

1	cup whipping cream	2	tablespoons butter, softened
1	pound light brown sugar	3	to 5 tablespoons bourbon
2	cups pecan halves		(optional)

Mix the cream and brown sugar in a 4-quart microwave-safe bowl. Microwave on High for 13 minutes. Quickly add the pecan halves, butter and bourbon and stir to mix well. Drop by teaspoonfuls onto a foil-lined surface.

Peppermint Swirl Bark

Makes 1 pound

6	squares semisweet baking chocolate or bittersweet baking chocolate	6	squares premium white baking chocolate
		1	cup crushed peppermint candies (about 50)

Microwave the semisweet chocolate and white chocolate in separate medium microwave-safe bowls on High for 2 minutes, stirring halfway through the cooking time. (The chocolate should be almost melted. Stir the chocolate until completely melted.) Stir 1/2 cup crushed peppermint candies into each bowl. Alternately spoon the melted chocolate mixture and white chocolate mixture onto a baking sheet lined with waxed paper. Swirl the chocolate mixture and white chocolate mixture together with a knife to marbleize. Chill for at least 1 hour or until firm. Break into pieces to serve.

Note: *Also, try another popular candy, Jungle Pieces, in* Settings on the Dock of the Bay, *page 253.*

Toffee Crunch

Makes 1 1/4 pounds

1	cup (2 sticks) butter	1	cup (6 ounces) semisweet chocolate chips
1 1/3	cups sugar		
1	tablespoon light corn syrup	1/2	cup pecans, walnuts or almonds
2	tablespoons water		
1	teaspoon vanilla extract		

Combine the butter, sugar, corn syrup and water in a 2 1/2-quart saucepan. Cook to 300 degrees on a candy thermometer, hard-crack stage, stirring constantly. Remove from the heat and stir in the vanilla. Pour into a 10×15-inch pan lined with heavy-duty foil. Sprinkle with the chocolate chips and let stand until softened. Spread the melted chocolate with a spatula evenly over the toffee. Sprinkle with the pecans and press into the chocolate. Chill until the chocolate is set. Break into pieces. Store in an airtight container or the freezer.

Peppermint Whipped Cream

Process enough peppermint candies in a food processor into a fine powder to measure 2 tablespoons. Beat 1/2 cup heavy whipping cream, the 2 tablespoons ground peppermint powder and 1 tablespoon confectioners' sugar in a mixing bowl until stiff peaks form. Pipe or spoon onto baking parchment and sprinkle with 1 tablespoon crushed peppermints. Freeze for 20 minutes. Remove from the freezer and place in an airtight container. Store in the freezer until needed. Use in hot cocoa or coffee drinks, or as a topping on chocolate desserts.

Almond Cheese Pie

Serves 6 to 8

1 1/2 cups chocolate wafer crumbs
1 cup chopped blanched almonds
1/3 cup sugar
1/2 cup (1 stick) butter, melted
8 ounces cream cheese, softened
1 cup sugar
3 egg yolks

1 tablespoon almond liqueur
3 egg whites, stiffly beaten
1 cup heavy whipping cream, whipped
• Butter
1/4 to 1/3 cup sliced almonds

Mix the wafer crumbs, 1 cup almonds, 1/3 cup sugar and 1/2 cup butter in a bowl. Press over the bottom of a lightly greased 9-inch springform pan. Cream the cream cheese and 1 cup sugar in a mixing bowl. Beat in the egg yolks and almond liqueur. Fold in the egg whites and whipped cream with a large whisk. Pour into the prepared pan. Cover with foil to seal and freeze. Sauté 1/4 to 1/3 cup sliced almonds in enough butter to cover the bottom of a sauté pan until toasted. Sprinkle over the frozen pie. Cut into slices and serve with additional almond liqueur.

Note: *If you are concerned about using raw egg yolks, use yolks from eggs pasteurized in their shells, which are sold at some specialty food stores, or use an equivalent amount of pasteurized egg substitute.*

Sweet Potato Pecan Pie

Serves 6 to 8

2 cups mashed cooked sweet potatoes
1/2 cup packed dark brown sugar
1/2 cup granulated sugar
3 tablespoons butter, softened
1/2 teaspoon ground cinnamon
1/2 teaspoon vanilla extract
1/2 teaspoon salt

1 tablespoon lemon juice
3 eggs
1 cup evaporated milk
1 unbaked (9-inch) deep-dish pie shell
3 tablespoons butter, melted
1/4 cup packed dark brown sugar
1 cup chopped pecans

Combine the sweet potatoes, 1/2 cup brown sugar, the granulated sugar, 3 tablespoons butter, the cinnamon, vanilla, salt and lemon juice in a bowl and mix well. Beat in the eggs and evaporated milk until smooth. Pour into the pie shell. Bake at 375 degrees for 35 to 40 minutes or until a knife inserted in the center comes out clean. Remove from the oven and cover the top with a mixture of 3 tablespoons butter, 1/4 cup dark brown sugar and the pecans. Bake for 20 minutes.

Holiday Coffee

Contributors

Patsy Abele
Atiya Abouleish*
Yvette Abouleish
Steve Acuna
Melissa Adam
Cynthia Aldape
Shirley Alderman
Rawia Ali
Donna Anderson*
Leslie Anslanian
Courtney Atchley*
Janet Atteberry
Janeane Bacon
Laine Bagby*
Sylvia Balionis*
Sheila Banovic*
Sherry Banta*
Salam Barazi
Cathy Barrentine*
Tammy Barrier*
Carol Base
Sandy Basso
Denise Beakey*
Ana Bearce*
Deborah Beard
Ruth Beecher*
Marilyn Bein
Carolyn Bennett
Sheryl Berg*
Carol Bergman*
Patricia Bertelli*
Neerja Bhardwaj*
Debbie Bonno*
Kristin Boozer*
Krista Borgen*
Annie Bourgeois
Anne Boussert
Ann Brady*
Kathy Braeuer

Patty Branch*
Nancy Brewer
Dana Brown*
Doris Brown*
Lynn Brown
Jennie Buderer
Pam Bungo*
Patricia Burnett*
Joan Burt*
Betsy Bush*
Kathryn McArthur Byrd
Linda Byrd*
Marion Callahan
Lane Callner*
Cindy Canino*
Cindy Castille*
Connie Chance
Nancy Chen*
Cheryl Chrisco
Peggy Clause*
Diane Coats
Sirena Collins
Tonya Collum*
Catherine Collura*
Jessie Cook
Ronda Cook*
Nelda Cooper
Janith Coutret*
Ebby Creden*
Pat Creech*
Peggy Creech
Susan Crowder
Gloria Cruz*
Pam Culpepper*
Georgette Curran
Kathie Curry*
Margaret Daniel
Darice Davis*
Barbara Decker

Sheila Dell'Osso
Emily Denesha
Loni Dennis
Belva Dewey*
Deborah Dewey
Terri Dieste*
Sharon Dillard*
Renee Ditta*
Renee Dollar
Liz Dooley*
Anne Dowbekin
Rebecca Doxey*
Linda DuBose
Barbara Dugat*
Carrie Dulmage*
Frances DuPlantis
Annette Dwyer*
Trish Early
Jailane Ebeid
JoLynn Falgout*
Stacy Fanning
Judie Ferguson*
Sue Ferguson*
Sheila Fichtner*
Edrina Fitting*
Marlive Fitzpatrick
Darlene Fore
Joyce Fornea
Alice Forsthoffer
Janelle Forsthoffer
Lynda Forsthoffer*
Tisa Foster*
Sheree Frede*
Mary Kay Gaido*
Carla Gandy
Karen Gandy*
Theresa Gardner*
Lisa Garrett-Garcia*
George Garris

230

Donna Gartner*
Fran Gentry*
Cathy Giesinger*
Dianne Gilbert*
Elizabeth Glenn*
Lil Glynn
Jeni Golden
Linda Goodman*
Sue Ann Goodwin*
Vicki Gorman
Dolores Gregory
Barbara Groh*
Cindy Grosmano
Dot Grovert
Lanette Hale*
Kayne Haley*
Lee Miori Hall
Sally Hammoud
Jennie Hampton*
Cheng Hang*
Rachel Hart
Octive Healey
Joe Hegyesi
Susie Heimbach
Peggy Heinrich*
Jo Herran
Jan Herzog
Melba Heselmeyer*
Rosie Hesse*
Linda Hicks
Julie Hill*
Melissa Hodge
Patty Hoffman*
Joanne Hogarth*
Lisa Holbrook
Katherine Holcomb
Anna Holder
Cherre House*
Leslie Huff*

Jana Hurzeler
John Hutchings, Jr.
Chieko Iida
Marie Inkofer*
Suzanne Jaax
Laurie Jachimiec*
Michele Jacobs*
Donna James*
Donna Jerz
Emily Johnson
Rita Johnson*
Skeets Johnson
Alice Jones*
Jeanne Jones*
Libby Jones*
Starla Jones*
Sherry Keimig*
Amina Khalil
Diedre Kidder
Faye R. Kidder*
Richard Kidder
Sharron Kifer
Misty Killebrew*
Kathie King*
Jeri Knapp*
Carl Konick
Diane Konick*
Stephanie Korenek*
Tracy Kubena*
Sheryl Lane*
Gloria LaPadre
Sherry LaPrade
Carol Latimer*
Nancy Laura
Nancy Leeper
Jeanine Levin
Joan Lindsay
Connie Lopez*
Judy Love*

Rebecca Lunney*
Teresa Macon
Charlene Magliolo
Jeana Magness*
Melinda Marcum*
Michelle Marrs
Lynette Mason-Gregg*
Johanna Mathera*
Pat McAllister*
Peggy McBarron*
Barbara McCollum
Linda McCormack*
Cathy McDaniel*
Michelle McKernan*
Kakie McKinney
Darla McKitrick*
Diane McLaughlin*
Laura McWater
Jeane Meller*
Sharon Mendelson*
Margie Miori
Sonya Moore*
Pam Morneau
Barbra Mouton*
Jim Mouton
Joy Muniz*
Sandra Munz*
Badiha Nassar*
Lyla Nettles
Marian Nickerson*
Hasnaa Nokta
Dewanna Norris
Jennifer Nutt*
Jan O'Dell
Nancy O'Dowd*
Rana O'Quinn*
Cathy Osoria*
Martha F. Owen
Laura Parker*

231

Jan Parks*
Edie Parsons
Eileen Parus
Tina Patterson*
Betsy Pennington*
Yvonne Perrin*
Wendy Peters*
Maryann Pilon
Antoinette Piperi
Georgia Piwonka*
Nancy Platt*
Sherry Pomykal
Cindy Porterfield*
Nancy Powers
Lavern Premeaux
Cindi Priebe*
Karl Priebe
Judy Raiford*
Lori Ray*
Joy W. Rayne*
Ann Reed
Melanie Reed
Tommie Reed
Debby Reichert*
Sylvia Resch*
Lisa Richards*
Lisa H. Richardson
Rebecca Richey*
Helene Ringer
Louie Roberts
Sylvia Robirds
Patty Rodgers*
Suzie Rogers*
Patty Romanko*
Metta Rone
Sandra Rooney
Missy Rorrer*
Lila Rosen*
Ann Rosenthal

Barbara Rosenthal*
Janet Rushing*
Betsy Salbilla
Barbara Samples
Sooky Sarabia
Sarah Sawin*
Belinda Scheurich*
June Schladenhauffen*
Doris Schoening
Lisa Schulte
Sandra Sellers*
Rhonda Seward*
Hasnaa Shafik
Gretchen Sheehan*
Glenda Sheffer
Carol Short*
Diana Shuman*
Sharon Siddons
Anita Sitter
Floy Smith
Mary Smith*
Melanie Smith
Re Smith
Jill Smitherman*
Joy Smitherman*
Susan Spalding
Betty Squyres*
Jackie Stallings
Patricia Stallings*
Abbey Standley
Pat Stouflet
Jill Strong*
Paula Stroumpos*
Laura Sukkar*
Patti Sulkin*
Kathleen Symons*
Meridy Tabackman
Lisa Tanzberger*
Sheila Tarbox

Lou Taylor
Charlotte Teeter*
Lucille Terraso*
Mary Todd
Emilie Toguri
Margaret Tramonte
Michelle Turner
Roslyn Turner*
Tracy Uehlinger*
Sandy Vail*
Deanna Vernon*
Diane Vest*
Barbara Visser*
Terrie Waddell*
Kathy Wade*
Pat Waldron
Doug Walt
Linda Walt*
Robin Rogers Ward
Nancy Warren*
Susan Weaver
Dawn Webb*
Elizabeth Webb*
Tehren Webb*
Tracey Webb*
Angie Weinman*
Sally Wigginton*
Jill Williams*
Robin Williams
Sandy Williams
Krista Williamson*

*denotes members of
Assistance League®
of the Bay Area

Index

Settings Sunrise to Sunset

A Medley of Flavors, Tastes, and Styles from the Texas Gulf Coast

AL assistance league® the Bay Area

ASSISTANCE LEAGUE®
OF THE BAY AREA
P.O. BOX 590153
HOUSTON, TEXAS 77259-0153

[} Mr.   [ ] Mrs.   [ ] Miss   [ ] Ms.

_____
Name

_____
Street Address

_____
City   State   Zip

_____
Daytime Telephone

_____
E-mail Address (optional)

Orders may be placed by phone, fax, order form, or by contacting us through our Web site.

Toll-Free
877-277-3452

Fax
281-326-6248

Web site
www.bayarea.assistance
league.org

Your Order	Qty	Total
Settings, Sunrise to Sunset at $27.95 per book		$
*Settings on the Dock of the Bay at $22.95 per book		$
Both *Settings, Sunrise to Sunset* and *Settings on the Dock of the Bay* at a special rate of $45.95 per gift set		$
Postage and handling: $4.00 for the first book		$
$2.00 for each additional book		$
$6.00 for each gift set		$
Subtotal		$
Texas residents add 8.25% sales tax		$
Grand Total		$

*Tabasco award-winner, now in its third printing

Proceeds from the sale of this cookbook are returned to the community through the projects of ASSISTANCE LEAGUE® OF THE BAY AREA.

Payment: [ ] American Express   [ ] MasterCard
                  [ ] VISA   [ ] Checks payable to ALBA Cookbook

_____
Account Number   Expiration Date

_____
Signature of Cardholder

Photocopies accepted